T0013536

HAPPY AF

Happy AF

SIMPLE STRATEGIES TO
GET UNSTUCK,
BOUNCE BACK,
AND LIVE YOUR BEST LIFE

Beth Romero

SHE WRITES PRESS

Published 2023
Printed in the United States of America
Print ISBN: 978-1-64742-589-0
E-ISBN: 978-1-64742-590-6
Library of Congress Control Number: 2023910020

For information, address:
She Writes Press
1569 Solano Ave #546
Berkeley, CA 94707

Interior design by Stacey Aaronson

She Writes Press is a division of SparkPoint Studio, LLC.

TO MIMI AND PAVIS

CONTENTS

Chapter 8:
Your Past Prepares You
193

Happy AF

From Crappy to Happy and Everything in Between

WHEN I WAS FIVE YEARS OLD, MY MOTHER ALWAYS TOLD ME
THAT HAPPINESS WAS THE KEY TO LIFE.
WHEN I WENT TO SCHOOL,
THEY ASKED ME WHAT I WANTED TO BE WHEN I GREW UP.
I WROTE DOWN "HAPPY."
THEY TOLD ME I DIDN'T UNDERSTAND THE ASSIGNMENT,
AND I TOLD THEM THEY DIDN'T UNDERSTAND LIFE.
—ATTRIBUTED TO JOHN LENNON

F*ck you, 2020. You seriously kicked my ass. Not just a passing beating, but a full-blown, take-you-out, can't-get-back-up, dear-God-someone-please-throw-the-white-towel-in-the-ring knockdown. When the clock struck midnight on December 31, silent tears coursed down my cheeks in gratitude that you were finally over.

I'm aware that millions around the world felt the same way, as 2020 was a brutal moment of reckoning that spared few in its path. Although every story is unique, each shares a common thread of loss whether in productivity, experiences, financial security, employment, or loved ones. And that was the tip of the iceberg. Below the waterline was an endless depth of grief, uncertainty, and fear that buoyed its crippling effects well beyond the New Year.

So, there's that.

I've experienced my fair share of personal and professional blessings, for which I'm grateful. But life can still throw a few ferocious curveballs that unexpectedly knock you on your ass and take your breath away, and 2020 was like a possessed pitching machine hurling fireballs that left many of us ducking for cover or staying down with our face in the dirt to avoid any more direct hits. *Like literal roadkill.*

Many people have experienced some sort of a "roadkill" moment at one time or another. Loss of a loved one. A breakup. A divorce. Loss of a job. Betrayal. Loneliness. Bullying. Assault. Loss of purpose. Addiction to alcohol, drugs, sex, pornography, gambling, food, etc. Loss of home. Bankruptcy. Sickness. Disease. The list could go on and on. Although the event may be different, the roadkill feeling in its aftermath is universal. Life just ran you over, and you're struggling to get back up.

I try never to measure my losses against those of others; I know there are personal stories far worse than mine out there. As I tell my teenage daughters, run the race of life against only yourself. Plus, I find "comparative suffering" to be particularly toxic and minimizing. Thus, the woes herein are mine and mine alone, and 2020 was the perfect shitstorm in every aspect of my life that didn't just knock the wind from my sails—it sank the entire ship. Rock bottom. Lowest of lows.

But that's only *part* of my story. The best part of the story is what it took to get to the other side. It is said that rock bottom will teach you lessons that mountaintops never will. *Rock bottom was my blessing.* A defining moment, really. Rock bottom served as my springboard to grow, to learn, to thrive, to soar. Falling apart actually allowed everything to fall together in a new way—a *better* way. And those profound lessons serve as the inspiration and foundation for *Happy AF*.

This book is about my hike back up that mountain. Every strategy that I employed to catapult from rock bottom to loftier heights of happiness is outlined in these pages. And to be clear, these methods and means are backed by clinical data, not simply my humble opinion or arrogant proclamation (I have a lot of those, too, but that's for another time—preferably over a bottle of wine).

Here's the kicker: They're simple strategies to be a better version of you, to be happier, to be awesome, even.

We all just want to be seen, to be understood, to know that we aren't alone during our rock-bottom moment, whatever that may look like. I see you. I get you. You may feel like you're falling apart. Let's make sure you fall forward. Take this journey with me to get back to your mountaintop and find your happy.

ROADKILL AVALANCHE

Sometimes it's hard to pinpoint exactly when and where the decline started. I think of mine as a slow decay that gained ferocious momentum during the pandemic of 2020, kind of like an avalanche; any given factor, in and of itself, might not be a big deal, but taken all together, the drifts can prove catastrophic. It's an insidious process, and "suddenly" you're in chaos when, in reality, there's nothing sudden about it.

My slide downhill started in the two years prior to 2020. One catalyst after another joined forces to become this demented chorus harmonizing the demise of my happiness—the kind of ominous soundtrack you'd hear in a low-budget slasher movie or *Sharknado.*

Let's start with a brutal romantic breakup in which I allowed my confidence to be fair game for a manipulative, cheating narcissist. I was emotional target practice for someone with unerring and deadly aim. For seven years, no less.

This man was my first significant relationship after my divorce, and he swept me off my feet. This was before I ever heard the term "love bomb." (If you've never heard of that concept, do yourself a favor and google it. You will thank me later!) The first night I met him, he admitted that he cheated on his wife, which led to his divorce. I thought, *How refreshing and vulnerable to own your mistakes and to have grown from them.* I should have realized he was merely telegraphing his punches, as this pattern also continued for most of our relationship.

This shiny new relationship was a welcome respite from the abject loneliness masquerading as a marriage that I had experienced with my ex. I relocated from Arizona to California (where the new boyfriend lived) with the undaunted, romantic optimism of J.Lo in pursuit of my happily ever after.

When we moved to California, my girls were six and seven years old, and I did not take uprooting them lightly. In retrospect, this was part of the reason that I stayed in the relationship far past its expiration date. I could not accept that I had overturned my life and that of my babies for a sham—a lie. To make matters worse, I had consuming guilt over filing for divorce from my previous marriage and not "sticking it out for the kids," so I was determined to be committed to the next relationship and make it work. *Ride or die.* And it was indeed a slow death—of my heart, trust, and confidence. From this relationship, I learned sex addiction was indeed a real thing and not simply the banal excuse of philandering celebrities. To add insult to injury, gaslighting often occurs hand in hand with the behavior, so not only is your body compromised, but your mind is as well. You start to doubt your own reality when faced with constant lies. That part was worse than the physical infidelity itself. After countless months of counseling and group therapy, the only thing that remained was my eroded confidence and blistered self esteem.

After finally ending that relationship—determined to start fresh after my seven years of hard time served—I purchased a new home, a haven in which to heal from the toxicity I'd just escaped. I was resolved to make California work, despite our lackluster origin story.

A week after I closed on the house, I lost my job. New management, a different direction, blah, blah, blah. My safe haven turned into a financial albatross. Single mom with two teenage daughters, no income, and a pricey mortgage with ridiculous California taxes? The Golden State had fully lost its shine, and my happily ever after seemed to be a lost cause.

Yet that was still child's play compared to what was to come.

As I was trying to reinvent myself personally and professionally in the early months of 2020, a new threat appeared on the horizon—one that many of us never saw coming, never even thought possible in today's day and age. As a country, we all became intimately and horrifyingly familiar with the term "coronavirus"—and in April of 2020, I lost my beloved father to the disease.

One could argue it was fortuitous that my dad even lived to the ripe age of eighty, as many do not get that privilege. (There's that comparative suffering crap again.) I *get* the circle of life. Yes, I was a daddy's girl and adored my father, but I realize no one lives forever, and Father Time is keeping tabs. What crushed me was the *way* he passed. He died in the initial, frenzied stages of the pandemic—when questions far outweighed any answers, when we all felt like we were actors in some far-fetched pandemic movie. Hospitalized twice with the virus, my dad went weeks and weeks without seeing a loved one before he passed.

Given that he had Alzheimer's, I imagine this period was even more confusing and terrifying for him. I tortured myself with this thought, seemingly helpless to do anything about it. I would imagine him alone and frightened, not understanding why his family was not there. What was he thinking? *"Where is my wife? Why am I alone? Why is everyone wearing what appears to be hazmat suits? Why can't I see anyone's face?"* The thought of him feeling abandoned, scared, and confused broke me.

As I lived across the country from my East Coast family, the telephone was my lifeline for getting health updates, which were extremely difficult to come by given the triage scenario in hospitals. It was chaos and confusion. Finally, the doctors told us that he was being released given his promising recovery. Relieved and grateful, for the first time in weeks I turned off my ringer and slept that night. I foolishly forgot that the virus was a master at evasion and could take multiple paths to wreak its fatalistic destruction. I woke up to seven missed calls. Instead of being released from the hospital, hospice was on its way instead. It was an emotional whiplash for which I wasn't prepared. That call took me to my knees, and I pretty much stayed there for several months.

I was old enough to know death is a part of life. I'd just never imagined it would unfold this way. My father alone. No one holding his hand.

During that time, my mother was in isolation at an assisted living facility in New Jersey. Whereas my father had difficulty with his cognitive faculties, my mother struggles in the physical realm. A three-time cancer survivor with multiple sclerosis, she requires a wheelchair but is mentally sharper than most people half her age. She was my dad's rock, and he adored her. Prior to my father's hospitalization, my parents had only been separated by a locked door disguised as a bookcase in the Alzheimer's wing, through which she could freely come and go. Now, a virus provided the ultimate and permanent barrier to their togetherness.

As the pandemic was in full swing, all residents at her facility had to take their meals alone in their rooms and were not allowed to receive visitors. My mother had to endure the loss of and grief for her husband of fifty-nine years in total isolation. I will never forget—*ever*—watching my mother's face on Zoom for my father's funeral. The pain and solitude. Typically, the community helps the bereaved to heal, enveloping them in its sympathetic embrace and providing a buffer during the mourning process. Not this time. My mother was alone in her pain. Not one comforting hug. I couldn't wrap my mind around that either. It felt like Stephen King himself had penned the awful surrealism of this moment.

My mother, MiMa, requires special living arrangements to accommodate her electric chariot. After my father passed, I'd fantasize about how I could break her out of assisted Alcatraz and bring her across the country to stay with me. Unfortunately, the distance, as well as the physical configuration of my house— namely, the stairs—made that an impossibility, for which I felt such incredible guilt. In fact, grief and guilt were my constant bedfellows during this time—essentially the shittiest slumber party you could imagine.

USE PAIN AS A STEPPING STONE, NOT A CAMP GROUND.
—ALAN COHEN

In retrospect, there's no doubt that these tragedies were exacerbated by the pandemic's isolating circumstances. I'd experienced loss, pain, and grief before, but I'd always managed to bounce back—often with the alacrity and impunity of a Teflon Don. This time, however, was different. Let's be honest, simply *living* during the pandemic was and continues to be challenging at times. California embraced shutdowns and stay-at-home orders more readily than other areas. My children were schooling from home—not always with success, I might add. And given what happened to my father, I was tangoing a bit with an agoraphobic mindset. Even going to the grocery store seemed like throwing myself into an episode of *Survivor* during those early days.

You don't realize how much you take for granted until it's taken away. Simple joys like hugging, walking next to people, seeing people smile, eating out, and going to the movies, gym, church, library, or concerts were out the window. Even rites of passage were robbed of their glory, including graduations, weddings, birthdays, orientations, ceremonies, and holidays. Yes, we all did our best to improvise and compensate, but there was still a poignant nostalgia for what had been. I recall taking my daughter to her high school freshman orientation in August and lamenting her limited ability to socialize, meet new people, or even see people beyond their masks. Badass goddess that she is, she asserted, "It's okay, Mom. Even with my mask, I'm *really* good at happy eyes."

That comment took my breath away, not only for its sweet optimism but for the harsh realization that I had indeed lost my happy eyes. There was nary a twinkle to be found.

So, yes, whereas I had triumphed over adversity before, this little constellation of challenges took me down—hard. That gradual decline had gained momentum with no guardrails in sight. I lost my security. I lost my solo sobriety. I lost my happiness. I essentially lost myself.

There were a few gains as well. I gained, for example, a staggering income tax debt and took to bed when given the news. Not kidding. Pulled the covers over my head and everything. I also gained twenty pounds thanks to perimenopause, lazy thyroid, the sedentary lifestyle inherent to the pandemic, and plain ole depression. Note to future self: baking isn't the wisest pastime during safer-at-home orders. I gained a rather disturbing chemical dependency, after finding that even the most diligently prescribed MAO inhibitors couldn't breach the firewall of my anxiety and depression.

I was approaching rock bottom—a fact that was further underscored the day I realized I was walking around the house with my head down. I mean literally, not figuratively. Walking. With. My. F*cking. Head. Down. In the privacy of my own home. By myself.

This realization was a rude awakening. I couldn't believe I'd let my circumstances defeat me in the way that they had. I know, I know, it's winning the war that matters most and not any one battle, but it was still shocking. This wasn't how I typically lived my life. I prided myself on taking the road less traveled, burning the ships, and choosing fire in the face of adversity.

IF YOU'RE SEARCHING FOR THAT ONE PERSON WHO WILL CHANGE
YOUR LIFE, TAKE A LOOK IN THE MIRROR.
—UNKNOWN

One day, I looked in the mirror and asked aloud, "Who are you?" I didn't even recognize her. I'm not just talking about the extra twenty pounds, lusterless eyes, or unkempt, wiry eyebrows. I'm talking deep down. *Inside.* Fire-in-the-belly stuff, not belly-be-hanging-over-the-waistband stuff. Where'd she go? I mean, come on. Nobody puts Baby in the corner! And yet, I'd managed to not just put her in the corner but shove her into forced isolation in a super scary, dark, and dingy basement. WTF.

No, really. WTF.

CHOOSING FIRE

I've always loved reading biographical stories of courage and bravery. Such great sources of inspiration, especially when in need of a motivational booyah. I've even used the phrase "burn the ships" as my can-do mantra when faced with obstacles—borrowed from Alexander the Great, undefeated in battle, considered one of the greatest conquerors of his time. His fabled strategy for winning one of his greatest battles was to do just that: burn down the ships. Literally. Upon reaching the impending battle's shores, he ordered all their ships to be burnt down. Retreat and failure were simply not an option. He and his soldiers had to be 100 percent committed and fight like their lives depended on it, because they did. Talk about major cojones. I have long aspired to be like him.

Imagine if we took that scorched-earth, no-turning-back, your-life-depends-on-it approach to every obstacle we encountered with 100 percent commitment, 100 percent of the time, and never half-assing it. Oh, what a wonderful world it would be. I have embraced this philosophy throughout my life—sometimes not always by choice, to be honest.

In my early thirties (think idealistic ingénue with pre-child-bearing hips), I was part of a company startup in an industry riddled with not just five-hundred-pound gorillas but *good ole boy* five-hundred-pound gorillas. This, of course, was many years before any type of #MeToo empowerment or actual repercussions for discriminating, bullying, or just plain shitty behavior in the workplace. The stories I could tell—many in that network would be unemployable by today's standards and professional guardrails.

These men didn't take too kindly to a li'l gal, too big for her britches, trying to play in their schoolyard. In those early salad days, we were frugal by necessity. We ran lean and mean. For one of our first national trade shows, we had an itty-bitty booth simply displaying our products on clothed tables, with no fanfare or chichi effects and surrounded—swallowed really—by the huge trade show exhibits of the five-hundred-pound gorillas replete with stages, seating, and sound systems. It was quintessential David and Goliath, and the only slingshot I had in my possession was my voice.

So, risking a carnival barker persona, I stood on an egg crate without microphone or fanfare and began a motivational rah-rah that rivaled Oprah Winfrey on the famous day she gave away 276 Pontiacs to her studio audience—"*You* get a car! *You* get a car!" In this case, it was our product. Who doesn't love a freebie? We quickly became a gathering hotspot, and the crowd's excited chants echoed throughout the trade show floor. I could only take stage once an hour, as I had to nurse cough drops and spray Chloraseptic down my throat in the interim to soothe my horribly abused vocal cords. I was vying against the loud music blaring from the neighboring sound systems. But I wasn't about to let a little hoarseness and discomfort stop me.

The crowds grew larger and larger in anticipation of my

giveaways—until, a few hours in, I was approached by the trade show general manager. I needed to stop my egg crate jubilees because all the magillas around me were complaining. "And they did pay significantly more for the space, blah, blah, blah. You understand, Beth, right? Great, thanks so much." In other words, thanks for playing, but it's time to cash out and let the big boys play.

Like clockwork, a very large crowd gathered at the top of the hour. Joining them now was the trade show GM and his staff, I guess to make sure I behaved. I didn't know what to do as I took to my crate. My palms sweating and subdued in tone, I informed the crowd of the reprimand by management. I explained how we were upsetting the competition with our boisterous enthusiasm and had to cease and desist from our hour of power get-togethers. The crowd booed their outrage and dissent. I told them that I could either go gently into the night, not make any waves and be a good girl, or I could go out in a ball of fire, consequences be damned.

I paused, briefly looked down, and then fiercely raised my arms in a victory salute and shouted, "I choose *fire!*" Clearly, I lean toward the dramatic, but it *was* an inspired Eva Perón–like moment. As you can imagine, the crowd went bat-shit crazy, the rallying cries of which could be heard throughout the convention center. It. Was. Awesome.

Whether it was our indefatigable spirit, commitment to product quality, or both, that company took off. Fast-forward seven years, and I was now chief brand management officer, not only for our little engine that could—*and did*—but also for the two largest industry gorillas that had formerly been our competition.

My point? I had a history of burning the ships. In fact, I could credit most of my professional and personal triumphs to that mindset. So, what the hell had happened to me? Yes, 2020 had been ripe with heartbreak, but how had I let myself become its roadkill? This wasn't a hill I was willing to die on. I couldn't recognize the girl in the mirror, but she was still in there. Of that much, I was sure. It was time to get back on my feet. It was time to live again.

It was time to once again choose fire.

CAN YOU POINT ME TO THE HAPPINESS AISLE?

Given my liberal arts studies, I was familiar with the law of polarity. I started googling what could potentially be the opposite of clinical depression. I mean, I had to find out. I wanted to go there because I just knew *here* sucked. I was determined to do whatever it took, whatever was recommended, whatever worked to move the needle from rock bottom to mountaintop.

One of the first hits to my frantic search was the term "chronic happiness." Again, WTF. I had a degree in psychology and yet never heard of such a far-fetched quixotic notion. Was that a thing? Was there a psychological paradise lost from which I'd banished myself? I started reading, googling, reading, googling. I was like a possessed Alice going down the keyboard rabbit hole in pursuit of my own wonderland—shopping for happiness.

WHEN YOU HAVE EXHAUSTED ALL POSSIBILITIES,
REMEMBER THIS—YOU HAVEN'T.
—THOMAS EDISON

Many references to chronic happiness are about being happy despite some sort of condition—a chronic illness, aging, etc. That wasn't the context I was seeking. I wasn't interested in finding happiness in response to something challenging; my original quest had morphed into something bigger than the moment. I wanted to peel back the onion even further and transcend circumstance. I was interested in happiness just for the sake of happiness, in its purest form.

I love, love, love the smell of babies. I know I'm not the only one—but I'm obsessed. When my girls were tiny, I loved to inhale my little swaddled burritos of joy. They were so pure, so unsullied by anything. If purity had a fragrance, it would be that of a newborn. Maybe that's why I always wore Love's Baby Soft perfume as a young teen, so that I could exude that baby-fresh scent for as long as possible. I was interested in *that* type of happiness. Pure. Unadulterated. A baby-soft kind of bliss.

And I wanted to know, once I'd grabbed hold of that happiness, how I could encourage it to grow. If my depression could grow to Incredible Hulk–like proportions, surely I could do the same with my happiness—and do so with intention. I'm talking committing, 100 percent, to the practice of being happy AF.

I needed to fast-track this road to redemption for many reasons: to be the best mother and role model for my daughters; to love myself as much as I loved them; to be about others; to fit into my jeans; to once again dance in my kitchen.

It was time to get at it, 2020 be damned.

POSITIVELY PSYCHO TO
POSITIVE PSYCHOLOGY

Much of historical psychology is rooted in disease, pathology, and treatment, often through a negative lens. As such, there is a plethora of naysayers, scholars, and research studies that eschew a deliberate pursuit of happiness. According to these researchers, happiness is largely determined by genetics, circumstance, or, even worse, chance. Too bad, so sad, right?

We then have the opposite faction, firmly grounded in fairy dust and drinking a bit too much from the woo-woo fountain: "Believe, and it will be." I wish I could insert my favorite eye-roll emoji here as that little guy can emanate more disdain than the most cutting prose. Clearly, my analytical nature can't take this Fisher-Price type of happiness theory either; I'm more of a moderate.

This is what I do believe: Nothing is possible without faith.

My ex-husband, baby daddy, and purveyor of a new wife I like even better than him has a favorite Bible verse that he has ingrained in those around him: "Faith is the substance of things hoped for, the evidence of things not seen." I love that. For me, it's not merely statistical data but also the substance of things not seen—*the possibility of yet*—that guides my happiness journey. A balance of science and belief. Make no mistake, any strategy suggested herein is grounded in research, but don't discount the power of your beliefs. As the saying goes, "Whether you think you can or think you can't, you're right." I would encourage you to "be right" about things that serve you. If you believe that intentional practices will help your happiness flex, then you're already halfway there.

≥\\//≤

EVERY EXPERIENCE, NO MATTER HOW BAD IT SEEMS, HOLDS
WITHIN IT A BLESSING OF SOME KIND. THE GOAL IS TO FIND IT.
—UNKNOWN

Thankfully, there was a welcome perspective shift in the late 1990s when positive psychology was introduced into the professional vernacular. [1] This school of thought encourages a focus on flourishing human function and not simply the treatment of pathology: to improve and not just repair, making good even better in pursuit of our best life. A slew of studies emerged from this psychological theory that offers hope and statistical support that happiness isn't merely random or predetermined. Seek and you shall find, right? Hallelujah! Suddenly, optimal human functioning was given a seat at the table.

What you focus on grows. Since my quest was about being happy AF, I decided I would play exclusively in the schoolyard of optimism and possibility. I drank from the fire hydrant of positive psychology and voraciously read articles, research papers, and books on the topic. Much of it was stuff I already knew—but I desperately needed a refresher course. A grief/depression/anxiety spiral can do that to you. It can make you forget everything you know to be true. I needed to remind myself that I was a queen and to straighten my f*cking crown.

For me, happy was now a verb, and I was going to verb the shit out of it. But there would be no crystal-froufrou ideology for me; I needed my happiness pursuit to be grounded in data and science. Luckily, modern positive psychology has produced compelling research on the efficacy of happiness pursuits, and I immersed myself in this work. Researchers determined that three primary factors affect chronic happiness levels, and only 10 percent of happiness is determined by external circumstances.

[2] Genetics (50 percent) and intentional activities (40 percent) make up the primary pieces of the pie.

This was a very powerful revelation for me. It suggests that *intentional* activities offer the most promising means to increase and sustain levels of happiness. Intentional activities underscore choice! My happiness isn't a helpless leaf subject to the capricious and often cruel winds of fate. It can be tethered to a tree of intention—of choice. Will, meet Way. How awesome is that? We get to *choose* happiness.

And I was ready to do just that.

CALL ME GRETCHEN

I'm sure most of you are familiar with Edvard Munch's expressionist work of art entitled *The Scream*. It's his homage to the desolate anxiety inherent to the human condition. Apparently, he was strolling with friends at sunset and experienced an overwhelming sense of anxiety and exhaustion. As the sky turned blood red in its glorious farewell salute to the day, he "sensed an infinite scream passing through nature." [3] That moment inspired and materialized itself into this eponymous icon of modern art. Such a profound description, right? Honestly, could any other artistic expression better embody 2020 than that? *Not even close.*

Ironically enough, it was my euphemistic scream that gave voice to the words you are now reading. Kinda cool, huh? "F*ck you, 2020" were the first words I typed. My middle school English teachers would be outraged, I'm sure, their rulers primed to rap my knuckles once again. But I like to consider myself the Helen of Troy of witty, practical wisdom. Hers was the face that launched a thousand ships; my "F*ck you" was the expletive that launched a thousand (okay, more than a thousand) words.

For some reason, recounting my journey from roadkill to redemption was important. I wanted to share the simple strategies that helped me escape from rock bottom. And once I started, the words poured from what felt like the floodgates of my soul. Corny, perhaps, but gutting yourself in black-and-white print can be even more harrowing than having lived it in Technicolor. Unsure where it was heading, I was willing to let the words lead.

One fine day, I was engaged in the never-ending job of chauffeuring my daughters. As I was carting my youngest somewhere and talking about something that I'm sure was *very* interesting, she interrupted me and said, "Mom, don't be such a Gretchen Weiners."

What? Since I couldn't take my eyes from the road and eviscerate her with a scathing glance, I replied, "I beg your pardon?"

"You know, Gretchen Weiners from *Mean Girls*. She knows everything about everyone. That's why her hair is so big. It's full of secrets."

Again, *what*?

"She pathetically tried to make 'that's so fetch' a thing—a new slang phrase. Stop trying to make fetch happen, Mom."

Umm, okay. In a not-so-subtle way, my fourteen-year-old was throwing some heavy shade my way.

I love and respect my daughters. Their fervent fight for inclusivity, activism, and enlightened perspective inspires and truly humbles me. They're my raison d'être and best accountability buddies ever. But that does not preclude me from seeing them exactly as they are in those occasionally less-than-perfect moments when their impassioned beliefs strangle polite discourse—when their self-righteous smugness and "OK Boomer" derision for anyone over twenty rears its ugly little head. It's *totally* annoying, especially since I'm the one who finances their hallowed little existences.

And furthermore, I was not about to have my fourteen-year-old Regina George me. I mean, *come on*. I saw *Mean Girls* before she was even born.

Ironically though, I rather did like the idea of championing a "happiness" happening—a crusade for hope. Was that so far-*fetched*? (Wink, wink or eye roll, your choice.) In that very moment, I decided that chronic happiness was going to be my magnum opus. I was determined to have something good come from 2020—to build a thriving lemonade stand on the foundations of the life lessons it had slapped me with.

And with that, my friends, the idea for this book was officially born, dropped by a snarky stork shapeshifting as my precocious teen. This inspired moment had the unshaven hair on my legs standing at full attention (in defense, your honor, grooming took a bit of a hit during the pandemic). I swear I could hear Beethoven's "Ode to Joy" in the background soundtrack of my mind—the motivational montage which morphed into a super mash-up with *Rocky*'s theme song "Gonna Fly Now." A John Mc-Clane meets Rocky Balboa surge of inspiration—it was fire.

$$\gtrless\!\backslash\!\big\vert\!/\!\lesssim$$

YOU ARE ALLOWED TO BE BOTH A MASTERPIECE AND A WORK IN PROGRESS, SIMULTANEOUSLY.
—SOPHIA BUSH

The common usage of chronic is "persistent, constantly recurring," most often in reference to an illness or something negative. I wanted this beleaguered little word to gain secondary fame as a ceaseless marathon of ooey-gooey awesomeness. In my Shangri-La of slang, chronic happiness came to refer to the constant state of play—i.e., specific habits, strategies, and mindset that keep you rooted in happiness.

Interestingly enough, I discovered during my research that "chronic" was also slang for good marijuana. Apparently, Snoop and Dre birthed the malapropism when partaking in some extraordinary hydro*ponic* variety. Well, I wasn't going to let that deter me in my quest for having chronic happiness *happen*. At least in their lexical usage, it means *really, really good* weed. And Snoop *is* dope. And apparently, I *am* Gretchen.

So, let's be hope dealers.

QUITTER TWITTER

As often the case with any vast undertaking (e.g., writing a book), the devil's advocate will not miss an opportunity to hiss in your ear all the doubts, fears, and fateful what-ifs in hopes of curtailing your endeavor. I mean: *Who are you anyway for anyone to even care about what you may have to say?* Bear in mind, this was a mere sampling of the lovely words of discouragement as slights to my abilities, body (particularly my ass), creativity, lovability, age, mothering, etc., were also part of the diatribe. My inner critic is incredibly thorough, I'll give her that.

$\geq\!\!\backslash\!\!\backslash\!\!/\!\!/\!\!_\angle$

NEVER GIVE UP, FOR THAT IS JUST THE PLACE AND TIME THAT THE
TIDE WILL TURN.
—HARRIET BEECHER STOWE

After spending an entire evening of wallowing in a soup of this relentless self-doubt—sprinkled with some wily hormones—I awoke the next morning feeling rather discouraged and ready to abandon ship. As I was mindlessly scrolling Instagram to numb out and self-soothe (not a recommended coping mechanism, by the way), a quote from Brené Brown popped up in my feed. Given that I was already a huge fan and had read several of her books, I instantly stopped mid-thumbing to read: "One day you will tell your story of how you overcame what you went through and it will be someone else's survival guide."

This was such a beautiful notion of paying it forward, removing any grandiose inklings of ego from the equation and instead focusing on what someone else may possibly gain from my story. It rendered the idea purposeful and far beyond any bossy autobiographical trope. I don't believe in coincidences—never have. I believe I was meant to read those very words at that very moment and was being prodded to continue forward with my dream. So, I did.

Every single happiness habit I've adopted since beginning this journey is backed by clinical research. Its efficacy is irrefutable. None of it is rocket science, yet it's one thing to know it and quite another thing to put it into practice—thus why New Year's resolutions quickly peter out by the end of January. You know why the road to hell is paved with good intentions? Because *intentions* are diddly-squat. *They mean nothing without action.* If you merely read all the strategies herein and never put them into play in your life, you've wasted your money and your time. Keep doing what you're doing, and you'll keep getting what you're getting.

Trust me. I didn't always want to make the changes I needed to make either. So, if that's where you are, I get it. Sometimes you really do have to fake it till you make it. There were days that I really, really had to grasp at things to put in my gratitude journal—it was a stretch. There were days I'd rather have been numbing with wine and sea-salt kettle chips than taking a walk outside or nourishing my body with whole foods. There were days I wanted to binge on Netflix under the covers instead of focusing on goals or a vision board. And sometimes it felt inauthentic. *Until it didn't.* Much like the descent into depression, the climb back up the mountain doesn't happen in the blink of an eye. It's a process. It's one foot in front of the other. Step by step. When suddenly, before you know it, the horizon comes into view.

And when it does, it's glorious.

SELF-HELP VS. SELF-HOPE

I adore words—the inherent beauty of language. Always have. As a child, I remember clocking six Nancy Drew books in one day. Books were the magical flying carpet ride for my imagination, hopes, and dreams. When I was in college, I worked part-time at a bookstore because of this love. During those halcyon days, I recall the droves of people who came into the store and headed straight for the self-help section located near the back.

I have a love/hate relationship with the term "self-help"—not because of the practice, mind you, but rather the stigma associated with the term. And I resent that stigma, to be quite honest. In my humble opinion, the stigma is propagated by small-minded cynics whose misguided superiority and lack of self-awareness will ultimately be their folly. They spew their derision toward any type of transformational theory through whatever bullshit platform that offers the loudest, jeering bullhorn.

When I see someone in the self-help section of a bookstore, I feel an instant kinship to them. I respect the fact that these individuals are not only open to optimizing their mind, body, or soul, but actively seeking it. I absolutely believe in the power of improvement, empowerment, and transformation, in seeking these for oneself, in *doing the work*. Studies suggest that people with favorable views of self-help books report greater life happiness. [4] And that's what we're here for—to be happy AF. So, while I may not like the vilified stigma of self-help, I realize this book falls under that umbrella. Do I wish we could rebrand the genre? Hell, yes. Something more along the lines of personal mastery, empowerment, or development, with the emphasis being strength as opposed to weakness—because isn't self-help really just self-hope put into action?

If you're sick, you go to a hospital. If you're injured, you go to rehabilitation. If you want to optimize, you go to a training/retreat. This book is essentially a rehabilitative training manual for the spirit and soul. It's an integrated model grounded in science to whip your mental ass and mojo back into shape—a modern-day parable in which you're provided with guideposts for your happiness journey. It's storytelling laced with contextual how-tos, all backed by clinical research. Because that's how we learn, really—through stories. Hopefully, you will laugh, relate, empathize, roll your eyes and, most importantly, come to realize that the quest for chronic happiness is attainable. It's not a place; it's a state of being.

So, who's this book for, you ask? This book is for anyone who's been knocked down. Who's lost their way. Who's had their ass kicked. It's also for anyone who simply wants to better themselves. Who wants to be happier. Who wants to up their game. Who loves mountaintops. Because, honestly, who the f*ck doesn't want to be happier?

We do this dance only once. Let's master the steps and boogie our asses off.

Just sayin'.

ROAD TRIP, ANYONE?

If you're like me, you like to plan out your trips so that you know what to expect along the way—to ensure that you stop at the most important landmarks and truly maximize the trip.

This journey will be no different. No flying by the seat of our pants here; we'll save that for Vegas trips and tequila shots. Being happy AF—and getting there in a reasonably efficient way—requires a predetermined roadmap.

So, what are the cool stops along the way? Think mind, body, and soul connection, as this is a holistic road trip. Otherwise, it's like going to the gym and only working out one arm. We've got to take on the total package—from head to toe, from EQ (emotional quotient) to IQ (intelligence quotient), and everything in between. Each stop is necessary. Take in the beauty of each one—no drive-bys.

MIND

- THOUGHTS: think, thank, thunk

- NEUROPLASTICITY: the brain's bionic superpower

- RESILIENCE: bounce, baby, bounce

- OPTIMISM: perception is everything

BODY

- DAILY HABITS: stepping stones to greatness

- STRESS RELIEVERS: happy endings all day long

- PHYSICAL HEALTH: if you ain't got it, you ain't got nothing

SOUL

- GRATITUDE/VISION: giving thanks for the here and now and the power of yet

- FAITH: your heart, not head, is in the clouds

- KINDNESS: random or purposeful acts; it's all good for the soul

- FOCUSING OUT: when in doubt

The chapters to come will build upon themselves, starting with the very foundational and moving up the esoteric ladder. The bullet points we've just run through are merely topical references as to what to expect, not necessarily when to expect it. For example, I consider gratitude a core building block for happiness, and that will be addressed early on.

At each chapter's end, there is a "happiness check." It consists of three tiers: a stretch, a challenge, and a double-dog-dare-ya. For each one, the most important question of all to ask yourself is, *Do I feel happy?*

Well, do ya? If not, don't wuss out, okay? We're crossing this finish line together. This journey is about being 100 percent committed to being happy AF. Nothing less. You'll get out of it only as much as you put in.

I've done my part. Are you ready to do yours?

CHAPTER ONE

The Art of Letting Go, Bouncing Back, and Being

> DO OR DO NOT.
> THERE IS NO TRY.
> —YODA

The concept of *tabula rasa* (clean slate) has been the subject of philosophical discussions from Aristotle and St. Thomas Aquinas to John Locke and Freud. According to this theory, the mind is a blank slate at birth without preconceived notions, ideas, or biases. We begin full of possibility, with nary a scar to mar our smooth surface.

After years of walking this earth, however, it's doubtful that your canvas is still blank or pristine. Chances are it is filled with a lotta crap—some good, some bad, some serving no purpose whatsoever. On a scale of one to ten, how would you rate your own slate at this point? Is it a field of dreams or a haystack of horrors?

In my favorite movie/life analogy, *Field of Dreams*, Ray has a vision of a baseball diamond while walking through the cornfields on his farm. To realize this vision, he must destroy part of his crops. He doesn't get rid of something bad; it is part of his livelihood. In fact, he risks financial ruin and ridicule to make space for this possibility. In daring to follow his vision, his dreams come true in more ways than one. It takes a certain type of bravery to let go of something fine or good enough to make room for the possibility of something great. It's a bird-in-hand mentality; we tend to hold on to things with a clenched fist whether they serve us or not.

Other times, the obstacles to our dreams are not benign cornfields but rather malignant, thorny vines. Either way, sometimes we must burn it all down before we can see the glorious vistas of what could be—before we can rebuild. That's kinda how I felt about 2020. My landscape was so riddled with cracks and holes—think Old Testament–style devastation—that I was constantly playing emotional whack-a-mole. And that kept me so busy that no matter how hard I tried, things only fell into further disrepair.

It was time to embrace "Burning Down the House" as my anthem and call-to-arms. I was ready to choose fire and get back to living my best life, but first I had to make space for that possibility. I had to get rid of anything that was holding me back or that wasn't serving me.

I had to Marie Kondo my life.

What's holding you back? Fear of failure? Money? Time? Unworthiness? Lack of confidence? What do you need to burn down to build back better?

In my case, I had to rid myself of all the negative thoughts and beliefs of self-doubt that I had been feeding myself. It was a starvation diet for healthy self-esteem. But that negativity of mine didn't go quietly. Having to feed on itself, it had morphed into fear of failure. Yes, I had been part of a successful start-up, followed by a lucrative acquisition, but what if that had been a fluke? Maybe I was a one-hit-wonder, and it was all a downhill luge from here. If I tried again and failed, it would be proof that I suck. Self-limiting beliefs are rarely relegated to only one aspect of your life. They are pervasive and wreak insidious havoc everywhere—career, relationships, family. Nothing is off-limits.

EVERYTHING YOU WANT IS ON THE OTHER SIDE OF FEAR.
—JACK CANFIELD

Fear really is the longest distance between you and everything you want. The answer? *Go the distance.* I actually whispered that while I typed it, trying to access the *Field of Dreams* juju on your behalf. (You're welcome.)

I needed to burn my fear the f*ck down. And fast.

LET GO OR BE DRAGGED

Do you remember that Halloween when all you saw were little Elsas everywhere? The little blue gossamer gown and blond braided wig? It was like an Elsa apocalypse. Not surprising, considering *Frozen* garnered $1.28 billion in sales between 2013 and 2014. [1] "Let It Go" won the Oscar for best original song, and little girls adopted it as their anthem.

I was conflicted about that song, to be honest. On the one hand, I was thankful that Disney heroines had moved beyond the "Some Day My Prince Will Come" lament. On the other hand, Elsa's let-it-go proclamation had a bit of a gnarly undertone. I applauded the letting go of expectations to be true to your authentic self, but did that freedom require forced isolation in an ice palace? How was that winning?

After doing my homework, I get it.

The Harvard Study of Adult Development, one of the longest-running studies on happiness, has been following 724 participants since 1938. [2] In that time, researchers have found that certain personality traits are associated with increased levels of happiness as participants aged. Letting go is one of those hallmark characteristics. Not shocking, right? At some point, we've all struggled with letting go—whether that be a relationship, dream, habit, guilt, forgiveness, way of thinking, or grief over the loss of a loved one.

IN THE PROCESS OF LETTING GO, YOU WILL LOSE MANY THINGS
FROM THE PAST, BUT YOU WILL FIND YOURSELF.
—DEEPAK CHOPRA

The boogeyman of fear makes letting go difficult. The unknown is well, *not known*, and some perceive that as a black hole of nothingness instead of a white space of possibility. It's almost easier to hold on to the devil you know. When channeling your inner Marie Kondo, letting go is integral to making space. It's okay to grieve whatever you're letting go of. I'm not suggesting you turn into a calculating narcissist without emotion. I would then have to date you (cue in canned TV audience laugh track; and don't worry—that dating pattern was at the top of my *Shit That's Gotta Go* list!). Seriously, grieving is part of letting go. It's comparable to Elisabeth Kübler-Ross's grief model in her studies on death and dying. [3] You often need to go through similar stages (denial, anger, bargaining, depression) before you can reach the stage of acceptance, which is your springboard to freedom. Think *Sound of Music*, spinning-with-your-arms-out-stretched-amidst-the-majestic-mountains type of freedom.

If the superpower of acceptance and its resulting freedom aren't incentive enough, I'm happy to negatively condition you as well. The longer you hold on to negative affect and let it linger, physical health and functioning suffer. Your immune system. Your cardiovascular system. Your digestive system. Chronic stress accelerates aging and is associated with premature death. [4] It's a fact.

Want to be healthier? Want to live a full life? Let whatever you're clinging to the f*ck go.

I get it. *I really do.* It's hard to let go—to give up that perceived control. Hi, my name is Beth, and I'm a controller. I'm reformed, but that inner dominatrix is always lurking beneath the surface if I'm not vigilant. Even the thought of not having control could put me into a tailspin. But that's the thing about control: it's an illusion.

Monitoring my cheating boyfriend on Find My Friends or constantly checking his call log was an absolute exercise in futility. I thought I had control over the situation when, in fact, it was controlling me—nay, consuming me. Being an internet and smartphone sleuth became my side hustle—an exhausting one at that. I couldn't control what he did—or *who* he did, for that matter. Letting go of that relationship took more than one do-si-do through those stages of grief, but on the other side of acceptance was exhilarating freedom. Sure, the sex may have taken my breath away (insert green vomiting emoji repeatedly), but now I can actually *breathe* again. Talk about waiting to exhale. I forgot what that felt like. Oxygen is the best "big O" out there; don't let anyone tell you otherwise.

My advice? Keep an *Oh-Hell-No* litmus test handy. For me, my two beautiful daughters became the ultimate litmus test for my own life. I would imagine what my advice would be if they were ever in similar situations as young adults. If *Oh-Hell-No* immediately comes to mind, then it's not okay for you, either. No do-as-I-say-not-as-I-do bullshit. It's an effective account-ability exercise. In a perfect world, I love and respect myself enough not to have to play the *Freaky Friday* mind swap to find my truth. I'm developing that muscle (so can you), but it's still a viable fallback when in doubt. If you wouldn't recommend something for your BFF, grown child, or loved ones, then it should be off-limits to you as well. Healthy choices are a two-way street.

Take inventory of your life, and identify what's gotta go. For many, it's the resulting space left behind that scares them into stuck submission. Rather than viewing it as a gaping hole of nothingness, embrace your tabula rasa. View it as potential and not a penalty. What would you like to put in its place? Write it all out—whatever that new masterpiece may be (partner, career, life change)—in detail. Be as specific as you can. It's incredibly beneficial. (FYI, the power of "vision" is explored in greater detail in Chapter 4, as it deserves a spot of honor in your primetime lineup.)

Focus on what you can control: your attitude; your daily habits—diet, exercise, etc. Keep them healthy. Don't underesti-mate the healing effects of gratitude. Focus on what you do have and give thanks for it. Gratitude is a total game-changer. Fall into the warm, supporting embrace of family and friends. A support system will help buoy you through the waves of grief.

My friends are the 911 on my emotional speed dial. One of my dearest friends, Sione, is my break-in-case-of-emergency friend. I can call him any time of the day or night, and he'd be there. No questions asked. He's saved me from a night of crying into my pillow more than a few times.

Stop being a martyr thinking you must face it all alone. There's nothing more beautiful than being lifted by the love of family and friends. It reminds you of what you do have and mitigates the sting of letting go.

> WHEN I LET GO OF WHAT I AM, I BECOME WHAT I MIGHT BE.
> WHEN I LET GO OF WHAT I HAVE, I RECEIVE WHAT I NEED.
> —UNKNOWN

Another effective letting-go strategy is to reframe the scenario. Shame and guilt are prisons of your own making and prevent you from moving forward, so rewrite the script on that failed pilot. Recreate the narrative through more compassionate eyes toward yourself and others. Forgive yourself and anyone else who needs a prison pardon. Forgiving my monogamously challenged ex was an extraordinary (with a capital "E") challenge, not gonna sugarcoat it. I had to view him through a totally different lens. Not as a tormentor, purveyor of pain, or total POS. My beloved brothers have a go-to phrase for my exes—"F*ck him. He was trash."—purloined from the movie *Jagged Edge*. (Gotta love protective brothers. I'm like a Jan, bookended between two hulks of righteous retribution. *It's awesome.*) But someone's trash can be another's treasure, right? Perspective is everything. I had to view my ex as a treasured child of God, wounded, vulnerable, a work in progress. *Just like me.* I had to go through several pairs of rose-colored glasses to get there, trust me, but it was worth it.

Forgiveness really is the gift that gives back.

Letting go as an actual ritual also can be a powerful experience. Years ago, my friends and I had a burn party where we pitched our major let-it-go items straight into a bonfire. I threw in my divorce papers. It was liberating. We totally disco-infernoed our way to a happier space that night.

Stay in the moment. Get your ass out of the past. Only ghosts live there, and they will haunt the crap out of you if you let them. Practice mindfulness. Take a walk. Notice your surroundings—like through a child's eyes. Even simple appreciation (not just gratitude) is associated with greater life satisfaction.

The technical term for this kind of appreciation is "savoring," and studies have found it positively associated with high self-esteem, resilience, happiness, and life satisfaction. [5] Savoring has also been shown to improve depressive symptoms and anxiety. Why then waste the skill on only food? If you can savor your favorite pizza, how about trying a moment or two?

Children are masters at savoring everything. Watch and relearn. As adults, we're so rushed trying to get a thousand things accomplished that we barely register our experiences, let alone savor them. Savoring requires slowing down and just being in it.

One evening, my youngest asked me to come snuggle in bed with her. She had redecorated her room and was enjoying the fruits of her labor. We're talking a Pete Davidson/John Mulaney poster, a candle, and a pride flag. Simple treasures are sometimes the happiest. She wanted me to lay there with her and just be in it. After about ten minutes, she said, "I'm so 100 percent happy right now. I wish I could bake this moment into a cookie, so I could take it out and eat it later when I'm feeling sad."

I mean, *can you even?* My. Heart. Exploded. It was the personification of savor at its finest.

My mother-in-law is the queen of savoring. (Yes, she's

technically my ex-mother-in-law, but I'm keeping her.) She has the uncanny ability to find joy and beauty in the smallest of things—a flower, a bird, a rain shower. She takes the time to take it all in. She views the ordinary through the lens of the extraordinary. All the time. It's like her superpower. And it shows in her face. Her smile. Like you want a puff of whatever she's smoking. Next to her faith, it's her greatest gift.

Savor. Even the word itself is cool. Do more of it.

If your letting-go space feels a little empty, fill it with some cool new stuff. Learn a new skill. I learned how to make homemade pasta. Not only did I do my heritage proud, but you have no idea how therapeutic pounding the shit out of dough can be. I kneaded my way to a happier self and became a culinary legend in my kids' eyes to boot. Take on a hobby. Go to a museum. Journal. Join a group of peers with shared interests and hobbies. Go on a bike ride. It doesn't have to be complicated. It was in one of those gaps that I found yoga. Seriously life-changing.

Stay the course and trust the process. Initially, the unknown may be a bit scary, but letting go creates the space you need to realize your dreams.

Go the distance.

ENTER THE GROWTH ZONE

What false security blankets are you clutching in your comfort zone, not realizing that they're dead weights holding you down? Gotta let these go, too, Linus.

I always found the term "comfort zone" so ironic. What the hell is comforting about mediocrity? The term was popularized in the '90s as a behavioral state, virtually free of risk and anxiety, that enables steady albeit not necessarily spectacular performance. [6] There's little incentive to reach higher, and it's safer not to. Entrepreneurs do not live in the comfort zone. Neither should you. I'm not telling you to go all Mark Cuban on me (*wouldn't that be amazing?*), but we can always reach higher to achieve our God-given potential.

IF YOU AIM AT NOTHING, YOU WILL HIT IT EVERY TIME.
—ZIG ZIGLAR

When we step out of the comfort zone, we pass through the fear and learning zones until finally reaching the Emerald City of the growth zone. [7] In these concentric circles, the fear zone is much smaller than the learning and growth zones, yet it's the hardest to traverse because of its uncertainty. That's how much we hate the unknown. Scholars theorize that "fear of the unknown" is the mothership and foundation of all fears. [8] It keeps us rooted in place despite better things being just around the corner.

I saw a funny meme a few years back that stated, "Why? Because I'm stardust. I do epic, cosmic shit. That's why." It so tickled me, I told my girls they had to start calling me Stardust—in the privacy of our own home, of course, because it sounded like a stripper name. They decided they, too, wanted cool cosmic names and were duly christened Moonbeam and Rainbow. We had bracelets made with our celestial monikers to remind ourselves that we're badasses who shoot for the moon. Nothing was going to hold us back. Embrace your epic, cosmic shit, move through the fear zone, and, as Les Brown so beautifully put it, "land among the stars." You can either stargaze from the fear zone or twinkle and sparkle in the growth zone. Bystander or go-getter; you get to decide. Me? I prefer to sparkle in all my stripper glory.

While you'll face challenges in the learning zone, you also acquire and hone new skills. You stretch, throw your neurons into an aerobics class, and learn, which is the golden ticket to the growth zone. This is where the magic happens: *purpose, dreams, actualization.*

Word of caution—the growth zone means nothing unless you put it into action. Unused, it's like buried treasure: rich in beauty but never seeing the light of day. I once listened to a radio show, and the pastor said something that stuck with me: cemeteries are our greatest source of buried treasure and unfound wealth. "Buried in the ground," he explained, "are businesses that were never formed, songs that were never sung, books that were never written, potential that was never realized, and dreams that never came to pass." [9] Ouch. How sad is that?

Listening to this pastor talk, I knew I didn't want to be buried one day still carrying around galaxies of unrealized potential inside me. I was going to leave it all on the field—give it everything I've got so there wouldn't be a single coulda, woulda, or shoulda at the end of my story. I plan to say, "I gave it absolutely everything. I didn't waste a single drop," as I dance through the pearly gates and straight into my dad's bear hug.

Conserve water. Conserve the rainforest. Conserve the climate. For the love of God, do not conserve your talents, treasures, and gifts. Use everything given to you. It was given for a reason.

BE A WEEBLE

When we were little, my brother and I had these awesome playsets called Weebles. These little roly-poly, egg-shaped characters would come in multiple settings, yielding hours of endless entertainment. I can still hear the jingle in my mind, "Weebles wobble, but they don't fall down." I would sit there and determinedly knock them over time after time, and they would always bounce right back up.

You see the metaphor coming here, right?

Embrace your inner Weeble. There will be missteps and slip-ups on the road back up the mountain. When you stumble, just get back up and keep on keepin' on. No need to despair over your footwork.

IF YOU CAN'T FLY THEN RUN, IF YOU CAN'T RUN THEN WALK,
IF YOU CAN'T WALK THEN CRAWL, BUT WHATEVER YOU DO
YOU HAVE TO KEEP MOVING FORWARD.
—MARTIN LUTHER KING JR.

Take baby steps. Be inspired by toddler temerity. A recent study found that during free play, toddlers fall seventeen times an hour. [10] New walkers fall sixty-nine times an hour. I experienced this firsthand with my little ones. And they were born a mere thirteen months apart, so I had toddlers falling everywhere. I had my house professionally baby-proofed and even went so far as to google little Evel Knievel–like helmets. (I didn't buy them in the end, but I did legit research them given my girls' constant kamikaze missions.) What I realized later is that there's such a profound lesson in infant locomotion. Toddlers realize what we, as adults, often forget: *you will not be able to walk, let alone run, unless you are willing to fall.*

There will be stumbles in this happiness journey. Expect them and acknowledge that these blips are part of the ultimate beauty. Forgive yourself and forge on. Remember that every setback is a setup for an even more remarkable comeback! When framed as such, it makes the recovery cha-cha part of a more significant, beautiful dance.

As I two-stepped my way toward happiness, I experienced several setbacks despite my determination. One particularly glorious one involved simply getting my mail—something I avoided doing for a full seven weeks, at which point the accumulated avalanche of bills crushed my avoidance ass into oblivion.

My brilliant solution to the problem was to down five Krispy Kremes and an entire bottle of chardonnay. Essentially, I chose to avoid my avoidance further. How do you think that worked out for me? The moral hangover the next day rivaled that of the physical. I had managed to kick myself even harder while I was down. That is often what these "feel good in the moment" coping mechanisms are—a false panacea, a wolf in lamb's clothing or, in my case, a bottled vintage from Napa masquerading as a temporary respite from anxiety and depression. I woke up in night sweats (hormones and alcohol do not mix), with a crushing headache, sandpaper for a tongue, and a gluten bloat portending the necessity for stretchy leggings. Oh, and all those tear-stained bills were still there lying in wait.

I laid there discouraged and quite puffy. Of course, the sniping symphony of self-loathing was in full force. Same old lyrics—you're pathetic, you're weak, you're a loser, *yada, yada, yada*. We've all been there. These are your moments of reckoning.

You need to immediately flip the script. This isn't the time to languish. So, I didn't. I fought the overwhelming urge to go back to bed and wallow in my learned helplessness. I told my inner critic to shut the hell up, and I started opening that mail.

There will be more than enough haters in your life willing to attempt an emotional coup on your behalf. You *must* be your own cheerleader and party-of-one stadium wave. Sometimes, charity really does begin at home.

COURAGE DOESN'T ALWAYS ROAR. SOMETIMES COURAGE IS THE LITTLE VOICE AT THE END OF THE DAY THAT SAYS I'LL TRY AGAIN TOMORROW.
—MARY ANNE RADMACHER

You slipped up. It happened. Move on. Martin Luther wisely wrote, "You cannot keep birds from flying over your head, but you can keep them from building a nest in your hair." So, save the wallowing for your triumphs, unexpected wins, and moments of happiness. Comb your hair (*no bird gonna nest here, mutha-fuckaaaaa*). Brush your teeth. Smile at yourself in the mirror. Shower.

Speaking of showering: after my dad's passing, I realized I was more vested in my puppy's grooming than my own. I rationalized I was saving water by wearing the same clothing twice or three times. Umm, in a row. I hate doing laundry, so saving the planet through water conservation seemed like a noble pursuit. I was letting my skin "breathe" by never wearing makeup. I was giving my highlighted hair a "rest" by not styling it. On more than one occasion, I had to ask myself if I brushed my teeth that day. *Blech.*

For all my fellow soap-challenged folks out there, here's some food for thought: water bathing, aka hydrotherapy, has been shown to decrease cortisol, balance serotonin, improve mood, and boost immunity. [11] So, rub-a-dub-dub for happiness, mental well-being, and, quite frankly, if you ever wanna have sex again.

Another way to boost your good feels is to *move*. Movement is the bane of stagnation. Psych yourself up with music. It works. (Try staying mopey while listening to Pharrell Williams's "Happy"; it takes some serious sad-face commitment!) Create an upbeat mix for your life's soundtrack. Easier yet, tell Alexa to play songs from the '70s, '80s, and '90s or whatever musical genre that is your motivational call-to-arms. I created a playlist and titled it "Happy." (Remember, we are verbing happy, so don't roll your eyes at me.) I listened to it every day while writing this book and often broke into dance. Added bonus: the unabashed cringey-ness of it would annoy the crap out of my kids. It was the gift that kept on giving.

Scientific studies provide backup support for the beneficial power of music. Since 2006, two UCF professors, neuroscientist Kiminobu Sugaya and violinist Ayako Yonetani, have offered the popular class, Music and the Brain, which, as you can guess, explores the effects of music on brain function. Music has been shown to reduce stress and depression while improving mood, cognitive skills, memory, and health. [12] According to Sugaya, music also increases dopamine release in a specific part of the brain, similar to that of illegal drugs. It's like a cerebral Woodstock, only with musical rather than chemical stimulants (and better hygiene).

In other words, it's time to tune into a happier you. Next to showering, it's one of the easiest things you can do to give yourself an immediate pick-me-up. (Disclaimer: please do not emotionally "cut" with music, as that defeats the purpose. Point in fact—when I was going through my divorce, an acquaintance once suggested I listen to this new vocal artist, Adele. "She will sing your pain," he advised. Well, he was right. I'm obsessed with Adele and find her talent astonishing, but repeatedly playing "Someone Like You" while sitting in the dark and drinking wine ranked up there with Top Ten Coping Mechanism Fails. So, choose wisely. Think Lizzo, not Billie Eilish!)

As therapeutic as background music may be, it's all for naught if your internal soundtrack sounds like something out of a haunted house of horrors. When you subject your brain to constant negative thoughts and emotions, you actually change its physical structure—and not in a good way. (Remember those "this is your brain on drugs" commercials from the '80s? The ones with the egg in the frying pan? They weren't so far off from the truth!)

Our internal airwaves are priority numero uno. Good news? You're the spin master; you're in charge. Let's take a moment to explore exactly what negativity does to your brain. Once you have all the information, I guarantee you will become more selective in your choice of soundtracks.

LET'S GET WIRED

In neuroscience circles, you often hear the phrase "neurons that fire together, wire together." [13] As clever as that may sound, it's true. Every experience, feeling, or thought triggers thousands of soldiering neurons which, in turn, forms a neural network. An army, if you will. It can be an army for good or a black op for bad.

Our natural inclination is to lean into the negative. It's called negativity bias. Our ancestors, ever vigilant, had to scan the horizon for threats to survival. As such, we're hardwired with a negativity bias: we innately look for threats instead of rewards. [14] While this may have worked well for Fred and Wilma, it doesn't so much for us now. We're looking to thrive, not just survive. In 1963, the Bronx Zoo had an exhibit hailed as "The Most Dangerous Animal in the World." What was inside? A *mirror*. Saber-toothed tiger be damned. Nowadays, your greatest threat often comes from within. You need to guard your thoughts.

From yourself.

Sadly, the brain can't differentiate between actual threats and perceived threats. Losing one's job and worrying about losing one's job can wreak the same neural and emotional havoc. Ironically, research suggests that approximately 85 percent of what we worry about never happens. [15] Think about how much of your time is wasted worrying about things that never come to pass. All that neural and emotional chaos—all for nothing. Harsh reality check. Worry-induced gray hair or deeply furrowed WTF lines are not badges of honor. It doesn't mean you care more or love more. It actually means you believe less and now just require more time at the salon. Be a warrior, not a worrier.

WORRY NEVER ROBS TOMORROW OF ITS SORROW,
IT ONLY SAPS TODAY OF ITS JOY.
—LEO F. BUSCAGLIA

I spent a good deal of my thirties worrying about whether I'd have kids or not. I was fine with waiting on the hubby part—the baby part, not so much. I wanted children, particularly daughters, more than anything. I spent countless hours agonizing over my biological clock, feeling sorry for my aging ovaries. Then, at thirty-seven, I married and became pregnant within two weeks of the ceremony—and three months after giving birth to my first child, I became pregnant again, and ended up with two beautiful girls.

I tell this story solely to underscore the fact that there's no greater time-killer or happiness-slayer than worry. I worried all that time for nothing. That's time that I can't get back—time that could've been spent on more productive pursuits than nonexistent reproductive angst.

Awareness is the first step to changing these downer thought patterns. The average person has between six thousand to sixty thousand thoughts per day. Of those thoughts, 90 percent are repetitive and up to 70 percent are negative in nature. [16] Granted, you can't stop the occasional negative thought from passing through, but that doesn't mean you have to allow it to live rent-free in your mind. You've got to slam the mental door shut on these negative little shits instead of inviting them to dinner because the only thing being served up is your happiness. Don't be that sacrificial lamb.

Ever notice that you may easily forget a compliment but can recall an insult from middle school as vividly as if it were yesterday? I still remember the mean things the kid three seats behind me in homeroom used to say to me—word for word.

Plainly stated, negative events produce more neural activity and affect us more than positive ones. It's unfortunate but true. It's the negative things that resonate the loudest, ingrain in your memories, and influence future decisions. [17] So, given that the negative carries more weight, we need to balance the happiness scales with much more positive stimuli to counteract its punch. In relationships, the ideal ratio is 5:1: five positive interactions to overcome the effects of only one negative interaction. *Yikes.* Makes you rethink every snarky criticism, doesn't it? [18] This is why positive affirmations can be so effective. The practice directly counteracts your negative internal loop from hell. Rather than playing positive catch-up, be proactive from the get-go: guard your thoughts, and watch what the hell comes out of your mouth.

THE FRYING PAN OF STRESS

Let's bring this all together. We're inclined to search out the negative and perceive it more readily than the positive. *Strike One.* The negative stimuli produce more neural activity and affect us more than positive stimuli. *Strike Two.* What happens in response to this overwhelming negativity filter? Our body releases the fight-or-flight hormone, cortisol. *Strike Three.*

Under normal conditions, cortisol is integral to your body's homeostasis and has many beneficial effects on the body. I think of these steroidal hormones kinda like those little furry Gremlins. Remember how cute they were—until they weren't? It took certain conditions (water, sunlight, midnight feedings) to unleash their inner demons, and suddenly adorable li'l Mogwai transformed into a creature of destruction. The same holds true for cortisol. Under conditions of prolonged stress, Captain Cortisol trades its white hat for a black one and is now a pinch hitter for Team Destruction. It can't turn itself off, and the resulting flood wreaks neural havoc.

Under times of severe or prolonged stress, cortisol [19]:

* Depletes your dopamine levels, the arsenal of happy hormones;

* Destroys the receptor sites for the happy transmitters;

* Breaks down the part of your brain that helps form new memories, making it more challenging to form new *positive* memories;

* Lowers serotonin, further reducing feelings of happiness and well-being; and

* Disrupts synapse regulation, which can result in antisocial and avoidance behaviors.

This should freak you out. It's like a neurological uphill battle to be happy. If that's not bad enough, cortisol (also called the obesity hormone) may be responsible for the muffin top that you can't seem to lose. That's right, *I'm playing the vanity card.* Chronic stress and cortisol overload are linked to weight gain, particularly around the belly. Watch your thoughts. Watch your waistline.

You can't surrender to this crap. Stress is an insidious attacker that threatens your mental *and* physical health—and, by extension, your happiness. It's associated with the six leading causes of death, and 75 percent of physician office visits are for stress-related ailments. Moreover, stress is known to increase vulnerability to drug use and addiction. [20] In other words, stress isn't just a frying pan, it's a f*cking double broiler!

CHANGE YOUR THOUGHTS AND YOU CHANGE THE WORLD.
—NORMAN VINCENT PEALE

I'm not trying to say you should avoid *all* negative experiences and thoughts, always. Those things are a part of life. They're normal. To claim to be a happy camper 24/7 would be disingenuous, exhausting, and just plain weird. Studies have found that trying to be constantly positive can make you unhappier, [21] not to mention annoying and unpopular. I can't stand people with a simpering smile no matter the circumstance. In Chapter 2, we'll address negative ruminations and how to reframe and redirect them. You can do this while still being authentic to yourself and not become some creepy Stepford wife or star in *The Truman Show*.

The negativity bias is actually beneficial. It protects us from perceived harm in the environment as well as helps us to learn from our mistakes and problem solve. The danger lies in the ruminating negative soundtrack, when the focus is off-kilter and you're caught in the negative feedback loop just digging its groove deeper and deeper and deeper, like a grave. It's when the glass is *always* half-empty. This is when guarding your thoughts becomes so critical.

There are a number of things you can do to boost your dopamine arsenal and mitigate the effects of stress until the cortisol squadron is under control. Best part? They're not that complicated. Simple daily practices and habits can be effective foot soldiers for happiness.

First up: get your zzzzzz's. Yep, eight to nine hours of restful sleep goes a very long way in balancing your hormones. Another great tool is to put yourself in time-out: fifteen minutes a day of quiet time, just you and you. What else? Deep breathing exercises. Cardio exercise. Yoga. Eating healthy whole foods. Eliminating sugar. Getting a massage. Reading a book that you enjoy (reading can reduce stress up to 68 percent!). [22] Have sex. Laugh. (Hopefully not while having sex.) *No, really*. Laugh.

Studies have found laughter lowers stress hormone levels. [23]

Do as many of these things as you can, as often as you can. Think of it as your grassroots happiness campaign. These little acts of self-care add up and provide opportunities to retrain your brain. These habits slowly become your new normal.

A happier normal.

CALLING ALL SUPERHEROES

It's really important that you get this shit as the empirical evidence is overwhelming. Excessive and ruminating negative thoughts and emotions are literal poison to your soul and use neural pathways as their means of attack. Your experiences and thoughts can alter the very structure of the brain, *changing you from the inside out.*

Luckily, all is not lost. Neuroplasticity is the brain's superpower ability to reform, reorganize, and modify synaptic connections through experience. You can build neural pathways for good too! Train the brain for happiness. In the next chapter, we're going to Glinda the Good Witch our neural pathways. Get ready for a deep dive into the pool of therapeutic thought.

HAPPINESS CHECK

Here we go—our first happiness check! We'll start with a stretch, then move on to a challenge, and, finally, a double-dog dare ya. Let's go!

STRETCH

Did you know the lungs are the largest source of waste removal for your body? That's right. The lungs. On average, we take seventeen thousand breaths per day, and 70 percent of the body's waste is eliminated in the carbon monoxide we exhale. Given that, surely we can give this powerhouse some extra love for at least five to ten minutes a day?

Deep breathing is the foundation of most relaxation practices and mindfulness. Let's give it a try together:

* Get comfortable. Sit with your back straight and supported or stretch out with a pillow under your head. Place one hand on your chest and the other on your stomach.

* Breathe in through your nose and inhale to the count of three-to-five, whichever count works best for you. Count slowly. Breathe out through your mouth by the same count, pushing out air until abdominals contract. The hand on your stomach should rise and fall in sync with your breathing. The hand on your chest should move very little.

* Continue to breathe in through your nose and out through your mouth.

CHALLENGE

Practice "Walking Empathy" for a person you need to forgive, need to let go, against whom you are holding some sort of grudge, etc. When *we* are in the wrong, we are more apt to forgive ourselves because we know the reasons behind our actions. Offer this person the opportunity to show you their reasons. Envision their life from childhood on. Every boo-boo. Every hurt. Try to understand their come-from. Not just for their sake but also for yours.

∖∣∕

WE JUDGE OURSELVES BY OUR INTENTIONS AND
OTHERS BY THEIR ACTIONS.
—STEPHEN M. R. COVEY

DOUBLE-DOG DARE YA

Do you think personal affirmations are stupid? Yeah, me too. *Until I didn't.* Studies show that affirmations work and offer numerous benefits. And hey, it can't get much easier than repeating a sentence. What do you have to lose?

Develop your own personal affirmation. Make it brief, specific, and present tense, focusing on the positive not the negative. Start with "I am." If you're struggling to get started, check out one of the many apps and websites that offer ideas and inspiration. My personal favorite is the "I am" app. It literally sends me reminders throughout the day. It's like passing love notes to myself. Choose whatever affirmation feels most authentic for you and repeat it to yourself every day at least once. Sweet-talk yourself. You totally deserve it!

CHAPTER TWO

Change Your Thoughts, Change Your Life

YESTERDAY I WAS CLEVER,
SO I WANTED TO CHANGE THE WORLD.
TODAY I AM WISE,
SO I AM CHANGING MYSELF.
—RUMI

*J*ust *don't think about it.*

Yeah, I'll get right on that.

If only life were that easy. Our brains don't work that way. And not only does thought suppression not work, it's also counterproductive to mental well-being. [1] One of the most  famous studies by Daniel Wegner, considered the founding father of thought suppression research, involved white bears. [2] Subjects were told to report their free thoughts verbally for five minutes. Prior to starting, however, they were told to *not* think of white bears, and if they did, to ring a bell. As you can guess, subjects reported thinking of white bears on average more than once a minute. What's even more interesting is that the initial thought suppression had a rebound effect when subjects were subsequently encouraged *to* think about white bears. They reported thinking of bears *significantly* more than the control group who had received the opposite instructions.

In a nutshell, what you resist, persists. And grows.

Okay, so you have these negative thoughts whirling in your mind. Let's do the math for a hypothetical shitstorm of a day where you're maxing out the negative (70 percent) and repetitive (90 percent) thought ceilings. Given forty thousand thoughts that day, approximately twenty-eight thousand are negative nellies. That's quite the mental assault. If you can't Jedi mind trick your negative thoughts into oblivion, then what?

Distracting yourself is just postponing the inevitable. Why not address things head-on (literally!) instead? Thoughts determine feelings. Change your thoughts, and your feelings will follow.

Your first move is to take a step back from your negative thoughts and gain perspective. It's called cognitive defusion. [3] View your thoughts for what they are: only thoughts and not reality. Instead of thinking, "I'm going to embarrass myself at the meeting," say to yourself, "I'm having the thought that I'm going to embarrass myself at the meeting."

Take it one step further and label the thought and emotion. Author and psychiatrist Daniel Siegel coined this practice, "Name it to tame it." [4] The thought is further defused by giving it a more generalized description and not giving oxygen to its specific content. So, instead of focusing on the specifics of "embarrassing myself at a meeting," drill it down further to its generalized form: "It's just worrying." Studies have found that putting feelings into words has therapeutic effects literally seen on MRIs of subjects' brains. [5] It's the adult version of "use your words." Now I say it to myself instead of to my kids.

Some experts advise taking it a step further and giving the

source of your negative self-talk a name. Preferably something silly or light-hearted to further distance yourself and underscore that you are *not* your thoughts. I went with "Harpy." According to mythology, harpies are monsters often depicted as a bird of prey with a woman's face. The modern-day definition is a foul, sharp-tongued woman. Seemed like the right fit for that nasty voice that fills my head with fear and doubt!

BE MINDFUL OF YOUR SELF–TALK.
IT'S A CONVERSATION WITH THE UNIVERSE.
—DAVID JAMES LEES

Now that you've got a handle on what's going on inside your mind, challenge those thoughts. That's right, put them on trial and Judge Judy them. This is one of my favorite tactics because who doesn't relish a good-natured argument? Evaluate its accuracy. What's the evidence? Are there alternatives? Be your own public defender.

Since they were little, I've instructed my daughters to have their words pass through three gates before they utter them. Is it kind? Is it true? Is it necessary? The "necessary" gate was always an effective *ahem*-moment for my rather precocious youngest—the one who tried to *Mean Girls* me. You can do the same with your thoughts. Instead of asking if the thought is true, ask yourself, "*Is it helpful?*" If not, toss it like last season's skinny jeans.

You can toss them *literally*. Write down the thought on a slip of paper and throw it away. Research has shown this is more effective than simply visualizing it. When subjects physically discarded the thought, they mentally discarded it as well. They were also less likely to use it in forming future judgments. [6]

Want to save paper? They found similar effects when subjects typed the text on a computer, then dragged the text into the trash/recycling bin. It's like defriending your thought and hitting the unfollow button. Oddly satisfying *and* effective.

THE HORSEMEN OF THE HAPPINESS APOCALYPSE

I think of thought distortions as the Horsemen of the Happiness Apocalypse, although there are far more than four, and they leave nothing but destructive thinking in their wake. Here are a few examples [7]:

- BLACK-AND-WHITE THINKING: A tendency to think in extremes, as one way or the other, offering no middle ground. It's all or nothing. We all need a little grey—a little in-between —in our lives.

- PERSONALIZATION: Internalizing and thinking you're to blame for everything, thinking everything people say or do is a direct reaction to you. Last I checked, the earth revolves around the sun. It's not all about you, so relax. I fall prey to this one if I allow my codependent beast to roar to life. Remember, *name it to tame it.*

- CATASTROPHIZING: Assuming the worst possible thing will happen. What if? What if? What if? Instead of "what if," ask yourself, "and then what?" to get to the root of your fear. State the situation aloud. After each successive answer, keep asking yourself, "and then what?" It typically diminishes the fear or whittles it down to ridiculousness. As Mr. Chow from *The Hangover* trilogy queried, "But did you die?" Typically, nothing is ever as bad as we fear it to be. When you break it down to its most common denominator, it's even less daunting.

- FILTERING: Only seeing the negative qualities of things/ experiences and discounting the positive. There's always a different side to a story!

WHEN YOU CHANGE THE WAY YOU LOOK AT THINGS,
THE THINGS YOU LOOK AT CHANGE.
—DR. WAYNE DYER

THE BEST DEFENSE IS A GOOD OFFENSE

The frame through which you view a situation determines your point of view. When you shift the frame, the meaning often changes. [8] Think of this as creating your own internal HGTV show. My favorite shows are never the ones with unrealistic budgets, partners who can apparently make *anything*, or those individuals who make complex DIY projects look easy-peasy. My favorites are the ones that take everything in the house and essentially repurpose or rearrange the items, with little to no expenditure, and *voilà*—the space is transformed into a design haven, and all it took was a different perspective.

Do the same for your experiences and thoughts. Put them in a better frame. It's literally the cheapest yet most valuable redesign you'll ever do.

Did you ever see the gameshow *Who Wants to Be a Millionaire?* Contestants are given lifelines in which they can request to phone a friend when unsure of the answer. This works wonders for the mental jackpot as well. Having a negative thought? Share it with someone! According to professor and author Brené Brown, calling a friend is an effective way to stop the shame cycle of negative thinking. Shine the light on it. Shame can't stand being spoken aloud or met with empathy, which is exactly what we receive from our friends. [9] (If not, it's also time to make new friends!)

Gratitude is another recommended practice for countering negative thoughts. I know we've already talked about gratitude, but y'all—it just keeps coming up *again* and *again* as having so many beneficial and therapeutic effects on our well-being. When you express gratitude, your brain releases dopamine and serotonin, those totally awesome feel-good neurotransmitters. Rather than the vicious cycle of negative thoughts, gratitude evokes a *virtuous* cycle in your brain. Since the brain searches for things that we already believe to be true, gratitude primes that pump. Once you start looking for things to be grateful for, your brain keeps it up. [10]

When barraged with negative thoughts, it's also important to focus on your strengths. Look in the mirror and notice your beautiful smile or sparkling eyes as opposed to wrinkles or blemishes. Instead of thinking about the things you're not great at, highlight your soul strengths. Character strengths are associated with a ton of well-being goodies such as positive affect, engagement, physical health, resilience, and healthy relationships. [11] And when you use those strengths to improve the world around you, you're setting yourself up for a happy, meaningful life.

Try some of these tactics the next time your internal record is stuck in the negative groove—and keep on trying them! Practice, after all, makes perfect.

RETRAIN THE BRAIN

I have such profound respect for the field of neuroscience, especially after my father's Alzheimer's diagnosis. You only need to hear your beloved daddy utter the heartbreaking words, "My brain is acting funny today," once to become a huge advocate of neuroscience research.

The brain truly is an extraordinary mechanism, with its billions of nerve cells and trillions of synaptic connections. Connections are maintained or removed based on their usage—a "use it or lose it" law of the land. With the brain's neuroplasticity, you can engage in behaviors that build new "happiness" pathways and dig existing "happiness" pathways even more deeply. In other words, you can train the brain for happiness. It reminds me of the line from one of my favorite shows from the late '70s, *The Six Million Dollar Man*: "Gentlemen, we can rebuild him." But this is even cooler because you're rewiring *your own brain*—talk about a superpower.

YOUR STRONGEST MUSCLE AND WORST ENEMY IS YOUR MIND.
TRAIN IT WELL.
—UNKNOWN

Think use-dependent cortical organization—a kind of self-directed neuroplasticity to turn Harpy into Happy. The answer isn't to suppress negative thoughts (*white bear! white bear!*) but to foster more positive experiences.

Let's look at some of the ways to rewire the brain to be positive. According to Shawn Achor, renowned happiness researcher and author, you can retrain your brain to be happier in a short period of time. Take two minutes a day and write three things for which you're grateful for. Do it for twenty-one days in a row. [12] Your brain retains this pattern of searching the world for positives instead of negatives. It's like a muscle that you flex and with continued use; it helps balance our inherent negativity bias.

This exercise achieves two things: 1) It encourages savoring. If you notice something positive but with a fleeting awareness, it leaves little imprint. If you hold something in your awareness for twenty seconds, your neurons fire together (to wire together), and its trace memory increases. 2) You're *writing* about it—and writing about positive experiences has been shown to increase their positive affect. It's astounding really—a mere two minutes a day of gratefulness can literally retrain and rewire your brain. As mentioned, gratitude has been shown to increase the release of dopamine and serotonin. [13] So not only does this exercise rewire neural pathways, it also showers you with those happy neurotransmitters.

Another practice shown to increase happy neural pathways is—drumroll, please—meditation. *I know*. I feel ya. I was the same way. In my mind, the only thing worse than meditation was perhaps burpees. Not only is meditation an integral tool in our happiness arsenal, it's also a proven means to rewire the brain. [14] Even the United States Marine Corps uses it to help reduce stress and increase focus. Corporate executives at Google, Target, and General Mills also embrace meditation's therapeutic effects on productivity. [15] If that's not enough for you, Oprah Winfrey, Hugh Jackman, Sting, Paul McCartney, Michael Jordan, Arianna Huffington, Arnold Schwarzenegger, Eva Mendez, Jerry Seinfeld, and Jennifer Aniston are all fans of the practice as well. [16]

Why not give it a shot? I realize the suggestion of meditation is often met with doubt and skepticism. *Thanks, but no thanks.* Like I said, I was the same way—but after much avoidance, I finally decided to give it a go. Total. Game. Changer. If you're still feeling resistant, do a guided meditation to take the brain-work out of it. There are amazing apps that make the pursuit easy and not nearly as intimidating. I personally use the Calm app every evening, quieting the mind through breathing. The good news? You don't need to carve out a huge chunk of your day to do it. In fact, as little as a few minutes a day has proven effective in harnessing its benefits. [17]

Setting goals is another simple yet incredibly effective tool for rewiring and building those happy neural pathways. When you set a goal, your amygdala (the brain's emotional center) evaluates the importance of the goal. The more you desire a goal, the brain perceives its obstacles as less significant or daunting. Apparently, where there's a will, there's a way in our neural universe. Your frontal lobe then identifies the specifics of the goal. Both parts work together, and the brain structure changes to optimize behaviors to achieve the goal. [18] It's the ultimate cerebral teamwork to materialize the dream. Accomplishing a goal, no matter how small, releases more serotonin and dopamine in the brain. It's like giving yourself a neurotransmitter cookie for a job well done.

$$\geqslant \!\!\backslash\!\!\mid\!\!/\!\!\leqslant$$

I HAVE LEARNED THAT THERE IS MORE POWER IN A GOOD STRONG HUG THAN IN A THOUSAND MEANINGFUL WORDS.
—ANN HOOD

I'm a hugger—so you can imagine how excited I was to learn that hugging is another great way to rewire the brain! A gentle, loving touch stimulates the production of serotonin and oxytocin in the brain. [19] And did you know that when you hug your children, you are helping their brains develop, especially from birth to three years of age? When babies are stimulated, it encourages synaptic connections as their brains are very malleable. I found this out when my first daughter was born eight weeks premature. The NICU was a huge proponent of kangaroo care (skin-to-skin contact between parent and infant) because touch is shown to hasten myelination and maturation of the brain in preterm babies. [20] Touch is one of my love languages, so let's just say I was Captain Kangaroo while she was in there.

Lifestyle choices such as diet, exercise, and sleep patterns also affect your brain's health and neuroplasticity. Even sunshine stimulates the release of serotonin. Healthy habits, happier brain. [21] It's not rocket science. And yet, more often than not, we eat fast food, drink sugary drinks, binge on Netflix instead of exercise, and believe caffeine is an adequate replacement for eight hours of sleep. At the beginning of the pandemic, I was guilty of all the above. No wonder I was emotional roadkill. On top of mourning my father, I had abdicated every healthy habit from my life. Postmates, Netflix, wine, and staying inside became my mainstays. *It was a spiral.* I'm so grateful I eventually clawed my way out of it.

Remember those affirmations we came up with for ourselves at the end of the last chapter? Well, evidence-based research shows that affirmations also rewire the brain on a cellular level. [22] Makes sense really. If shitty self-talk can adversely wire the brain, then positive affirmations can interrupt those maladaptive neuro-nets from hell and rewire your brain for happiness. The more you engage in positive affirmations, the "fire together, wire together" magic happens. Remember how the brain can't tell the difference between a real threat and a perceived threat? The sword cuts both ways and works to your benefit with positive affirmations. Since the mind can't tell the difference between real or pretend, affirmations can program your mind into believing a stated concept. Ah-mazing!

I AM THE GREATEST, I SAID THAT EVEN BEFORE I KNEW I WAS.

—MUHAMMAD ALI

Case in point: Muhammad Ali, the greatest boxer of all times and the absolute *master* of positive affirmations. He would tell everyone and anyone that he was the greatest of all time. His boxing matches began in his mind, before he even stepped foot into the ring. In his autobiography, Ali said, "It's the repetition of affirmations that leads to belief. And once that belief becomes a deep conviction, things begin to happen." [23] And indeed, they did. Ali won the Olympic gold medal and went on to win the heavyweight championship three times. His speeches and interviews were master classes in affirmation. While you may not float like a butterfly or sting like a bee, you've this amazing superpower to literally rewire your brain by repeating a few positive sentences to yourself.

You. Can. Rebuild. Him.

GO WITH THE FLOW

Another great way to maximize and build happy neural pathways is to be in the zone, otherwise known as "flow," a term coined by famed positive psychologist Mihaly Csikszentmihalyi. Flow is a state of mind when you're fully immersed in an activity in which your skill set matches the task at hand. You derive absolute pleasure from the experience itself and "lose" yourself in the moment. Time becomes almost transcendent. [24]

When in the zone, people feel greater happiness, energy, and engagement. According to Csikszentmihalyi, "The ego falls away. Time flies. Every action, movement, and thought follow inevitably from the previous one, like playing jazz. Your whole being is involved, and you're using your skills to the utmost." [25]

The coolest part about flow is what happens to your brain, as evidenced by neuroimaging techniques. There are distinct changes in brain activity during episodes of flow. People assume being in the zone requires more brain activity, when the opposite is true. Your brain essentially turns off whatever is not needed for the task at hand and gives it a much-needed breather. Higher cognitive functions turn off, and you often lose sense of time and sense of self—the place that houses your inner critic. It's the ultimate mute button for Harpy. While in flow, your spikey beta wave activity calms to a steady, smooth alpha wave. Think of it as calm waters versus choppy waves. The quieting of the neuron firing enables a more relaxed and creative cognitive state, as well as enhanced focus and attention. Better yet, flow stimulates the release of several happy neurochemicals such as dopamine, anandamide, norepinephrine, serotonin, and endorphins. It's the ultimate feel-good cocktail. [26]

Flow is often referenced in sports, arts, music, and gaming. Athletes and artists actively strive to harvest it. Sports psychologist and meditation teacher George Mumford has coached Michael Jordan, Shaquille O'Neal, and the late Kobe Bryant to be flow-ready and in the zone. [27] The greatest talents are well aware of the optimized performance found in the zone. Not just limited to sports or the arts, flow promotes creativity and innovative thinking in the workplace as well. Flow can also be found in common activities such as yoga, swimming, cycling, running, table tennis, and yes, even baking. [28]

In what activities do you lose track of time? Where hours seem like minutes? More likely than not, you're experiencing episodes of flow. Do more of these activities. Flow is associated with greater self-actualization, which makes sense as you're maximizing your skill sets. [29] Use the gifts that God gave you and showcase your light to the world. *No buried treasure here.*

Years ago, I read an excellent book called *StrengthsFinder 2.0*, by Tom Rath, which helps you find your flow. [30] Definitely recommended reading. Based on Gallup's forty-year study of human strengths, the Clifton StrengthsFinder online assessment helps people identify their talents. It also offers an action-planning guide to best maximize these talents through career choices and day-to-day activities. According to their studies, when you're engaged in your core talents daily, you're three times more likely to report an excellent quality of life. *Sounds happy AF to me.* In an ideal world, everyone would pursue their flow every single day.

While I'm a big believer in the American dream, I also believe that the best dreams are rooted in reality. That's why I like that Rath—like the Clifton StrengthsFinder—doesn't claim that you can be whatever your little heart desires. He just says you should focus on activities that make your heart sing. When I took the test in February of 2017, I discovered that my top five strengths are associated with the following career pursuits: coaching, teaching, journalism/media, and psychology. It was such an *aha* moment to revisit the assessment results as I wrote this book. It helped me understand why the days raced by as I wrote—because I was constantly in the zone. I would look up from writing this book to find six hours had passed. It was almost disconcerting.

I've had the opposite happen at work, as I'm sure you have as well—times when I've watched the clock all day, feeling like time is moving through sludge. That's honestly the worst. I've had many well-intentioned friends and family opine that careers that don't seem like work are unicorns, and the daily grind is the real deal. I know that's their reality. It doesn't have to be yours. It's your truth only if you allow it to be your truth. I knew from an early age that I never wanted to fall prey to daily monotony, the mundane. And once I had kids, I certainly knew I wanted flow to be the norm and not the exception in *their* lives.

Want the same for yourself.

Before you start thinking this is all pie in the sky crap, let's give this a go. Your inner critic is probably already shooting this down as improbable and impossible. *Yeah, right. I have bills. Responsibilities. Passion doesn't pay my mortgage.* But not so fast.

First, I want to distinguish between passion and talents. I have a passion for music, but I can't sing worth a hill of beans. In fact, you'd probably rather eat a hill of beans than hear me sing. Flow is when your skill set matches the task at hand.

Our goal is to find meaning and happiness in what we do, to be in the zone. It's estimated that 80 percent of people are dissatisfied with their jobs, yet one-third of your life is spent at work. One-third! Approximately ninety thousand hours throughout your lifetime. That's a f*ckload of time not to love or even like what you do. Why do you think the two have to be mutually exclusive? Happiness or a paycheck? There is a difference between a job, a career, and a calling. And yes, you may have to work a few jobs in pursuit of your calling.

But there's a way.

I'm not saying quit your current job and throw caution and

your bills to the wind. In most instances, it takes a gradual and thoughtful approach. As I said at the beginning, if you believe you can, then you're halfway there.

Now for the second half. First, don't forget that misery really does love company, and you living your best life will intimidate some people. Stay away from the haters and negative nellies who will just shoot down your dreams.

Now that you've tuned out the naysayers, focus on your strengths and talents. Dig deep and identify them. Which of those talents do you love to do? Marry those favored talents with a career. Not all talents are created equal. For example, I'm really good at cooking when I make an effort, but I hate doing it. Like, dread it. Choosing a culinary career would therefore be an epic mistake in my case. But helping other people find their flow? *That* I love!

Once you ascertain which talents of yours also light a fire in your belly, explore various careers with that skill set. Talents + Love = Career. TLC. A little TLC goes a long way in your happy AF journey. Here are some ways to get there:

* BUILD ON YOUR CORE TALENTS AND STRENGTHS. RESEARCH, STUDY, TAKE A CLASS. Candace Nelson left her career as an investment banker to go to pastry school, and Sprinkles Cupcakes was the resulting offspring—the world's first cupcake bakery. Pretty ballsy considering the bakery industry was in a no-carb slump at the time. Fast-forward to thirty-one locations coast-to-coast. She turned her sugar rush into a gold rush.

* FIND A JOB IN A RELATED FIELD WHERE YOU CAN DEVELOP ADDITIONAL SKILLS TO ENHANCE YOUR CORE STRENGTHS. Ava DuVernay was originally a publicist for filmmakers. She learned from being in their company and

realized she, too, could make films. She launched her first short film in her thirties. In 2017, DuVernay was included in *Time's* annual 100 list of the world's most influential people.

- START A SIDE HUSTLE. Sara Blakely sold fax machines during the day (for seven years) and ran Spanx out of her apartment in the evenings. She went from hating panty lines in white pants to a net worth of over $600 million. Nike founder Phil Knight sold running shoes out of his car at track meets while working as a CPA. An accountant! That's what I call walking the talk or "just doing it."

- FREELANCE OR VOLUNTEER WORK ON THE SIDE CAN HONE YOUR CORE STRENGTHS, HELP GET YOUR FEET WET, AND BUILD CLIENTELE. Volunteer and network with people in your desired career path. Find a mentor. Steven Spielberg started as a full-time, unpaid intern at Universal Studios to get his foot in the door. Many years later, Steven was a mentor for J. J. Abrams and hired him when he was sixteen years old to clean up old movies.

THE PEOPLE WHO GET ON IN THIS WORLD ARE THE PEOPLE WHO GET UP AND LOOK FOR THE CIRCUMSTANCES THEY WANT AND IF THEY CAN'T FIND THEM, THEY MAKE THEM.
—GEORGE BERNARD SHAW

To be clear, there's no *luck* here. As Seneca, the Roman philosopher and renowned Stoic, wisely opined, "Luck is what happens when preparation meets opportunity." Overnight success is mythical bullshit. For example, James Dyson is now worth almost $10 billion—but he had to create 5,126 prototypes of his vacuum cleaner before finding success. How many people would have quit after the first few dozen attempts? Colonel Sanders, meanwhile, had his recipe rejected more than a thousand times (that's a lot of finger-licking FUs) and had to take on various odd jobs to sustain him until his chicken franchise took off. And did I mention that he started this journey at sixty-five, when most people retire? Then there's Stephen King, whose first published novel was rejected thirty times. He was so frustrated, he chucked poor *Carrie* in the trash. Can you imagine a world without Stephen King? That would be an actual nightmare.

It's preparation and *perseverance*. And a whole lotta sweat. But worth it. So find your flow, yo. Your brain will love you for it.

BOUNCE, BABY, BOUNCE

When my girls were still little, I realized that a solid self-esteem was one of the most important gifts I could bestow upon them as a parent. If successful in that endeavor, I was convinced, it would help circumvent a world of hurt as they grew older. I mean, *come on*. There's practically a direct line between low self-esteem and shitty/abusive/controlling emotional partners since vultures always search out and prey on wounded sparrows. So, the best way to thwart these birds of prey? Do not be quarry. Self-esteem, enter stage right.

To advance this mission, I wrote a children's book—just for my girls, not for public consumption—during a summer vacation in 2012. In it, I reinvented the whole happily-ever-after saga and outlined principles for my little princesses-in-training that not only totally eschewed the whole damsel-in-distress BS but actually suited them in armors of strength, courage, and conviction.

My youngest daughter particularly loved the story and would request it as bedtime reading night after night. Every time—especially because it was merely printed copy paper stapled together, with not even a measly picture or two to augment it—my heart did a little jig of happiness. I confess to casting more than one condescending gloat at *Fancy Nancy*, *Junie B. Jones*, and *Pinky Dinky Doo* sitting idle on the bookshelf.

I titled the last and hence most important principle in the story, "Bounce, Baby, Bounce." Why am I dragging you down this memory lane? Because *bounce* is what you need to do in those low times; you need to elevate and propel yourself forward from that psychological *SPLAT*.

Just bounce back? you're probably thinking. *Yeah, thanks for nothing. Waiter—check please.* But hold on; I wouldn't be that trite, I promise—at least, not intentionally! A lot goes into bounce.

A more sophisticated term for this idea can be found in resilience theory, a tenet of positive psychology. *Psychology Today* defines resilience as that indomitable quality "that allows some people to be knocked down by the adversities of life and come back at least as strong as before. Rather than letting difficulties, traumatic events, or failure overcome them and drain their resolve, highly resilient people find a way to change course, emotionally heal, and continue moving toward their goals." [31]

I'm obsessed with people who excel at bouncing. I mean, seriously, who doesn't like a good comeback story? Please tell me you've seen at least one of the *Rocky* movies! But actually even more inspirational than the films themselves is their writer and star, Sylvester Stallone.

Much like the down-on-his-luck character, Stallone was

struggling, broke, and nearly homeless. He had to sell his beloved dog, Butkus, for fifty bucks because he couldn't even afford to feed him. But instead of giving up, he used this rock-bottom moment as a springboard to create his own possibility. He wrote a script about a down-and-out fighter because he could do that particular role. He essentially wrote it for himself.

When Stallone ran *Rocky* by some studios that expressed interest, it was with one caveat: he wanted to star in the film. The studios loved the script but wanted a more prominent name on the marquee. But Stallone, though broke, refused. He stood by his convictions. According to Hollywood lore, he was offered $300,000 for the script and still refused. And finally, the studio United Artists agreed to let him be the star, and they paid him for the script.

The rest is history. In addition to winning the Oscar for best picture, *Rocky* was the highest-grossing film of 1976. Stallone was able to buy Butkus back (for much, much more), and he put his beloved canine in the first two movies.

OUR GREATEST GLORY IS NOT IN NEVER FALLING BUT IN RISING
EVERY TIME WE FALL.
—UNKNOWN

Stallone's ability to bounce under extraordinarily trying circumstances is incredible. And he's not the only famous person to have done something like this. Daniel Craig, Halle Berry, Tiffany Haddish, Jim Carrey, Steve Harvey, David Letterman, Jewel, and Steve Jobs—did you know these incredibly successful people were homeless at some point as well? [32] I could go on and on, but you get the point. Being knocked down doesn't define you.

It's our bounce that defines us. The good news is that resilience can be learned, and you can optimize your natural resiliency reserves. [33] How? Start flexing that resiliency muscle. Instead of being devastated by setbacks, view them as temporary; think of them as a setup for a comeback. Be like Nelson Mandela, who so masterfully stated, "I never lose. I either win or I learn." Imagine if everyone had that mindset. When you're able to look at everything, good or bad, as a growth opportunity, it's life changing.

Learning from mistakes doesn't require firsthand experience. You can learn from *others'* life lessons too! I love this for my daughters; I'm not looking to be anyone's martyr, but if my girls can glean insight and understanding from my past stumbles, then I'm here for it.

Smith College, a prestigious all-women's college, launched a program entitled "Failing Well" in 2016 to destigmatize failure and teach resiliency to its students. [34] Failing is a part of learning and not an anathema to it. One must prepare to fail to learn. The most successful CEOs are well-aware of this fact. Netflix, Amazon, and Coca-Cola encourage failure because they're constantly pushing the envelope of creativity and innovation and know you can't have one without the other. Intuit, an accounting software company, gives awards and parties for failure. "At Intuit we celebrate failure," explains cofounder Scott Cook, "because every failure teaches something important that can be the seed for the next great idea." [35]

Resilient people don't view themselves as victims but rather as survivors of trying times. This is a key character trait of resilient people—not playing the victim card. Studies have found that resilient people are six times more likely to have an internal locus of control. [36] Meaning, they believe their actions and choices can help influence outcomes instead of believing they're powerless. When you think you're powerless, you really abdicate taking responsibility for the situation.

You're not a victim of your circumstances. You're a product of your decisions. Really look at your perspective in every situation. Is it empowering or disempowering? I don't think the wildly popular reality series *Survivor* would have celebrated forty seasons if it were called "Victims." Nobody wants to see that shit, let alone *be* it!

Positive self-talk is just one of the ways to help build and encourage a resilient mindset. According to the Bounce Back Project—a collaborative of physicians, nurses, hospital leaders, and staff that promotes "health through happiness"—there are five pillars of resilience: self-awareness, mindfulness, self-care, positive relationships, and purpose. [37] According to this movement, we become more resilient when we strengthen these pillars.

I encourage you to look at your pillars. If they seem shaky, it's time to fortify. Strengthen your pillars and turn your emotional house of cards into a fortress of resiliency. As Sheryl Sandberg, American business executive, billionaire, and philanthropist, told the graduating class of UC Berkeley, "You are not born with a fixed amount of resilience. Like a muscle, you can build it up, draw on it when you need it. In that process you will figure out who you really are—and you just might become the very best version of yourself." [38]

In other words, bounce your way to a better you!

HAPPINESS CHECK

STRETCH

Name your inner critic. When you give it a name, it's no longer you saying it, it's them. Mine, if you'll recall, is called Harpy. I encourage you to come up with something similarly fun and light-hearted, to show that you're not taking that beotch seriously. And when that inner critic starts its negative diatribe, it's time to tell it to STFU. Call it out. Challenge it.

CHALLENGE

Take a Gratitude Walk. This doesn't have to be any more involved than taking fifteen minutes and walking around your neighborhood, park, or somewhere in nature. While walking, think of everything that you are grateful for: your relationships, your family, your friends, your health, your job, your creature comforts—shelter, food, etc. Even the fact that you are walking and breathing. Embrace the total sensory experience of it and pay attention to what you are seeing, hearing, smelling, and touching (going barefoot in the grass is an added bonus!). I know it sounds simple—and it is. But it can also be an extraordinary experience in gratitude, savoring, and grounding if you allow it to be!

DOUBLE-DOG DARE YA

The only reason this exercise is in the dare category is because I'm asking you to do it for twenty-one days in a row—not for some arbitrary reason but because lore has it that it takes twenty-one days to make or break a habit. So each day, simply write down three things you are grateful for. Give it some thought and do not just jot something down in under thirty seconds. Let it imprint. Let's rewire that bad boy and have our neural "confirmation bias" be biased for good.

CHAPTER THREE

The Game-Changing Trifecta— Gratitude, Faith, and Grace

I'VE MISSED MORE THAN 9,000 SHOTS IN MY CAREER.
I'VE LOST ALMOST 300 GAMES.
TWENTY-SIX TIMES, I'VE BEEN TRUSTED TO MAKE THE GAME'S
WINNING SHOT, AND MISSED.
I'VE FAILED OVER AND OVER AND OVER AGAIN IN MY LIFE.
AND THAT IS WHY I SUCCEED.
—MICHAEL JORDAN

Gratitude is the foundation on which to realize your visions and dreams. As Dr. Michael Bernard Beckwith, spiritual guru and author, observed, "Nothing new can come into your life unless you are grateful for what you already have." [1] We've already touched on gratitude briefly, but let's dig deeper to fully unearth its treasure.

BE A GRATITUDE BALLER

Gratitude is defined as the quality of being thankful; a readiness to show appreciation and return kindness. It comes from the Latin word *"gratus,"* meaning pleasing and thankful. Harvard Medical School provides slightly more color and defines gratitude as ". . . a thankful appreciation for what an individual receives, whether tangible or intangible. With gratitude, people acknowledge the goodness in their lives. In the process, people usually recognize that the source of that goodness lies at least partially outside themselves. As a result, gratitude also helps people connect to something larger than themselves as individuals—whether to other people, nature, or a higher power." [2]

Yes, gratitude already has its own holiday—but while Thanksgiving rocks, our goal is to turn gratitude into a 365-day-a-year affair and not just one of the busiest travel weekends of the year. We take so many things for granted that it's well past the time to flip the script to gratitude instead. I truly believe it's one of the greatest distinctions to a happy life.

I didn't realize how much I took something as simple as walking for granted until I had two ankle surgeries. For three decades, I didn't even question or give thanks for the ability. "These boots were made for walking," right? Once that ability was taken away, I experienced a total wake-up call. I didn't give a hoot about high heels anymore—my former wardrobe staple. I just wanted to be able to walk again without pain. I was relegated to a scooter and an orthopedic boot for months on end, not to mention physical therapy out the wazoo. I remember the first time I took a step without pain, and I started to cry. I was so grateful. More importantly, I was grateful for the life lesson as it profoundly changed me. I no longer took what I'd considered the "basics" for granted—vision, hearing, walking, breathing.

After that experience, I started thanking God first thing in the morning for even waking, viewing it as a gift as opposed to an entitlement. As Maya Angelou wrote, "This a wonderful day. I've never seen this one before." She tweeted that one year before she passed at the age of eighty-six—a true spiritual warrior and teacher to the end. We often take the gift of a new day for granted when some aren't afforded that luxury. You need only ask someone with a terminal illness how they view each day to put it in perspective.

I think a lot about my mom in her wheelchair and how something as commonplace as using the restroom is instead an ordeal for her—maneuvering the wheelchair, getting in and out with absolute care and concentration, the toilet rails, etc., having to be careful not to drink too much fluid if she's away from the facility as there may not be handicap restrooms that meet her needs. Imagine having to give that much thought to a simple bodily function. And yet she utters not one word of complaint. The woman survived three types of cancer, multiple sclerosis, and now COVID-19 while living in an assisted living facility in New Jersey—practically ground zero for the virus. She is resiliency on wheels. We tease her that she's too stubborn to go. I'm not entirely kidding. I genuinely believe it's her mindset, rather than her body (which has often failed her) that enabled her to ring in her eightieth birthday during the pandemic. Barely five feet tall, she's a giant in fortitude.

In addition to health, there are so many modern conveniences and simple creature comforts that we take for granted, especially in this country. The COVID-19 pandemic was an effective magnifying glass. I mean, did you ever think there would be a run on toilet paper, hand sanitizer, or Clorox wipes? I know I never did. I remember driving to five different grocery stores just to find beef. The aisles were virtually cleared out. I didn't realize how much I had taken convenience stores for granted. It was the most surreal experience—like being in a post-apocalyptic television series where airborne particles were the enemy. They're even more insidious than walking zombies—invisible and everywhere. There was so much confusion, panic, and misinformation. It was the ultimate wake-up call. We'd been taking simple daily life for granted. Never again.

If I were to find a silver lining, I think that was the gift of the pandemic: a finer appreciation for what we do have. I will never take certain things for granted again, like hugging, being at family gatherings, seeing friends, going to church service, the movies, a concert—and yes, even toilet paper. I realized that I had let my gratitude lapse during the spiral, along with everything else. Epic mistake. I started thanking the Big Guy again every day. It was a gratitude reboot.

WHEN I STARTED COUNTING MY BLESSINGS,
MY WHOLE LIFE TURNED AROUND.
—WILLIE NELSON

Helen Keller was the ultimate gratitude baller. Born in 1880, Helen developed an illness when she was nineteen months old, leaving her deaf and blind. Given her inability to communicate, she became a frustrated, uncontrollable child, and many relatives thought she should be institutionalized.

Refusing to give up, her parents sought the advice of Alexander Graham Bell, who recommended Anne Sullivan as a mentor and teacher for the six-year-old child. Anne would ulti-mately teach Helen to write, speak, and read Braille. And what a voice Helen would become. She was the first deaf-blind person to earn a bachelor of arts degree. She became a renowned author, political activist, lecturer, and advocate for people with disabili-ties. She was awarded the Presidential Medal of Freedom and elected to the National Women's Hall of Fame, proving to all that true vision manifests in the heart and not with sight. "So much has been given to me, I have not time to ponder over that which has been denied," she observed. I aspire to *that* type of gratitude.

THANK U, NEXT

Having a gratitude reboot was essential to my redemptive journey. To be quite honest, the only thing that had changed *was* my perspective. The arguably crappy circumstances were still the same. I just changed the channel on that poor-me melodrama. It was time to take that shit off the airwaves already. I started being grateful for what I did have. God. My family. My friends. A roof. Sustenance. Love. Sunshine. A bounty of blessings, really. I became grateful even for the hard-earned lessons during my time at rock bottom. When you're a total emotional face-plant, let's just say your view of the world changes. I was no longer afraid of falling—of failure. I was already on my knees. Now, I just stayed there in gratitude.

Gratitude casts out fear, doubt, and worry. They really are mutually exclusive. Scarcity can't survive in an abundant mindset. Seriously. *That's a thing.* It's worth reiterating the importance of gratitude and its virtuous cycle—it pays off in spades. Author and psychologist Dan Baker argues that you can't be in a state of appreciation and fear or anxiety at the same time. During active appreciation, the threatening and anxious messages from the amygdala (fear center) and brain stem are cut off from accessing your neocortex. [3] Alex Korb, famed neuroscientist, offers a less technical interpretation: "Gratitude can have such a powerful impact on your life because it engages your brain in a virtuous cycle. Your brain only has so much power to focus its attention. It cannot easily focus on both positive and negative stimuli." [4] So, you can essentially distract your brain with gratitude, kinda like a mother does with her toddler.

For me, this discovery was empowering. Fear and worry had thrived in the darkness of my spiral but couldn't survive in the light of gratitude. In that light, other things grew in its place. My empathy and compassion increased tenfold. Grief stretches you in your heart. Carl Jung, founder of analytical psychology, wrote, "Embrace your grief. For there, your soul will grow." I get that. *I felt that.* The grief/fear/anxiety spiral hadn't diminished me. In so many ways, I emerged stronger. Wiser. Softer. More present. Grateful.

My hope for you is that you start last chapter's double dog dare-ya if you haven't already: three things for which you're grateful, twenty-one days in a row. *Give this gift to yourself.* You deserve it. You may even find you don't want to stop after three weeks. Like with meditation and affirmations, there are amazing apps for everything now. I never had my gratitude journal handy, but I *always* have my phone handy (so do you). I use the Gratitude app. It's free and always at my fingertips. Remember in *How the Grinch Stole Christmas* (my fave of faves) when his heart grew three times that day because Whoville was giving thanks even without all the presents and trimmings? That can be you! I'll be your Cindy Lou Who fangirl singing, "Fahoo fores dahoo dores" in solidarity. One hundred percent committed to being happy AF starts with gratitude.

GRATITUDE IS NOT ONLY THE GREATEST OF VIRTUES, BUT THE PARENT OF ALL OTHERS.
—MARCUS TULLIUS CICERO

Philosophers have suggested that gratitude is the greatest of virtues and serves as a "gateway" for other positive emotions. Empirical research has supported this ideology. *More and less.* Gratitude is associated with more and less of the following emotions [5]:

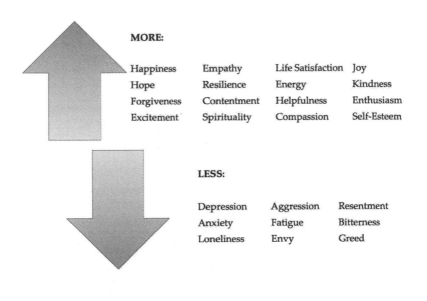

MORE:

Happiness	Empathy	Life Satisfaction	Joy
Hope	Resilience	Energy	Kindness
Forgiveness	Contentment	Helpfulness	Enthusiasm
Excitement	Spirituality	Compassion	Self-Esteem

LESS:

Depression	Aggression	Resentment
Anxiety	Fatigue	Bitterness
Loneliness	Envy	Greed

Read that list again, please. All that good stuff. Just from being grateful. I mean, it's harder to give up carbs than to practice gratitude, for the love of Pete (Davidson, of course). If you can keto, you can say thank you.

Taking five minutes a day to journal what you're grateful for can enhance long-term happiness by over 10 percent. [6] Robert Emmons, American psychologist, author, professor at UC Davis, and gratitude guru, has indicated that gratitude can increase happiness by as much as 25 percent. [7] This is based on empirical research and not merely spouted opinion.

So many people think the good life means the goods, possessions, bling, Benjamins, blah-blah bullshit. This misguided mindset has blown up even more given that the media, especially social media, constantly bombards us with this messaging. Researchers have found that while living in an economically developed versus a poor nation does factor into one's overall happiness, that's where the distinction ends. Once individuals have enough money to pay for their basic creature comforts, money does little to enhance happiness. [8]

Moreover, people who buy into this consumer culture of "more, more, more" report lower life satisfaction and more depression and anxiety. [9] Money, popularity, and image are the golden calves of modern times, and far too many people pray at that altar. I see it with my teens and their morbid fascination with TikTok, YouTube, and Instagram. *Thankfully*, gratitude reduces materialism, insecurity, and our tendency to compare ourselves to others. [10]

True success has nothing to do with material possessions. It's making a difference, having an impact. Focus on *that*. Steve Jobs profoundly said, "Being the richest man in the cemetery doesn't matter to me. Going to bed at night saying we've done something wonderful . . . that's what matters to me." [11] Jack Ma, founder of the e-commerce site Alibaba, has publicly stated that the $28 billion (*that's with a B*) from his IPO hasn't made him happy and instead finds himself more stressed and tired. In fact, he said that his time after college, as an English teacher making $12 a month, was the "best life I had." [12] He received a lot of online pushback and flack for saying that—people don't like hearing others' truth if it counters their narrative or conception of how things "should" be—but I believe him, and I applaud his honesty.

Don't get me wrong. I appreciate the finer things in life. But it's not my true north. I've learned to choose happiness over increasing the balance of my bank account. The payoff is bigger than any amount of money ever could be.

THE GRATITUDE GOODY BAG

While the practice of gratitude is clearly associated with psychological well-being, the literature on its effects on physical well-being is somewhat limited and still emerging. It's promising, though. Studies suggest, for example, that gratitude may have an upward spiral effect on physical health. "If [thankfulness] were a drug, it would be the world's best-selling product with a health maintenance indication for every major organ system," said Dr. P. Murali Doraiswamy, head of biologic psychology at Duke University Medical Center. [13]

Grateful people enjoy better physical health, in part because their better psychological health means they are more likely to take care of their health, exercise, and get regular check-ups. A systematic review of literature has found gratitude associated with stronger immunity, improved sleep and vitality, lower blood pressure and reduced inflammation. [14] Mind-body connection. As Napoleon Hill said, the body achieves what the mind believes.

FEELING GRATITUDE AND NOT EXPRESSING IT IS LIKE
WRAPPING A PRESENT AND NOT GIVING IT.
—WILLIAM ARTHUR WARD

Want more friends? Be grateful. Want a better intimate relationship? Be grateful. Gratitude makes us nicer, kinder, and more compassionate, which—wait for it—makes us more likeable. So, yes, gratitude has a definite social component as well. It helps build new relationships. Studies have shown that saying thank you to an acquaintance makes them more likely to want to hang out with you on an ongoing basis. [15] It helps deepen and maintain existing relationships too; partners are more likely to stay committed and maintain intimate connections when there's reciprocal gratitude.

One of the greatest things about gratitude is that it's even better when given away. An exponential ripple of well-being can manifest in amazing ways. Doug Conant can attest to that fact. In 2001, he became the CEO of the Campbell Soup Company, which was failing at the time—think kick-the-can rock bottom. He described the culture as very toxic, with low morale and little employee engagement. Doug decided to walk the talk. He wore a pedometer and vowed to walk ten thousand steps daily around the facilities to actively engage with his employees. Secondly, he wrote personalized thank-you notes every single day to his employees. He wrote over thirty thousand thank-you notes. *By hand.* By the end of his tenure, the company was the perennial winner of Gallup's "Great Workplace Award" and was outperforming both the S&P Food Group and the S&P 500. [16] This isn't an anomaly. Expressing gratitude in the workplace is associated with improved productivity, enhanced mood, and happier employees. [17] *Mmm, mmm, good*, indeed.

A few years ago, friends and I volunteered at a veterans' halfway house that helps homeless veterans get back on their feet. We raised money, planted a vegetable garden, cleaned and overhauled their property, facilitated life and career courses, etc. It was an incredibly fulfilling experience. My favorite memory was when we held a gratitude circle, in which we told each veteran present what we appreciated about them. I remember seeing tears roll down a veteran's face. I will never forget that. *Ever.* It was so humbling and such a profound life lesson. Words matter. So, express gratitude and appreciation. To loved ones. Friends. Coworkers. Acquaintances. Strangers.

Remember early in the COVID-19 pandemic when cities across the country had gratitude showers every evening? People stood on their front porch, balcony, or sidewalk and applauded the essential workers for their dedication, hard work, and sacrifice. There was something so beautiful about it. So human. So united. It doesn't have to take a pandemic or an orchestrated group effort to show appreciation. When was the last time you told your loved ones how much you appreciate them and how grateful you are for having them in your life? Out of the blue. Not because they did something, took the trash out, fixed your car, or rubbed your back. Just because. Try it. *Pay love forward.*

EMBRACE YOUR UPPIE

It would be disingenuous to have a chapter on gratitude without discussing faith. Robert Emmons believes that gratitude consists of two parts. The first part is the affirmation of the goodness in our life and in the world. The second part is determining the source of that goodness as it's often outside of ourselves—other people or a higher power. [18]

I'm not looking to proselytize. I avoid people who do that like the plague. But there's just no getting around the fact that studies have determined faith to be an integral and significant predictor of happiness. And by faith, I'm not talking about confidence in Tom Brady's throwing arm or J.Lo's unparalleled ability to twerk. I'm talking about the Big Guy (or Girl), Universe, Spirit, Supreme Being, or whomever that higher power may be to you. For me, it's God.

When I was growing up, my mother had a copy of the poem "Footprints in the Sand" hanging in our kitchen. Even at a young age, this poem spoke to me. In a nutshell, it's about a person reflecting upon their life and seeing two pairs of footprints in the sand—one belonging to them and one belonging to God. They notice that there was only one set of prints during the low points in their life. Bothered, they ask God why He abandoned them during those low times. Long story short, the loving reply was, "My precious child . . . it was then that I carried you." In those times in my life that have really bitten the big one, I've always taken comfort in that fact that I'm never alone. At my lowest lows, the Big Guy was carrying me.

Never did I embrace that belief more than during the pandemic when I was totally isolated for extended periods, especially when my daughters were with their dad. We were essentially under stay-at-home orders, and for many people that meant hours and days of enforced solitude. My family was across the country, and everyone else was socially distancing. My father had just died from COVID-19. I had never felt more alone.

My coping mechanism during that bleak period was a master class in F*ck Ups. Isolation; ruminating thoughts of my father dying by himself, alone and scared, surrounded only by occasional strangers in hazmat-like PPE clothing (this was a particularly effective form of emotional cutting and torture); junk food; not getting out of bed or showering; not answering my phone; and lots of wine—like red Solo cups full. Wine glasses were amateur sippy cups at that point and required too many trips to the fridge for constant replenishment.

THE DARKER THE NIGHT, THE BRIGHTER THE STARS.
THE DEEPER THE GRIEF, THE CLOSER IS GOD!
—DOSTOYEVSKY

My primary life preserver during that dark time was a spiritual one. Thank God for God, right? I prayed. I wept. I railed. I begged. I gave thanks. I asked forgiveness. All to God. I'm not quite sure what would've happened if I didn't have the Big Guy carrying and loving me—no matter what. And I wasn't an easy load to carry. In all my epic messiness. All my brokenness.

But there's beauty in brokenness.

I love the Japanese art of *kintsugi* ("golden repair"), a centuries-old form of pottery repair in which the damaged parts of broken artifacts are mended with lacquer resin or precious metals such as gold, silver, or platinum. This repair method highlights the cracks—the beautifully broken pieces—as opposed to hiding them. By accentuating the fault lines and celebrating its history, each piece is transformed into something even more magnificent and inspired, unique to its own cracks. In other words, the scars become the art.

If *The Scream* personified 2020, *kintsugi* embodies its recovery and redemption. Much like the potter's house, I, too, am clay in God's hands. Flawed. Forged by fire and shaped by my experiences, both good and bad. Sustained by faith. I purchased a *kintsugi* bowl to hold a treasured trinket of my father's that my mom sent me after he passed. I also put my "Stardust" namesake bracelet in the bowl to remind myself that although broken, I'd come through the fire and was more beautiful for the scars.

Knowing that my father was in heaven happily doing the hustle with God comforted me as I grieved, as did knowing that I would one day see him again. When we were little, my dad would always jingle his car keys while coming up the front walk from work so that my little brother and I could hear. It was like our Pavlovian papa bell. When we heard the car keys jingle, we'd excitedly race for the door to jump into his arms. It was our daily ritual, and a memory that I cherish. I know when my time comes (not too, too soon, mind you), my dad will be there jingling the keys to the Kingdom to welcome me home.

When my children were little and in need of some extra love, they'd stand in front of us with their little chubby arms raised and say, "Uppie." That was their not-so-subtle clue for us to sweep them up into the safe harbor of our arms. It was their happy place. Just like faith is my happy place.

By "faith," I'm referring to spirituality in all its forms, not any type of organized religion. Spirituality is universal, really. The specifics may vary, but all cultures have the concept of a sacred, divine force. [19] Brené Brown offers a beautiful, inclusive definition: "Spirituality is recognizing and celebrating that we are all inextricably connected to each other by a power greater than all of us, and that our connection to that power and to one another is grounded in love and compassion. Practicing spirituality brings a sense of perspective, meaning and purpose to our lives." [20]

When you look at the research literature, there's no single definition of "spirituality," and this ambiguity has contributed to mixed empirical results. [21] It's hard to hit a moving target. I'm not looking to get into an analysis on the varying degrees of religiosity/spirituality, and that's not the point, anyway. The point is what spirituality can do for you, however you practice it. A meta-analysis of research indicates that people who engage in spiritual practices are less likely to engage in drug abuse, unprotected sex, and smoking; have fewer incidents of alcoholism, depression, and anxiety; and have better physical health. [22] Spirituality, in its myriad forms, is associated with greater happiness, subjective well-being, and life satisfaction.

Spirituality acts like a lamp, a guidepost. It lights your path during life's darkest moments and allows the joyous moments to shine even brighter. Arthur Brooks, who teaches a course on happiness at Harvard Business School, believes that faith provides a definitive "happiness edge." Specifically, he wrote, ". . . the research is clear that many different faiths and secular life philosophies can provide this happiness edge. The key is to find a structure through which you can ponder life's deeper questions and transcend a focus on your narrow self-interests to serve others." [23]

Believing in something bigger than you; being about something more than you—embrace your Uppie, my friends.

IN GRACE, FREEDOM

On one of the many occasions I have done something *so outrageous* that *totally mortified* my girls in recent memory, they went into full-blown incognito mode—slouching all the way down in their seats—to avoid being seen in the car with me, after which they elaborated in great detail how lucky I was there were no video receipts of my behavior, or I'd be "totally canceled."

After laughing about it (raising teenagers requires humor, forced as it may be at times), it got me thinking: What else in my life would call for a "cancellation"? No doubt about it, I've had my fair share of missteps and mistakes on this journey of life. Some will haunt me until I reach those pearly gates. Others just "mortify" me upon recollection. Gaffes. Unintended hurts. Indiscretions. Harsh words. Infidelity. Social insensitivity. Gross judginess. Jealousy. Intemperate temper. Planet carelessness. Big breaches to little hiccups, like having too salty a tongue (never met a curse word I didn't like). I mean, the list could go on and on (let's not forget root perms!).

MISTAKES HAVE THE POWER TO TURN YOU INTO SOMETHING
BETTER THAN YOU WERE BEFORE.
—UNKNOWN

We all have our proverbial crap. For my part, I can honestly say that my missteps are never choreographed with malice or ill intent. Not that this absolves me, but I do like to think that I'm quick to apologize for any errant behaviors (although I'm sure some of my exes may beg to differ). I do make a point to legit apologize to my children when I make a mistake, and I try to teach them that changed behavior is the best "I'm sorry" you can give.

All in all, it's a powerful redemptive cycle: F*ck-up → Acknowledgment → Apology → Grace → Forgiveness → Redemption → Growth. That forgiveness hurdle can be a tough one, however, and many of us have trouble clearing it—whether as the givers or the receivers.

Notice what comes before forgiveness in the process I just laid out: grace. You can't fully appreciate the beauty of gratitude without taking in the scenic majesty of grace. They're intertwined. As theologian Karl Barth observed, "Grace and gratitude belong together like heaven and earth. Gratitude evokes grace like the voice and echo. Gratitude follows grace as thunder follows lightning." [24]

There are so many exquisite literary explanations of grace and its place in theology and life. One of my favorite no-nonsense takes on grace comes from Bono, whose profound words aren't solely limited to his super-cool lyrics. He's quite the philosopher, all-around badass, and champion for good. He said, "You see, at the center of all religions is the idea of Karma. You know, what you put out comes back to you: an eye for an eye, a tooth for a tooth, or in physics; in physical laws every action is met by an equal or an opposite one. It's clear to me that Karma is at the very heart of the universe. I'm absolutely sure of it. And yet, along comes this idea called Grace to upend all that 'as you reap, so you will sow' stuff. Grace defies reason and logic. Love interrupts, if you like, the consequences of your actions, which in my case is very good news indeed, because I've done a lot of stupid stuff." [25]

Haven't we all? Back in the day, I think I did some at a U2

concert. And a Stones concert. Definitely at some Grateful Dead shows. (No judging!)

I love how Bono worded his explanation of grace. *Love interrupts the consequences.* I think about that often. I count so much on God's grace, yet at times struggle with extending it to others. I really struggled extending grace to my cheating boyfriend, making forgiveness even more difficult. I mistakenly conflated grace with tolerance—felt that if I truly extended grace, there would be no consequences for his cheating. I gave great "I forgive you" lip service without really meaning it or practicing it. Meanwhile, my passive-aggressive words and actions were constantly reiterating that he was a cheater. It was like constant background music. Literally, I sang "Bed of Lies" by Nicki Minaj to him. *On more than one occasion.*

GRACE IS THE VOICE THAT CALLS US TO CHANGE AND THEN GIVES
US THE POWER TO PULL IT OFF.
—MAX LUCADO

When you don't extend grace, it serves as a kind of prison to the person seeking forgiveness, never allowing them to step out of the narrative, out of the label, out of the mistake. And when you are boxed in, you can't grow, be different, or be better. You can never reach the redemptive part of the cycle. Think about it. If you plant a tree in a small container and keep it in that container, the roots begin to circle around the pot until there is no potting soil left. Eventually the tree can girdle/strangle itself and die due to lack of space. Boxed in, it can never thrive and flourish. The same holds true for people. Whether you "hold" someone big or small, they will meet that space.

Grace sees beyond our mistakes. And thank goodness—because do you want to be defined by your mistakes? God knows, I don't. The theologian and clergyman who wrote the beloved hymn "Amazing Grace" had previously been a slave trader. He went on to become an ardent abolitionist. Grace redeems.

Every time you don't extend grace, you're withholding love.

I read a Pinterest post (gotta love Pinterest) that stated: "Grace means that all of your mistakes now serve a purpose instead of serving shame." Just sit with that for a sec. I love, love, love that. Grace transforms and recontextualizes. Mistakes are now your teacher, not attacker. You can't fall from grace. In actuality, grace catches you when you fall in its loving embrace.

Given my litany of screw-ups, flaws, and mistakes, I'm so grateful for God's grace. Whereas His love carries me, it's His grace that sets me free. It allows me to move past and forgive myself as opposed to being held bondage by those inner demons of guilt and regret. Grace escorts any guilt or shame out the back door, thus opening the possibility for transformation.

Grace allows people to step out of the shadows of their mistakes and missteps—and *become.*

HAPPINESS CHECK

STRETCH

Create your own Hallmark moment and write a thank-you note to someone in your life: a loved one, a friend, a coworker. Write it by hand. Make it specific. Express gratitude and appreciation for who they are to you. Don't wait for a holiday or occasion. Do it out of the blue. It makes a difference. Random acts of kindness, no matter how little, make the biggest impact.

CHALLENGE

Volunteer. Making a difference in someone else's life increases your sense of purpose. It can be super simple like going grocery shopping for a homebound neighbor or writing a letter to the troops abroad. I volunteered at a senior center for a while, and it was a hoot. They had weekly dances with an orchestra, and those dance partners wore me out. It was almost embarrassing. You think you can dance? Try it with someone who grew up on Fred Astaire.

Take time out of your life to be about other people. It does the heart good.

DOUBLE-DOG DARE YA

The Naikan Reflection is a structured method of self-reflection. Naikan means "looking within." The process involves reflecting on the following three questions while focusing your attention on a particular person.

* What have I received from _____?
* What have I given to _____?
* What troubles and difficulties have I caused _____?

The beauty is in its simplicity. It allows you to see things for how they really are while harkening feelings of gratitude and appreciation for others. You discover how much you take versus give in personal relationships.

CHAPTER FOUR

Your Why Is the Way— Goals, Vision, and Purpose

JUDGE NOTHING;
YOU WILL BE HAPPY.
FORGIVE EVERYTHING;
YOU WILL BE HAPPIER.
LOVE EVERYTHING;
YOU WILL BE HAPPIEST.
—SRI CHINMOY

I f gratitude grounds us, vision is the wind beneath our wings. What does vision have to do with happiness? I guess it depends on how you look at it. To me, it's much more than picturing myself in a Porsche Taycan Turbo S, although that'd be cool. I think of it as an upward spiral for happiness that gains momentum with practice: Goals, vision, purpose. Walk, run, fly.

It's time to start living on purpose instead of autopilot. We're on a vision mission, and shit's about to get real.

In a good way.

GET GOAL RICH

☆

I was first introduced to the importance of goal setting from Napoleon Hill's *Think and Grow Rich*, which I read well over twenty-five years ago. Every few years, I reread it as a refresher course. Not many nonfiction books are worthy of that personal distinction, with a few notable exceptions (e.g., *The Four Agreements, Man's Search for Meaning, Meditations by Marcus Aurelius, The Purpose Driven Life, The 5 Love Languages*). Often called the granddaddy of motivational literature, *Think and Grow Rich* has sold a staggering one hundred million copies worldwide since it was initially published in 1937. It's on more recommended book lists than you can count and still relevant today because its principles are timeless.

Over twenty years, Hill interviewed over five hundred of the wealthiest men in America to unlock the secret of success, which he outlined in thirteen principles. According to Hill, thoughts become things (*sounds familiar*); hence, the iconic title of the book. The starting point of all achievement is knowing what you want and detailing it. In a nutshell (you *really* should read the book), Hill outlined six practical steps for turning desires into reality, aka goal setting [1]:

- STEP ONE: Write down your goals.
- STEP TWO: Determine how will you achieve your goals.
- STEP THREE: Set a deadline.
- STEP FOUR: Create a plan and get into action immediately.
- STEP FIVE: Write a concise statement of the aforementioned four steps.
- STEP SIX: Review your goals twice daily.

The key to the above is persistence, day in and day out. Gotta be all in, much like being 100 percent committed to being happy AF. Half-assery won't do it. Another key trait of Hill's successful subjects was the unshakable belief they had about themselves and their goals. This still holds true today. To wit, Warren Buffet famously asserted, "I always knew I was going to be rich. I don't think I ever doubted it for a minute." Barack Obama said he was going to be president—when he was in elementary school.

This is the reason why we address thoughts and beliefs prior to vision and goals: they're your building blocks. Your thoughts and beliefs must be in alignment for goals and visions to manifest. Let's face it. People who think they'll fail, fail.

People who think they'll succeed, do.

> LIFE IS A MIRROR AND WILL REFLECT BACK TO THE
> THINKER WHAT HE THINKS INTO IT.
> —ERNEST HOLMES

Modern neuroscience further supports the tenets put forth in Hill's book. As stated earlier, the more you desire a goal, the harder your brain works to achieve it, even subconsciously. I like to picture little neurons with hard hats working underground together to achieve my goals; in my daydream, they look very much like those adorable little yellow Minions from *Despicable Me*. I'm probably giving the more scientifically minded a conniption—but hang on, the reticular activating system (RAS) is a real thing.

RAS is a bundle of nerves at our brainstem that filters out information so that only the important stuff gets through. It takes direction from your conscious mind and then passes it on to your unconscious. Like a bouncer at the best club ever, it only allows in what's on the list. When you consciously pay attention to something, the RAS puts it on the list. It will then start unconsciously noticing things relevant to the list.

For example, a pregnant woman will suddenly start noticing pregnant women and babies everywhere. When you learn a new word, you suddenly read or hear it much more often. You buy a new car, and suddenly you notice that car everywhere. Jeep literally turned the RAS into a marketing program. No joke. For years, Jeep enthusiasts have noted that Jeep owners wave to each other on the road. It was their thing, their nod of solidarity to being in the Jeep club. They call it the Jeep Wave. Fast forward, and Jeep branded the phenomenon into the Jeep Wave premium owner loyalty program. Reticular activating system, at work on and off the road.

Goal setting is like hitting the ignition switch on your RAS. When you set your goals and actively visualize them, the brain picks up the torch to help carry it across the finish line. We've already established that the brain can't distinguish between what's real and what we *think* may be real, and this is why the RAS is so integral to goal setting and attainment. Your brain will believe what you tell it and, in doing so, will influence your actions. It's the law of attraction manifested. It's not mystical. It's neuroscience.

Keeping your goals in focus allows your RAS to continue its heavy lifting. That's why it's recommended to write them down, visualize them, and go over them every day—so you keep them top of mind. Brands pay millions and millions of advertising dollars for top-of-mind consumer awareness. That's an actual marketing metric—the first brand that comes to mind when you think of a category. Soda? Coca-Cola. Tissue? Kleenex. Greeting card? Hallmark. Fast food restaurant? McDonalds. I mean, top-of-mind awareness even has its own game show, for heaven's sake—*Family Feud!* Top-of-mind awareness is a thing, clearly, and its inherent value is huge. The pay-off for companies is that the consumer buys into what they're selling. The pay-off for you?

Your mind buys into the goals you want to achieve!

In 2010, Demi Lovato tweeted that she would perform the national anthem at the Super Bowl one day. Demi was a teenager at the time. Ten years later, she did. Lady Gaga said she pictured her name in lights on the marquee and claimed her fame through daily affirmations. Tom Holland said he wanted to play Spider-Man someday down the line, and it happened three years later. In 2011, prior to launching her solo career, Ariana Grande tweeted that her dream role is to play Glinda in Wicked. Guess who was cast to play Glinda in the movie version of Wicked. . . over ten years later?

While I love, love, love anecdotal stories, there's a wealth of empirical data to walk the talk here too. Setting goals is linked with higher self-esteem, confidence, motivation, autonomy, and success. Moreover, a meta-analysis of studies links goal progress to improved positive affect, the boring technical term for . . . feeling happy. [2] Not sure why we need a meta-analysis to prove that, but good to know that science backs common sense!

A GOAL IS A DREAM WITH A DEADLINE.
—NAPOLEON HILL

Notice how most goal setting involves *writing* your goals, not just saying them, whether out loud or in your head—committing to it in black and white, whether by hand or Helvetica font. Studies show that goal setters achieve their goals. According to a recent study, you're 42 percent more likely to achieve your goals when they're written and well-defined, with a plan of action. [3] It also found that subjects who shared their written goals and progress with friends on an ongoing basis accomplished significantly more.

Never underestimate the power of the written word and an accountability buddy. They're important drivers of goal attainment and success. Research links writing out personal goals to improved health, finding purpose, and living a meaningful life. [4]

Throughout the years, my friends and I have gotten together on many a New Year's Day to have dinner and write letters to ourselves enumerating our goals and dreams for the year to come, to start the New Year off with intention, love, and good food. One year, I was honored to give a joint toast at my girlfriend's wedding. I read aloud a portion of the intentional goal letter she'd written three years prior, before she even met her future husband. It had been in safekeeping at my house. She described her yet-unknown husband to a T in the letter. It was freaky. And proves, once again, that fairy tales written on the heart and put to paper really can come true.

What's written on your heart? Are you ready to translate it into words on the page?

MAKE EVERY GOAL COUNT

Not all goals are created equal. Let's just acknowledge that from the get-go. When my kids say they just want to be famous, I inwardly cringe. And then I sit them down for a heart-to-heart reckoning. I guess you could call me a fame-shamer in that respect, but I'm okay with that if that's the extent of the goal—

fame—without any substance, meaning, or purpose behind it. This is different from fame being a byproduct of a goal or talent. I'm talking about when fame *is* the goal. Well, then, you're not just missing the mark—the target itself is the problem.

This is a burgeoning problem thanks to modern technology, social media, and people achieving overnight fame for the most bizarre things. A phrase, "howbow dah." Yodeling. Crazy pranks or stunts. An egg. Seriously, an egg? Fame has replaced talent in many cases. It's kinda sad. Listen, I'm not about to tediously drone, "Back in my day, we walked thirty miles to school in a blistering blizzard without shoes"—blah, blah, blah. But there does need to be some sort of goal/purpose reset for impressionable minds. *Because it matters.* Studies show that not all goals are created equal and they can have differing effects on subjective happiness and self-esteem.

Research indicates that goals around commitment to family, friends, and social and political involvement (intrinsic goals) promote life satisfaction and happiness. In contrast, goals committed to success, prestige, fame, and material gains (extrinsic goals) appear detrimental to life satisfaction. [5] Researchers speculate that intrinsic goals lead to greater happiness because positive life experiences occur while in pursuit of these goals. [6] Makes total sense. While hedonistic Vegas getaways are always fun and make for cool Instagram snaps, watch people tell stories about their mission trips, volunteering, or meaningful work. Their eyes light up with a sparkle that comes from within and can't be wiped off like caked-on nightclub glitter. The patina of meaningful pursuits never loses its luster.

Researchers further distinguish between two types of happiness: those derived from meaningful pursuits (eudaimonic happiness) versus pleasure-seeking pursuits (hedonic happiness). [7] Most agree that we require both to flourish. While both types are associated with lower depression, data indicates people with meaningful happiness have a better immune response profile, suggesting that a life of meaning may be better for our health at a cellular level. [8]

There's another important distinction to note in our goal quest: it's best to have a mix of process and outcome goals. Data backs this up as well. [9] If you only focus on results, results, results, your happiness could take a hit if the result isn't achieved. Process goals focus on the activities that help achieve the desired result. Here's an example to help you understand the difference: Outcome goal—I will lose thirty pounds. Process goal—I will walk twenty minutes a day. You're engaging in activities that support the goal while detaching your happiness from the specific outcome. Enjoy the journey!

An analysis of eighty-five studies found that happiness is greater when measured as goal progress rather than goal attainment. [10] Progress over perfection. You want to really fall in love with the process—the journey—not just the destination. When we were little, my brother and I would have as much fun on our road trips to the beach as we did when we got there. We'd have snack bags, car games, snuggly pillows. We'd sing songs, stop at cool spots along the way, and beat the hell outta "I spy with my little eye"—you get the idea. The trip was as much fun as the destination. Don't ignore the little wins. They add up.

VISION QUEST

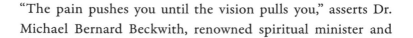

"The pain pushes you until the vision pulls you," asserts Dr. Michael Bernard Beckwith, renowned spiritual minister and author. [11] I love that. It's the ultimate spiritual soundbite. Life is progressive, and we're always growing. The growing pains push us until our vision pulls us. Steve Jobs said, "If you are working on something exciting that you really care about, you don't have to be pushed. The vision pulls you." [12]

I believe both statements. Chances are you picked up this book because of some discomfort or growing pains. Maybe a heartbreak, or perhaps just a little heart fracture. Maybe a case of the blahs or boredom. Maybe it's something you can't quite put your finger on: A feeling that there's something more. Something better. Like someone tapping on your heart. Or maybe you just thought the cover looked cool. Regardless of its origin (pain or inspiration), the common denominator is that vision pulls. Vision is the "running" portion of our upward spiral. Let's get swept up.

AND, WHEN YOU WANT SOMETHING, ALL THE UNIVERSE
CONSPIRES IN HELPING YOU TO ACHIEVE IT.
—PAULO COELHO

The art of imagination—seeing with the mind's eye—is essential to goal setting. Studies have shown that visualization of your goals leads to greater brain activation. Actively visualizing your goals stimulates your RAS. [13] You're constantly tipping the RAS bouncer to let the cool peeps in. To reiterate (I know, *again!*), the brain can't differentiate between the real and the imagined, so visualize your goals in as much glorious technicolor detail as you can. Mental imagery helps drive motivation. [14]

After one of the many breakups with my cheating ex, my girlfriend and I went to lunch and the sweet darling took on the role of consoler-in-chief. Lucky for me, Victoria is a master at it and a literal coaching badass. Anyway, she asked me to describe my ideal, picture-perfect day from the moment I would open my eyes in the morning until I went to sleep that night. She kept probing, having me go into deeper and deeper detail, using all my senses to give as much nuance to the vision as possible. It became almost tangible. The dream *is* in the details. The stark contrast between my perfect day and the present reality was glaringly apparent. My reality wasn't anywhere close to my vision, so why the hell would I mourn the loss of it? I later discovered this exercise is called a "vision walk," and it's an incredibly powerful tool. The vision literally pulled me out of the wah-wah-wah melodrama and redirected my attention to possibility instead of the problem.

If you can dream it, you can be it. In 1984, Mary Lou Retton became the first American woman to win the gold medal in the gymnastics all-around competition. Her use of visualization is well-known. She would lay in bed and visualize the perfect ten performance step-by-step. She would imagine hitting every move perfectly. She'd even visualize receiving the gold medal with the national anthem playing in the background. She won the gold repeatedly in her mind before stepping foot on the Olympic stage. [15] Lindsay Vonn, fellow gold medalist and one of the most successful skiers in history, also credits her mental practice as significant to her competitive edge. "I always visualize the run before I do it. By the time I get to the start gate, I've run that race 100 times already in my head, picturing how I'll take the turns." [16]

EVERYTHING IS CREATED TWICE, THE FIRST TIME IN THE MIND
AND THEN IN REALITY.
—ROBIN SHARMA

My favorite take on this is from Jack Nicklaus, one of the greatest golfers of all time, who said, "Before every shot, I go to the movies." [17] Imagine if we all did that. An image reel in our mind—winning each time. A literal cinema verité for our goals and dreams. You can be the writer, director, *and* star of your very own blockbuster movie—happy ending and all.

A PICTURE REALLY IS WORTH A THOUSAND WORDS

While the pen may be mightier than the sword, it looks like the Polaroid out-champs the ballpoint—at least from a neuroscientific perspective. Pictures speak far more effectively to the brain's subconscious than language. Images can bypass the cerebral cortex, where language is processed, and engage directly with the intuitive and visual parts of the brain. In other words, they skip the line and head straight to VIP.

Images speak louder than words. Given our social media–obsessed world where the mantra is "pics or it didn't happen," let's apply that same philosophy to images far more significant than the well-plated dinner, gym workout, or the endless summer of selfies—images not of the here-and-now, but of our visions for the future. Let's invest some time and imagery in the power of *yet*. It's far more fulfilling than pics of your manicure, promise.

I've been doing vision boards for years. I like the term "action board" better—not just a daydreamer's collage but an image-oriented call-to-action. Dr. Tara Swart, psychiatrist, neuroscientist, senior lecturer at MIT, and author of *The Source: The Secrets of the Universe, the Science of the Brain*, extols the effectiveness of action boards. [18] According to Swart, the brain engages in "value-tagging" and imprints important things on your subconscious. The brain assigns higher value to images than written words. The more you look at the images, the more they move up the importance ladder. Swart also states if you look at the action board right before bedtime, it will imprint even more.

This phenomenon—and all you gamers out there are gonna like this one—is called the Tetris Effect. That's because people who played this incredibly popular, tile-matching puzzle video game on a frequent basis started seeing the pattern of the game's shapes reflected in their day-to-day activities and dreams. They imagined how they could fit objects in the real world together— like boxes on a grocery store shelf or buildings on a street—much like they did with the tiles in the video game. In other words, they began to see the world through the lens of the video game. Subsequent neuroscience studies found that advanced usage of the game made the brain more efficient in this "automation," increased its gray matter/cortical thickness, and positively affected its plasticity. [19]

The Tetris Effect occurs outside of gaming when we focus on a particular thing for extended periods and that pattern starts appearing in our thoughts, mental images, and dreams. I have experienced this so often throughout my life. As I've been writing this book, for example, I've found myself constantly dreaming about the chapter topics and all the relevant content

I've been researching. That's not surprising, as it's always on my mind. That time before sleep is particularly sensitive to suggestion. That's why you often hear people say not to watch the news right before bed. It's why I usually listen to a gratitude meditation on the Calm app while I fall asleep. I'm priming my brain, just like going over your goals and visions before bedtime primes your brain.

It's common sense, really. What you focus your time on influences the way you see the world. (Note: the sword can cut both ways, so pay attention to what you pay attention to!) As best-selling author and leadership expert Robin Sharma asserted, "What you focus on grows, what you think about expands, and what you dwell upon determines your destiny." [20]

ONLY THOSE WHO WILL RISK GOING TOO FAR CAN
POSSIBLY FIND OUT HOW FAR ONE CAN GO.
—T. S. ELIOT

According to a recent TD Bank survey, one in five small business owners used some form of an action/vision board when they started their business. Of these respondents, 76 percent say their business is what they envisioned at the beginning. [21] Sometimes a vision board can take the shape of a check, as was the case with Jim Carey. In 1985, while a broke and struggling comedian, he wrote himself a $10 million check for "acting services rendered" and post-dated it for Thanksgiving, 1995. In November of 1995, Carrey found out he was cast in the movie *Dumb and Dumber* for—$10 million. [22] (*So, you're telling me there's a chance . . .*) Not so dumb after all, hmm?

I practice what I preach. I designed the cover and wrote the dedication for this book when I only had one chapter written; then I made the book cover the desktop image on my computer and the home screen on my phone. I kept it as top of mind as possible, shy of tattooing it on my body. Of course, I still had to act on the vision—had to put in the work. But that visual cover art greeting me every morning, throughout the day, and before bedtime made it seem even more real. I spoke about the published success of the book as a fait accompli and even started talking about the next book topic. The thought of failure wasn't even an option.

Oprah Winfrey, Beyoncè, and Steve Harvey are famous vision board enthusiasts. [23] Recently, I was watching footage of Steve speaking informally to his studio audience about the power of goal setting and vision boards and was just blown away. He said the practice was biblical and referenced a Bible passage: Habakkuk 2:2–3. Intrigued, I looked it up. Sure enough:

Write the vision; make it plain on tablets, so he may run who reads it. For still the vision awaits its appointed time; it hastens to the end—it will not lie. If it seems slow, wait for it; it will surely come; it will not delay.

Seriously, do yourself a favor and google the video. It's on his website, steveharvey.com. The man just doesn't teach—he preaches and extols the practice of goals and vision in a way that elevates the conversation like no other. He speaks from faith. He speaks from experience. And, more importantly, he speaks from the heart.

Action boards are effective—if they're actually put into action. That's the real secret. There are no free rides. If you just put some cool images and phrases together and expect some mystical genie of the universe to pump out your wishes, you're in for a disappointment. But good news: it's never too late. As the saying goes, the best time to plant a tree was twenty years ago. The second-best time is now. It's never too late to get clear on your goals and visions and put them into action. There's no statute of limitation on potential. Vision/action/dream boards are inspiring and help prime the pump.

Let's Tetris our way to destiny, my friends.

A REASON FOR BEING

Perspective is everything. The higher the view, the broader the perspective. Just as Earth looks different from land, from air, and from space, so do our lives look different from various angles.

Rick Warren's *The Purpose Driven Life* was a game-changing book for me. [24] Pastor Rick details the importance of giving back—making a contribution to others—as one of our divine purposes. It's not just the highest view; it's *the* view, broadening my perspective on life and giving inspired meaning to the term "the big picture."

While I believe the end of our human life is really just the beginning (God, eternity, my dad, cool angel singing where I sound like Adele, etc.), I also believe we're given our time here on Earth for a reason. God just didn't put us here to kill some time in the interim. So, I think it's a helpful idea to read your life story backward from time to time in case you need to pivot or add a plot twist to make sure the ending is as fulfilling, robust, and as rich as you would want it to be—to ensure there's no treasure left unburied.

The point of this mental exercise isn't to stir up the regret, shame, and guilt demons. The point is to get perspective on our life in case it needs tweaking. In his bestselling book, *The Untethered Soul: The Journey Beyond Yourself*, Michael Singer asks the reader, "Are you going to wait until that last moment for death to be your teacher? The mere possibility of death has the power to teach us at any moment." [25]

Singer dedicates an entire chapter to the benefit of contemplating death. Not in a morose or morbid way, but rather to raise your awareness and challenge you to live at your highest potential. To be bolder. To live bigger. So that when death does come, there are no regrets. And hey—studies in social psychology have indicated that people tend to regret what they *didn't* do or do *more* of than regret what they did do. [26] Steve Jobs said it best: "Remembering that you are going to die is the best way I know to avoid the trap of thinking you have something to lose. You are already naked. There is no reason not to follow your heart." [27]

THE PURPOSE OF LIFE IS TO DISCOVER YOUR GIFT;
THE WORK OF LIFE IS TO DEVELOP IT;
AND THE MEANING OF LIFE IS TO GIVE YOUR GIFT AWAY.
—DAVID VISCOTT

You have this beautiful gift, just waiting to be unwrapped. Some call it following your bliss, your God-given calling, your purpose, the reason you're on this Earth. It's when you finally start living the life that has been waiting patiently for you. Nudging. Tapping on your heart. Every heart has a song to sing. And this is one song you can't sing off-key.

According to Deepak Chopra, the law of dharma states the divine essence takes human form to fulfill a purpose. It's the seventh spiritual law in his seminal book, *The Seven Spiritual Laws of Success*. [28] I read that chapter a few times to make sure my RAS put it on the list, and here's what I learned—essentially, there are three components to this law: to discover our higher self, to express our unique talents, and to be of service to humanity. These are the keys to living a life of meaning.

In his modern classic *The Alchemist*, Paulo Coelho calls this identification of your purpose in life and pursuing it your "personal legend." [29] I loved that he used the word "legend," as it implies a call to greatness. You sure as heck don't want to be an anecdote. Or a footnote. Or worse yet, an untold story. That would be a true tragedy.

Getting even more granular, author Daniel Pink suggests that to help find our life's purpose, we get to decide what we want our "sentence" to be, [30] implying that a strong purpose can be summed up in a powerful sentence.

$$\geq \backslash ! / \angle$$

THE TWO MOST IMPORTANT DAYS IN YOUR LIFE ARE THE DAY YOU
ARE BORN AND THE DAY YOU FIND OUT WHY.
—ANONYMOUS

In *A Man's Search for Meaning*, neuropsychiatrist Dr. Viktor Frankl chronicles his time as a prisoner in Nazi concentration camps and its lessons for spiritual survival. [31] He quotes Nietzsche—"He who has a *why* to live can bear almost any *how*"—and credits his own "why" as being what helped him survive the atrocities he suffered at the camps. He writes about his therapeutic method, logotherapy, which posits that the pursuit of meaning, not pleasure, is what matters most.

A Man's Search for Meaning has been translated into fifty languages for good reason: it's one of the most deeply profound books ever written. The Afterword of the edition I have shares, "Frankl was once asked to express in one sentence the meaning of his own life. He wrote the response on paper and asked his students to guess what he had written. After some moments of quiet reflection, a student surprised Frankl by saying, 'The meaning of your life is to help others find the meaning of theirs.' 'That was it, exactly,' Frankl said. 'Those are the very words I had written.'"

What's your sentence? What's your *why*?

"The only person you are destined to become is the person you decide to be," said Ralph Waldo Emerson. Notice how he doesn't say fate, circumstance, luck, or genetics; it's the person *you* decide to be, created in your mind and manifested in your action.

Hopefully, by now, you've burned down some shit to make room on your canvas and cleaned up the workspace for your masterpiece. We're not just aspiring to be less cluttered, although that does give us joy (*thanks, Marie*). We really want our tabula rasa to be a tabula *fabulosa*—Latin for fabulous and legendary. We're all about our personal legend, our purpose, our bliss, our personal mission statement, our sentence—our *why*.

Why ask why, you ask? Let's start here: a growing body of research shows that people with a strong sense of life purpose tend to do better across a variety of measures. A life of purpose and meaning is associated with [32]:

* Greater longevity
* Better health such as fewer strokes and heart attacks, and lower risk of dementia and disabilities

- Enhanced memory, executive functioning, and overall cognition

- Better stress management

- Lower depression, anxiety, and other psychological problems

- Engagement in healthier behaviors (i.e., exercise, preventive health measures)

- Better self-image

- Greater life satisfaction and overall well-being

Ka-ching.

Now, don't get all freaked out because you're not sure yet what your purpose is. And especially don't worry that yours isn't "big" enough. Not all life purposes are the same, yet all are equally important. A mother's purpose in raising her children is just as important as that of a missionary. It has often been said that if you want to change the world, go home and love your family.

There was an image of a schoolteacher's funeral service that went viral on social media. In lieu of flowers, the deceased had requested backpacks filled with school supplies for children in need. The funeral parlor was filled with backpacks. It was such a beautiful tribute to a life well-lived. That person embraced their purpose as an educator even in death. It was beyond inspiring.

That said, don't compare purposes! All purposes matter. If it gives meaning to your life, harnesses your talents, and is of service to this world, you're on point. You can make a difference with your family, friends, neighborhood, church, or industry. You can make a difference to a stranger.

I read about *ikigai*, which is Japanese for "a reason for being" or purpose in life, while reading the landmark book, *The Blue Zones*. [33] Dan Buettner identified five places in the world where people live the longest and are healthiest. These longevity hot spots were dubbed blue zones. The researchers found that all blue zones share specific lifestyle habits that they called the Power 9. Having a purpose, a "why I wake up in the morning," was one of those powerful lifestyles, and apparently life-sustaining habits. Simply put, having a "why" leads to longer and happier lives. (As a rule of thumb, the only person you should ask why is yourself. But we'll get more into that later during our EQ vs. IQ discussion.)

Start giving it some thought. Your mission statement. Your sentence. Your why.

Your why is the way.

HAPPINESS CHECK

STRETCH

Ideally, I want you to get clear on your goals in all aspects of your life (physical, career, relationships, etc.) and create an action plan for each as soon as possible. For this exercise, however, we will focus on one macro-goal, and eat that elephant one bite at a time through the merciful, yet incredibly effective, power of micro-goals.

Micro-goals are easy, actionable steps that help you achieve your macro-goal. For example, let's say the ultimate goal is to lose ten pounds. Write out the micro-goals and behaviors that will support this. Examples:

* Clean out the fridge and pantry of unhealthy food and drink items.

- Walk twenty minutes a day, three days a week.

- Prep my meals two days in advance.

- Drink eight glasses of water a day.

- Keep a daily food log on myfitnesspal.com.

- Limit wine to two times a week with dinner, only one glass.

- No TV or phone while eating meals.

- Do not skip meals.

Get the idea? Each goal in itself is doable and not Herculean in scope or intimidation. They are building blocks to success.

CHALLENGE

Perfect Day Exercise: Take yourself on a vision walk and imagine your ideal day. Find a quiet spot, choice of writing instrument in hand. Imagine it's three to five years from now and you're waking up to your perfect day. Write down every detail from when you open your eyes to when you go to sleep at night. Be as specific as you can. Involve all your senses. Don't scrimp on the details. It's your perfect day! Where are you? What does it look like? Who are you with? What activities are you doing? What are you eating and drinking? What's the weather like? What do you do before bed? How are you feeling? Put it all in there, sweetie. Every. Last. Drop.

DOUBLE-DOG DARE YA

Create a Vision/Action Board: Seeing is being. You want to imprint and keep your goals in top-of-mind awareness. Write a list of your goals you'd like to achieve in the next year and find images that reflect those goals. Years ago, I'd gather tons of old magazines to create an action board. That's still a popular method. Nowadays, I simply Google search my images, phrases, and quotes. I do the entire vision board electronically and print it out. It's actually quite artistic given the plethora of design websites. Pinterest has some cool inspiration too. Put the vision board where you will see it every day, especially before bedtime. We wanna put Mr. Sandman to work on your goals as well. Sweet dreams indeed . . .

CHAPTER FIVE

Mind Over Matter and Choosing the Right Hard

WATCH YOUR THOUGHTS;
THEY BECOME YOUR WORDS.
WATCH YOUR WORDS;
THEY BECOME YOUR ACTIONS.
WATCH YOUR ACTIONS;
THEY BECOME YOUR HABITS.
WATCH YOUR HABITS;
THEY BECOME YOUR CHARACTER.
WATCH YOUR CHARACTER;
IT BECOMES YOUR DESTINY.

—LAO TZU

*A*rthur Herbert Fonzarelli. He was my first big crush. While my brothers had the iconic Farrah Fawcett swimsuit poster splayed across their wall, I had the Fonz from *Happy Days* giving me the thumbs up with a swaggering smile meant only for me. I remember it like it was yesterday. My little brother and I would huddle around the television every Tuesday at 8:00 p.m. to see what antics the gang would get into at Arnold's.

One of the extraordinary things about the Fonz was his innate ability to make anything cool, even the unlikeliest of persons, places, or things. If the Fonz gave it the thumbs up, it was instantly relegated to the cool side. He even managed to make a restaurant public restroom cool. As a series ritual, he would often tell the gang to "step into my office," which, in actuality, was the guys' restroom at Arnold's. My germaphobia aside, this struck me as extraordinary. Now *that* was power!

Perception really is everything.

Your perception literally filters everything in your life. How do you perceive your world? Do you see the world through rose-colored glasses, mirrored lenses, or lenses so opaque and dark you can barely find your way out of the darkness? As we dig deeper, you'll see how perception can significantly impact your happiness—for better or worse. The cool thing? You're not married to your perception, and you can swap it out for a brand-new model any time. Make optimism your new pair of aviators; not only will you be more attractive, but so will your view of the entire world.

Remember how children teach us to savor? They can school us with their perspective powers as well. Their sweet little minds aren't sullied by judgments, critiques, biases, or various negative filters. It's why they can play for hours in an empty box, ignoring whatever treasure trove it transported. It's why matchbox cars are the best set of wheels in town. It's why goldfish snacks are literal gold in their stock market portfolio. They perceive everything as magical. Wondrous.

WHAT IS BEHIND YOUR EYES HOLDS MORE POWER
THAN WHAT IS IN FRONT OF THEM.
—GARY ZUKAV

Perhaps your perception can use a recalibration. An injection of wonder. Or at the very least, neutrality. I know mine needs a tune-up from time to time. It's like when we take our car for an oil change, and our filters are all mucked up and full of gunk. Same thing happens with our perceptions—our internal filters—and they, too, need a cleaning. A tune-up. So we can run better. Be better. A bit more wonder-ful.

SWIPE ON, SWIPE OFF

Perception is not reality. I repeat, perception is not reality. Perception is the lens through which we view reality. Part genetic predisposition, our perception is derived mainly from our past experiences, values, beliefs, stereotypes, biases, and cognitive distortions, much of which we learned from childhood. *Real men don't cry. Girls shouldn't be loud or bossy.* We view our experiences of the world through this lens, this filter. Our perception influences how we behave, how we respond, and how we react.

Perception is our subjective interpretation of an objective event. Everyone has two eyes, yet no one shares the same view. Every single event that happens has many different interpretations. You see that played out everywhere. Between spouses. Between siblings. Between political parties. The television series *The Affair* highlighted this concept at its premise. The series was told through alternative perspectives. The first half of the show would tell the story from one character's perspective, while the second half of the show reiterated the same event through the perspective of another character. It was so thought-provoking and compelling in that respect—a cinematic study of memory bias and the subjective interpretation of events. Not surprisingly, our memories tend to portray ourselves in a more flattering or victimized light, which can often be in stark contrast to how the other person remembers the event.

We run all day long on our programmed perceptions, automatically. Your interpretation is part of your larger narrative. Remember, the brain collects evidence to support what you believe to be true. Your interpretation of events feeds and confirms that bias, that narrative.

I remember years ago walking around town with my guy friend. Bummed over a failed relationship, I said, "Geez, I only see happy couples everywhere, argh!" He said, "Really? All I see is gorgeous women." We walked the same path, saw the same things, yet perceived the experience differently through the lenses of our confirmation bias. We do this all the time; we operate on cognitive biases. Our brain takes these unconscious mental shortcuts when processing information to make snap decisions or judgments.

I once attended a personal development workshop in which the participants engaged in feedback arcs. Essentially, we ascribed descriptive adjectives to each other based on perceptions of our looks, dress, or mannerisms as no one had interacted directly. It was seriously the most enlightening experience ever. How many times do you get to hear the thoughts of strangers vocalized out loud based solely on their perception of you?

THERE IS NO TRUTH. THERE IS ONLY PERCEPTION.
—GUSTAVE FLAUBERT

I was judged on my clothing (a participant said I look like one of those housewives of Orange County—I don't watch the franchise, but let's just say it didn't sound like a compliment). Bear in mind, I was in jeans and a blouse. Ironically, I even wore pink so I'd appear more approachable. I was judged because I nodded my head when the speaker said something that resonated (know-it-all). I was judged on my body language because I had my arms wrapped around me as I was chilly (closed-off, lonely). I was judged on how I smiled (charming, but not said in a good way).

Guess what? I was guilty of the same automatic biases in my estimation of people. It was a very humbling moment for me. I realized how I operate on these unconscious biases, these filters, these preconceived notions of reality that affect my perception of people, experiences, and events. It reminded me of the famous quote by Anaïs Nin, "We don't see things as they are, we see them as we are." This is so true. Rather than actually see the people in front of us, we often see nothing more than a reflection of ourselves—of our biases.

I mean, I'd judge people on their handshake as do a slew of other people, as studies attest. [1] Limp and feeble or strong and confident, that's how I had a handshake categorized in my mind. My snap judgment would then color the rest of the interaction. And if the handshake was sweaty and clammy, I'd have yet another judgment to throw the person's way. Given the pandemic and people's reluctance to shake hands, this rather common social judgment may fall to the wayside. Unfortunately, human nature seems talented at maintaining biases even if we must switch it up slightly. I'm sure elbow bumps will now be judged somehow. It's all so ridiculous when you think about it.

Happy AF

*A GREAT MANY PEOPLE THINK THEY ARE THINKING
WHEN THEY ARE MERELY REARRANGING THEIR PREJUDICES.*
—WILLIAM JAMES

Y'all, Tinder has existed for thousands of years—it just operated as an unconscious cognitive bias before it materialized into a dating app. We swipe left or right all day long in our minds. Through the feedback exercise I just described, I realized how often I unconsciously shut myself off from meaningful engagement with people based on my assumptions. I'd assume that I'd have little in common with the person based on a superficial assessment of their person. And I think that . . . sucks. So let's cut it out. Seriously, we need to stop swiping. Not just in dating, but in life.

I'm so thankful for that aha moment. After the bias reckoning, I met one of my best friends and favorite people in the world in that workshop. Twenty years younger. Different gender. Different sexual orientation. Different culture. No kids. We couldn't appear more different on the surface, yet my soul feels at home in his presence. I would have missed out on the gift of his friendship. Because of f*cking swiping. As Carl Jung proclaimed, "Until you make the unconscious conscious, it will direct your life, and you will call it fate." How do we do that? I can think of one way: the power of the pause.

STAND IN THE GAP

⇒ ⇐

That BFF that I just mentioned? He's the master of the pause. It's his legit superpower. He grew up in an environment that was often saturated with reckless words, and he was committed to showing up differently. Some people really don't get the power words can have to hurt or to heal. I've been guilty of that throughout the years, and it's not something of which I'm proud. I strive to be better with my words and reactions. *Constantly.*

My friend is the most thoughtful person that I've ever encountered. And when I say thoughtful, I mean measured in the expression of his thoughts. No matter what the topic or question, he'll always take a pause and collect his thoughts before answering. It's an incredible thing for an emotive, East Coast Italian like myself to witness; it leaves me in awe.

I recently saw a meme that made me laugh, well, because it resonated a bit: *I don't like to think before I speak. I like to be just as surprised as everyone else about what comes out of my mouth.*

You could say I hail from a family of reactors, with not always pretty results. I mean, they call it a nuclear reactor not a nuclear responder for a reason. It blows shit up. Some of my past reactions have had that unfortunate distinction. I'd make excuses and rationalize that hey, I'm passionate. I have a big, ebullient personality. I live big and love big. Looking back, I can see that all I was doing was rationalizing my lack of self-control. I can embrace the power of the pause and still have a big personality, and I think that's the greatest way to love big.

Love lives in the pause.

Mindfulness creates space between events and your reactions, between thoughts and your words. It creates a layer. A buffer, if you will. One of my favorite quotes, probably because it addresses my struggle, is attributed to Viktor Frankl: "Between stimulus and response, there is a space. And in that space is our power to choose our response. In our response lies our growth and our freedom."

Response versus reaction. Freedom versus being held hostage by your emotions. Let's look at the difference between the two. A reaction tends to be instinctual: an instantaneous response to a person or situation without much thought given to the outcome or consequence of the interaction. It's largely unconscious. It could be favorable or not, depending on your feelings, depending on your mood.

WHATEVER IS BEGUN IN ANGER, ENDS IN SHAME.
—BENJAMIN FRANKLIN

Some reactions are necessary. Survival instinct, defense mechanisms, all that good stuff. I'm not talking about those scenarios. Of course, react away in those instances. I'm talking about everyday events and challenges, when it's not life or death or necessary to react quickly: conversations with loved ones, colleagues, friends. A response is a reaction all grown up. Matured. Tempered by the conscious as well as the unconscious. It takes the outcome into consideration and responds according to the desired result. It harnesses the power of the pause and transforms itself from an emotional crapshoot to emotional intelligence.

A reaction is about the **moment**, whereas a response is about the **outcome**. Yep, I did the corny bolding of letters to underscore the point. The reaction is all about me (hint: you) in the moment, while a response takes into consideration the consequences to others (outside of me) as well. A response is the thinking person's reaction.

So how do you learn to respond rather than react? *Mindfulness.*

I know, I know—for some of us this sounds so esoteric, so *out there.* My Virgo mind tends to like concrete solutions, easily definable. How the f*ck do you quantify mindfulness? You can't. Yet the things that tend to be the biggest stretch/challenge for me (meditation, affirmations, mindfulness) are ironically the very mechanisms by which I see the greatest results.

Again, it's not that difficult. It just takes awareness and practice. And before you claim that you're stuck in your ways and can't learn new tricks like mindfulness, I call bullshit. And I was thoughtful in that response, *promise.* Recent research supports the effectiveness of mindfulness training in teaching older adults how to respond and not react. Findings suggest that mindfulness can simultaneously improve cognitive and emotional regulation, which may be particularly beneficial for older adults. [2] And that's really what a response is: self-regulation. It's not a reactional free-for-all. So, buckle up buttercup, you, too, can learn to harness this superpower. Your heart and health will thank you.

And your loved ones will too.

Mindfulness is paying attention to the present moment—noticing your thoughts, feelings, body sensations, and the world around you. Mindfulness is the stopgap to your reaction when you're feeling triggered (e.g., someone cuts you off in traffic; a coworker sends a snarky email; your spouse forgets your anniversary). Before being triggered though, let's start practicing mindfulness a few times throughout the day. *Just because.* Why wait for the shit to hit the fan? By practicing mindfulness throughout the day, you're priming the pump for when the inevitable trigger hits. Kinda like a dry run.

Mindful pauses are wonderful for your peace of mind, triggered or not. By simply taking a minute or two to check in with your body and mind, breathe, and notice your environment, you're setting yourself up for success later down the line as well. Habitual practice enables its natural occurrence when faced with triggering stimuli. Our goal is to dial down the unconscious autopilot of emotions and tap into the conscious response—which I promise is a way better driver. Fewer bumps and harrowing curves.

DON'T GET UPSET WITH PEOPLE OR SITUATIONS;
BOTH ARE POWERLESS WITHOUT YOUR REACTION.
—UNKNOWN

Triggering stimulus alert. What do you do? Take a mindful pause. Breathe and buy yourself some more time. Allow yourself to feel the emotion and take a step back from it, like an observer. The distance allows you to contemplate a response. Examine the circumstances and all possible explanations. Research indicates that mindfulness encourages cognitive flexibility, a fancy term for generating alternative explanations. [3] It's seeing the big picture, not just your narrow view.

What are your thoughts? What are you feeling? Label that emotion. Notice any sensations in your body. For me, it's like I can literally feel the blood pressure rising like a tsunami on the inside. Some feel a tightness in their chest or throat. Continue to breathe. Count to five. Now throw a throat punch. *Kidding.* Just wanted to see if you were paying attention.

Pausing. Checking in. Noticing self and surroundings. Breathing. Contemplating the response. Considering the outcome you desire. Getting perspective.

If there's time, you could even play the movie in your mind. Visualize your potential responses and how the resulting scenarios may play out. It's not rocket science. Your emotions don't have to control the show. You get to choose your response. No one can make you angry, resentful, or sad without your permission. Think about that. I mean, *really* think about that. There's power in that—an even greater power than there is in convincing your friends that hanging out in a public restroom is cool.

EQ OVER IQ

A reaction is emotional. A response is emotional intelligence (EI). EI (also called EQ) has been gaining more and more attention in recent years. If you're unclear on the distinction between IQ and EQ, IQ is a metric of one's intellectual ability and potential (reasoning, logic, problem-solving, etc.) and EQ is the ability to recognize and manage your emotions to express feelings appropriately.

EQ encompasses the ability to recognize and understand the emotions of others. Can't "manage" those bad boys because you can only control yourself, right? Repeat after me—"I can only control myself." But you can recognize and understand the emotion of others—that's called empathy. That's a good thing. And in doing so, you can help manage the situation. Crisis interventionists do it for a career. You can do it for a conversation.

In his book *Emotional Intelligence,* Dr. Daniel Goleman theorizes that EQ is the largest single predictor of success in the workplace. [4] Largest. Single. Predictor. Subsequent studies have quantified it even further, showing that individuals with high EQs make approximately $29,000 more annually than people with low EQs. It's directly linear too. On average, each incremental point of EQ equates to an additional $1,300 in annual salary. [5] Here's the really cool thing: unlike IQ, we can improve our EQ with effort and practice.

I put that little fun fact first because so many people often view success through the lens of income. We've already established that money can't buy happiness. It's nice to know, though, that being in touch with your own emotions can pay off financially as well as in a host of other categories. High EQ is associated with [6]:

* Better social relationships
* Higher academic achievement
* Better job performance and leadership abilities
* Emotional well-being
* Life satisfaction
* Self-actualization

I'd take that over being a Mensa member any day of the week.

Emotional regulation begins with self-awareness, the ability to understand your emotions and recognize your own tendencies and triggers. It's not enough to know better. That means nothing if you still go nuclear in your reactions. You get to *do* better as well and harness that awareness to regulate and direct your behaviors, your responses—to dial it down a notch, shift gears, and appropriately express yourself. Basically, to think before you act.

Psychologist Marc Brackett, founder of the Yale Center for Emotional Intelligence, developed an evidence-based approach for teaching EQ to children and teenagers. It's been used in nearly two thousand schools across the world. It hails by the acronym RULER, which I have to say is a full-circle moment for me. When I was in elementary and middle school, the teachers would rap our knuckles with a ruler as a means of reprimand. This esteemed psychologist and research staff now use RULER as an instrument to teach social and emotional skills. If that's not progress, I'm not sure what is. Of course, RULER can be applied to adults as well [7] (and it doesn't even sting). RULER is:

* RECOGNIZING emotions in oneself and others.

* UNDERSTANDING the cause and consequences of the emotion. Ask yourself, "Why am I feeling this way?"

* LABELING the emotion. We've been here before. Name it to tame it.

* EXPRESSING emotions appropriately in accordance with social norms and contexts, taking the when, how, who, and where into consideration. I'm a big believer in timing. Timing is everything. Ideally, you'd address an issue privately with your partner and not at a dinner party amidst onlookers. Moreover, you'd express feeling differently with a coworker than your spouse. Essentially, tune into the time, place, and appropriate tone for every situation.

* REGULATING emotions with helpful strategies; finding what works best for you. Breathing. Mindfulness. Visualization. How would my "best self" react in this situation? Take a five-minute timeout. Exercise. It could be as simple as splashing cold water on your face.

Always have your "emotion regulation" tool kit readily available. When my kids were little, I had a de-stress sitting area for when they were feeling stressed out or upset. There was a basket with a calming sound machine, coloring books and crayons, picture books about emotions and feelings, stress balls in the shape of cute animals, a snuggly blanket, and, of course, stuffed animals. You get the idea. These were things to help them regulate their emotions in a healthy fashion.

Adults need an emotional regulation tool kit too. Journaling, exercising, calling a friend, yoga, meditation. I even have adult coloring books—it's as relaxing now as it was back then. Otherwise, it's too easy to use vices as a means of emotional regulation (e.g., alcohol, drugs, food, porn, etc.). If I'd turned to my tool kit during my time as roadkill instead of burying it deep in the garage of self-loathing, I would have lifted myself out of my funk a helluva lot sooner. Keep your emotional regulation tool kit handy, my friends. Doing so will save you a lot of pain.

AS MUCH AS 80% OF ADULT "SUCCESS" COMES FROM EQ.
—DANIEL GOLEMAN

Individuals with high EQs tend to be to more intrinsically motivated and work towards their personal goals. This influences their interactions with people and situations and is reflected in their responses. For example, if your goal is to create a healthy, loving relationship, "f*ck off" is probably not an effective response in a disagreement.

We can be so committed to "being right" in an argument that we really miss the forest (*happiness*) for the trees (*I'm right*). Next time you are in a heated debate, ask yourself, "What's my goal in this relationship?" or "What is my end goal in this situation?" Then try out these four words: "You may be right." Dial down the temperature. I believe people want to be heard more than anything. Acknowledging their voice and perspective can do wonders. This isn't necessarily agreeing or condoning, mind you. It's creating space through the grace of acknowledgment.

Another word to the wise—be wary of using the word "why" if you can help it. *Why, you ask?* Often, when you ask a person "why," it immediately puts them on the defensive. It sounds accusatory (implying something wrong) and, as such, increases the chances of receiving a defensive reply. Think football. Defense blocks the play. It doesn't move the ball down the field. In a dialogue, we're looking to move the ball down the field—make progress, gain ground. That doesn't mean don't inquire. To the contrary. But do so in a way that moves the ball down the field. Remember, it's never what you say, it's how you say it that matters most. "How did you arrive at that decision?" or "What are your thoughts behind that?" are more effective means to a positive outcome.

EQ involves recognizing and understanding other people's emotions and perspectives, being in tune and not tuned out. My eldest daughter was born a Jedi master in this respect. Whereas my youngest daughter is my twin soul, my eldest daughter is my heart and the kindest person I've ever met. Her EQ is off the charts. She can walk into a room, just look at you, and be able to tell if something is wrong (despite diligent efforts to hide it, may I add). She picks up on emotional cues that most people are clueless about or impervious to recognizing. It's one of her greatest gifts. She makes me want to be a better person, and I can think of no compliment greater than that.

Empathy is a skill and is more innate for some than others. It's being able to see things from the other person's perspective—seeking to understand the "why" behind their feelings. It's checking in to see if your understanding is on track with their perspective—taking the time to see through their eyes, their understanding, their perspective.

THE BIGGEST COMMUNICATION PROBLEM IS
WE DO NOT LISTEN TO UNDERSTAND. WE LISTEN TO REPLY.
—STEPHEN COVEY

I hope you're not skipping the quotes I've been including throughout these chapters. They're meant to strike a chord in your heart, like arrows from a philosophical Cupid. And that one from Stephen Covey? It's worth internalizing until your RAS puts it on the permanent VIP list.

We're all so guilty of listening for our cue to reply, our turn, our time in the sun rather than listening to really understand the other person. You can totally *feel* the difference. When someone is really listening, seeking to understand your perspective, it's an energy, like an auditory hug that reaches into your heart. Similarly, you can feel the closed energy when someone is paying you ear service, without really taking in a single nuance of your perspective.

When we were little, my brother and I watched *Mr. Rogers' Neighborhood* every day. In times of childhood chaos, Mr. Rogers was the calming figure in the storm—a kind-spirited man, with the sweater and puppets, wanting to be our friend, making us feel special just as we were. He understood children because he really listened to them, and kids felt that. It's why they responded so overwhelmingly with love and adoration. He was the ultimate safe space. According to Mr. Rogers, "Listening is where love begins: listening to ourselves and to our neighbor. . . In easy times and in tough times, what seems to matter most is the way we show those nearest us that we've been listening to their needs, their joys, and to their challenges." [8] He called himself an emotional archeologist, and his EQ is what made him beloved by millions of children (and adults too).

Be like Mr. Rogers. Listen more.

I BELIEVE THREE OF THE MOST IMPORTANT WORDS ANYONE CAN SAY ARE NOT I LOVE YOU, BUT I HEAR YOU.

—OPRAH WINFREY

Individuals high in EQ tend to have more developed social skills and can interact with people and navigate situations more harmoniously. It's why people in leadership positions tend to have higher EQ—they can read the room and act in accordance with the desired outcome. This is otherwise known as "plays well with others." It works in the boardroom as well as the playground. Active listening, verbal and nonverbal communication skills, developing rapport and trust—all are indicators of high EQ. Hint: an eye roll is the antithesis of EQ, as is the passive-aggressive sigh.

Really look at your communications skills. Up your game. Life is better when *everyone* is winning.

GREAT EXPECTATIONS

Emotional intelligence checklist:

Perception is not reality? *Check.*

Respond, not react? *Check.*

Emotional regulation tool kit? *Check.*

Expectations? Expectations? . . . *and we have a runner.*

You may have heard the saying, "Happiness is reality minus expectations." Our expectations often influence our perception of the world. These "prior beliefs" influence how we interpret present events. Unrealistic expectation is often the main villain in my personal narrative. I'll have these Kodak moment images of how things should be in my head, and when reality doesn't reflect that perfect image, I'm disappointed—sometimes bitterly so. Expectation is premeditated disappointment, plain and simple. I know this. *I know better.* And yet, I still can engage in expectation traps if I'm not mindful.

DISAPPOINTMENT IS THE GAP THAT EXISTS
BETWEEN EXPECTATION AND REALITY.
—JOHN C. MAXWELL

This was particularly true with the birth of my firstborn. I had all these images of how beautiful and magical the day would be. I'd played the Hallmark movie version several times in my head. Instead, my water broke eight weeks early, and I was helicoptered (trauma-ridden and by myself) to a county hospital across town—supposedly because that hospital was known to have the most advanced neonatal care in the area.

As I was being wheeled in, they asked me if I spoke English, very slowly and very loudly, may I add, as if being a brunette (back then, anyway) had addled my senses in addition to whatever other biases they were operating under. A number of my compatriots there were pregnant female inmates from the local prison in wheelchairs with shackles and police escorts. The birthing room had cockroaches. The nurses told me I was just lucky there was a working TV with two channels. Dim, dismal, and somewhat dilapidated, it wasn't exactly the birthing suite I was expecting.

After I gave birth to my precious four-pound baby girl, the medical staff rushed her to emergency to check her vitals. My family, of course, went with the baby. Not thinking, the nurse turned off the light. I laid there in the dark, temporarily paralyzed from the waist down, by myself, not even having held my baby before they took her away. Talk about surreal. WTF had just happened? Was this a nightmare? Did I even really give birth?

Did you ever see *Poltergeist*, where the teenager Dana comes home at the end of the movie, and the entire house is being sucked into a crazy, demonic vortex and she just starts screaming over and over again, "What's happening?!" That was me in my mind. I almost couldn't process my reality versus my expectations.

Days later, I was discharged without my baby. She spent a few more weeks in the NICU. Every night, I sat in her empty nursery and just cried. This wasn't how I'd imagined it to be. Long story short, despite the fact that my daughter was discharged from the hospital with a clean bill of health not long after, I couldn't stave off the postpartum depression, and that rift—the deep chasm between my expectations of my birthing experience and its reality—played a huge part in sparking that depression, not to mention my elevated-to-epic-proportions anxiety over a delicate preemie baby, risk of SIDS, etc. Thank goodness for therapy and medication.

Moral of the story? Expectations can really f*ck you up.

Think of all the expectations you have operating at any given moment. Expectations of your significant other. Coworkers. Children. Expectations of events. Holidays. Birthdays. Date night. There's nothing *great* about expectations. It's a psychological setup that you perpetrate on yourself—setting yourself and others up for failure because, God forbid, reality doesn't meet your expectations. It's the *Should Shitshow*. Do yourself a favor and remove "should" from your thinking.

How do you avoid the expectation pitfall? Again, the first step is awareness. Always check in with yourself. What are your expectations of this person or situation? Are they realistic? What are they based on? Communicate instead. People aren't mind readers or privy to your laundry list of expectations. Instead of getting mad at your partner because they "should" have taken out the garbage, simply ask them to please take out the trash. Instead of being disappointed with birthday plans, express what you'd like to do. We expect people to be mind readers and then get disappointed when it turns out that people can't read minds. Why be an intentional saboteur? You, too, can be an emotional archeologist and happiness architect. It's a choice.

Have you ever heard the phrase "choose your hard"? It's prevalent in social media, and I'm slightly obsessed with it. It's a quick filter tune-up that works when I need it the most.

MARRIAGE IS HARD. DIVORCE IS HARD.

CHOOSE YOUR HARD.

OBESITY IS HARD. BEING FIT IS HARD.

CHOOSE YOUR HARD.

BEING IN DEBT IS HARD. BEING FINANCIALLY DISCIPLINED IS HARD.

CHOOSE YOUR HARD.

COMMUNICATION IS HARD. NOT COMMUNICATING IS HARD.

CHOOSE YOUR HARD.

LIFE WILL NEVER BE EASY. IT WILL ALWAYS BE HARD.

CHOOSE YOUR HARD.

—ANONYMOUS

You get to choose: your response over a reaction; acknowledgment over being right; communication over expectation. When you're mindful and aware, *you choose the right hard.*

A recent study suggests the key to happiness is lowering your expectations. Researchers found that it didn't matter how well things were going, as long as they were going *better* than expected. [9] I'm conflicted here. In general, to lower your expectations sounds like weary resignation, like the mediocrity/comfort zone crap. But I think it's more nuanced than that. It doesn't mean your ceiling is now the ground or that you must yield your boundaries, aspirations, or dreams. It doesn't mean aim low in life. It's about being mindful and recognizing the unrealistic thought patterns and distortions that can sabotage your happiness; not letting rigid expectations undermine the beauty of all that is currently around you; being grateful for what's right in front of you.

Expectations can be positive without being unrealistic. And *positive* expectations—well, now that's a different story. With a happier ending.

STOICISM, OPTIMISM, AND WINNIE THE POOH

I have a crush on a dude from the second century. My heartthrob happens to be the badass Roman emperor and preeminent Stoic philosopher Marcus Aurelius. During his reign, he journaled lessons, thoughts, and insights to himself that are immortalized in the modern-day translation *Meditations*. [10] It's one of my most favorite books, primarily because I aspire to his views of life. I love the way he thinks. It's like an antidote to my overly emotional tendencies.

Stoicism teaches us to live in the moment, focus only on what we can control, and treat others fairly and justly. If I were to summarize Stoicism (for me) in one sentence, it would be the following quote by Marcus Aurelius: "We can't control everything that happens to us but we can control how we interpret what happens to us and how we respond." Stoicism pretty much encapsulates the power of the pause, objective interpretation, response versus reaction, and neutrality. There are other virtues outlined in Stoicism (courage, self-control, justice, wisdom), but I'm not looking to get into a thesis dissertation here. I love Stoicism because it isn't armchair philosophy—one of those theories that's so convoluted, you can't figure out what the hell they're saying—but rather an actionable and understandable operating system for making yourself better. And happier.

Another one of my most favorite philosophers? Winnie the Pooh. Legit. I even have a Winnie the Pooh canvas hanging above my desk, reminding my daughters and myself that we are braver, stronger, smarter, and more loved than we'll ever know. I've always adored Pooh's simplistic optimism and his love of friends (and honey). When I think about it, there are many similarities between the musings of my two favorite philosophers. [11] To support this premise, I created this handy-dandy comparison chart for your viewing pleasure.

EACH DAY PROVIDES ITS OWN GIFTS.	ANY DAY SPENT WITH YOU IS MY FAVORITE DAY. SO, TODAY IS MY NEW FAVORITE DAY.
A PERSON'S WORTH IS MEASURED BY THE WORTH OF WHAT HE VALUES.	HOW LUCKY AM I TO HAVE SOMETHING THAT MAKES SAYING GOODBYE SO HARD.
A WRONGDOER IS OFTEN A MAN WHO HAS LEFT SOMETHING UNDONE, NOT ALWAYS ONE WHO HAS DONE SOMETHING.	IF PEOPLE ARE UPSET BECAUSE YOU'VE FORGOTTEN SOMETHING, CONSOLE THEM BY LETTING THEM KNOW YOU DIDN'T FORGET—YOU JUST WEREN'T REMEMBERING.
THE HAPPINESS OF YOUR LIFE DEPENDS UPON THE QUALITY OF YOUR THOUGHTS.	THINK IT OVER, THINK IT UNDER.
REMEMBER THAT VERY LITTLE IS NEEDED TO MAKE A HAPPY LIFE.	SOMETIMES THE SMALLEST THINGS TAKE UP THE MOST ROOM IN YOUR HEART.
TIME IS SORT OF A RIVER OF PASSING EVENTS, AND STRONG IS ITS CURRENT; NO SOONER IS A THING BROUGHT TO SIGHT THAT IT IS SWEPT BY AND ANOTHER TAKES ITS PLACE, AND THIS TOO WILL BE SWEPT AWAY.	RIVERS KNOW THIS: THERE IS NO HURRY. WE SHALL GET THERE SOME DAY.

THE IMPEDIMENT TO ACTION ADVANCES ACTION. WHAT STANDS IN THE WAY BECOMES THE WAY.	I ALWAYS GET TO WHERE I'M GOING BY WALKING AWAY FROM WHERE I HAVE BEEN.
MEN EXIST FOR THE SAKE OF THE OTHER.	IF THERE EVER COMES A DAY WHEN WE CAN'T BE TOGETHER, KEEP ME IN YOUR HEART, I'LL STAY THERE FOREVER.
ANGER CANNOT BE DISHONEST.	OH BOTHER.

Tell me you don't see it, right?! I've decided to embrace both, and that's why I consider myself a Stoic optimist—an optimist with a healthy dose of realism added to the mix to stave off any *Unbreakable Kimmy Schmidt* vibes.

Optimism is the belief that the outcomes of events or things will generally turn out positively. These positive expectations are not tied to a specific result, outcome, or narrow view of what "should" be. It's much different than the other rigid expectations we just touched on.

CHOOSE TO BE OPTIMISTIC, IT FEELS BETTER.
—DALAI LAMA

Like emotional intelligence, optimism can be learned. Learned optimism isn't being an annoying Pollyanna, but rather acknowledging our struggles and engaging in an explanatory style that boosts our self-control and promotes growth. In his book *Learned Optimism,* Martin Seligman distinguishes between pessimists and optimists in how they manage the "three P's" of emotional resilience when a setback or challenge occurs [12]:

* PERMANENCE: Optimists view setbacks as temporary as opposed to a fatalistic, things-are-never-going-to-get-better mindset. It's why optimists keep on keepin' on and why pessimists throw in the towel. Words matter, so watch the self-talk. Get rid of "can't," "always," and "never." Think in terms of "not yet," "this time," or "next time."

* PERSONALIZATION: Optimists view setbacks as due to circumstances or external forces and do not blame themselves like their contrarian counterparts. They separate the performance from the person and shift from "I" to "my." "My performance could use improvement" is much better than "I'm terrible," don't ya think?

* PERVASIVENESS: Optimists view a setback as just a setback, an occurrence, and not an indictment of their entire existence like good ole Eeyore. Setbacks aren't contagious. A speeding ticket only ruins your whole day if *you* let it. A failed test doesn't mean you suck at school. Keep the setback in its own lane.

This works both ways. When good things happen, the situation reverses itself. Pessimists think good things will be temporary, are uncommon, and are random in nature. Optimists believe good things will last, are universal, and of their own doing. Same event. Two different ways of interpretation. Which way sounds healthier? Happier?

Don't stand in the way of your own sunshine.

∖\|/∕

THE PESSIMIST SEES THE DIFFICULTY IN EVERY OPPORTUNITY; AN
OPTIMIST SEES THE OPPORTUNITY IN EVERY DIFFICULTY.
—WINSTON CHURCHILL

As far as I'm concerned, pessimists can take their half-empty glass and sit far, far away from me. I'm not interested in hanging with people like that. The famed Stoic philosopher Seneca asserted, "Associate with people who are likely to improve you." Pessimists aren't those peeps. Water seeks its own level, so stay away from pessimistic puddles.

Not surprisingly, an optimistic attitude is linked to numerous benefits, including [13]:

- Better mental health, resilience, and coping
- Happiness and higher self-esteem
- Lower stress levels and depression
- Better physical health
- Increased success in sports and work
- Increased life expectancy

Optimists view setbacks as a challenge or a learning opportunity—a teachable moment. Remember, no failures—just learning opportunities. Lean into it. When you really try, you can reframe even difficult setbacks in a positive fashion. I can't even begin to count how many of my own heartbreaks (perceived as such in the moment) have turned into "Phew, dodged that bullet!" with 20/20 hindsight.

You really never know till you know.

HAPPINESS CHECK

STRETCH

Press your pause button. *Mindfulness.* Remember, we want to practice with some dry runs and not wait until the shit hits the fan and we're triggered like the Incredible Hulk. So, commit to one day of practice. Commit to three mindful pauses throughout the day where you take a few minutes and just check in. Breathe. Notice your surroundings, your thoughts, what you may be feeling. Just be in the present moment. If you're game, try taking a slight pause before your responses that day as well. Just three seconds to breathe and collect your thoughts before you speak or respond. Measured responses are a recipe for success.

CHALLENGE

Ask for feedback (the constructive kind!). Constructive feedback goes a long way toward increased self-awareness. I used to ask my kids for feedback all the time (a little less frequently now given the snarky teenage years). Ask someone you trust and respect to give you honest feedback. How are you showing up? What's working? What's not working? What's missing? Don't get defensive. Take it in and reflect upon it. As Stephen Covey observed, "It takes humility to seek feedback. It takes wisdom to understand it, analyze it and appropriately act on it."

DOUBLE-DOG DARE YA

Turn that frown upside down and find the good in a failure. Stoicism advises to actively seek the positive in all negative events.

A closed door often leads to a better opportunity and growth. Reflect on a setback in your life, something you previously viewed as a failure. Find the benefit in it. What did you learn from the experience? Did it build character? Faith? Perseverance? Empathy? What would you do differently next time? What was its lesson? How are you better for it?

CHAPTER SIX

All You Need Is Love

IF YOU WANT TO BE HAPPY, BE.
—LEO TOLSTOY

R emember the seventy-five-year longitudinal study of adult development from
Harvard mentioned at the beginning of the
book? The longest study on health, happiness,
and well-being? The principal investigator and
psychologist, Dr. George Valliant, summarized
the results of this $20-million study as, "Happi-
ness is love. Full stop." [1]

When the study came out, a newspaper editor challenged
Dr. Valliant's conclusion as perhaps being overly sentimental. I
picture Mr. Potter, the embittered villain from *It's a Wonderful
Life*, shouting, "Sentimental hogwash!" The good doctor didn't
get defensive; he just brought the receipts. He went back and
spent a month reviewing the data to ensure there was no senti-
mentality in its interpretation. Once again, he analyzed all the
predicting variables and results through a scientific lens. The
conclusion? Still L-O-V-E. [2]

Family and friends are, without a doubt, my greatest gifts.
Honestly, I think it was the limited access to my peeps during
the pandemic that hastened my descent to roadkill. I sorely

missed being in their presence. Yes, we spoke on the phone (*when I picked up, that is*), but I kept my emotional distress under wraps. I know if they'd seen me in person, they'd have slapped some sense into me, but they didn't, and so my slump dragged on.

A FRIEND IS SOMEONE WHO KNOWS THE SONG IN YOUR HEART
AND CAN SING IT BACK TO YOU WHEN YOU
HAVE FORGOTTEN THE WORDS.
—SHANIA TWAIN

THE FAMILY WE CHOOSE

My friends refresh my very being. They view me—and hence my highs, lows, antics, missteps, etc.—through a filter of grace. A filter of love. Kinda like the filter used in the old Doris Day/ Rock Hudson movies. Ever notice how all the close-up shots of Doris are with a soft-focus lens? Almost fuzzy, like a visual angora sweater. The satiny focus made her appear even softer. Sweeter. Those are my friends. They're my Doris Day filter.

And they're my rock too.

The universe gave us friends as a second chance for family— just in case. The lucky ones have the best of both worlds, and I count myself among the fortunate. I have the best brothers in the entire world, a mom who is my biggest cheerleader, and a dad who gave miniature empty gift-wrapped boxes to his teenage children one Christmas. The boxes represented his love for us— which really could never be seen or contained. He was *that* dad. Loving, kind, proud beyond belief.

There's a different kind of unconditional love that is found purely in the free will and choice of friendship, however. We get to pick each other. Our relationships are baptized not by birth but by fire. I chose my friends once, and I'd choose them over and over again—each and every time.

And to be clear, I consider myself quite the discriminating connoisseur of friends. My girls-on-fire are the Katniss Everdeens of kick-ass fabulosity—and not by accident. In fact, I have developed certain nonnegotiables throughout the years and have become more and more particular with age.

MY PRIMARY LITMUS TEST OF FRIEND NONNEGOTIABLES

- Character, character, character
- Truly a good person
- Loving
- Word is their bond
- Royalty of loyalty
- No drama
- Brilliant (British lexicon version)
- Funny as hell
- Forever young at heart
- Edifiers
- Will laugh, cry, cackle, and cocktail with you at a moment's notice

Those are my deal-breakers or makers. Yours may be different from mine—but remember, there's a flock for everyone. Just be careful who you choose. It will determine how high you fly.

SOCIAL SUPPORT, NOT SOCIAL MEDIA

Let's clarify something. Your social network, especially your social media network, is not the same as social support. So many people are obsessed with how many followers they have on any given social media platform, yet "likes" and smiley face emojis are a hollow replacement for actual intimacy. True social support is having a network of family and friends that you can turn to—an emotional net to catch you, embrace you, propel your bounce. To be your Doris Day filter and rock. To stop you from doing something dumb, like drunk dialing or texting. To listen, advise, laugh, celebrate, mourn, and, most importantly, make you realize you're not alone.

They're your happy place.

IF YOU GO LOOKING FOR A FRIEND, YOU'RE GOING TO FIND THEY'RE VERY SCARCE. IF YOU GO OUT TO BE A FRIEND, YOU'LL FIND THEM EVERYWHERE.
—ZIG ZIGLAR

Our pioneering papas of positive psychology, Ed Diener and Martin Seligman, found similar results to the Harvard study in their study of college students. They examined students with the highest scores of personal happiness and found the most significant characteristic shared by these very happy peeps was "strong ties to friends and family and commitment to spending time with them." [3]

Social support is the psychological and material resources provided by your significant other, family, friends, and peers, through good times and bad. It comes in many different shapes and sizes [4]:

- EMOTIONAL SUPPORT: People who help fill your love, trust, and intimacy tank. They're the shoulder you lean on, cry on, and laugh on, those with whom you can be your vulnerable self. These peeps are particularly important during times of stress or loneliness.

- TANGIBLE/INSTRUMENTAL SUPPORT: People who offer you physical assistance: a hand to help with babysitting, go with you to the doctor, borrow money, give you a ride, help you move, etc. They show up.

- APPRAISAL SUPPORT: People you trust to give you honest feedback. "Tell me the honest-to-God truth . . ." and they do so in a way that supports your growth, not hinders it. The unsolicited critical cacklers can take a hike, thank you very much.

- INFORMATIONAL SUPPORT: People you trust for expert advice, guidance, and opinion, such as doctors, clergy, accountants, teachers, etc.

- COMPANIONSHIP/BELONGING SUPPORT: People with whom you share activities and enjoyment such as a social group, book club, cycling peloton, church group, etc.

Social support provides a type of insulation, a protective barrier. Whether in calm or choppy waters, social support is there buoying you through it all. It's kinda like an inner tube in your river of life but better because it doesn't let your ass hang out. A review of the happiness research clearly indicates that it's not simply the quantity but rather the quality of the relationship that matters most. [5] And no, Alexa or Siri are not adequate replacements for human contact.

Research and studies on the positive effects of social support are plentiful, and high levels of social support are linked to enhanced levels of [6]:

- Happiness

- Life satisfaction

- Longevity

- Immunity

- Mental health

- Physical health

Moreover, a meta-analysis of studies from researchers at Brigham Young University found that lack of social connections/loneliness carries the same health risk as smoking, obesity, not exercising, and alcoholism. [7] In fact, loneliness is even more dangerous than obesity and as bad for your health as smoking fifteen cigarettes a day. In 2019, a CIGNA study surveyed ten thousand adults and found that three out of five Americans are lonely. [8] A recent report through the Harvard Graduate School of Education indicates that loneliness substantially increased during the pandemic. [9] Researchers believe that loneliness could reach epidemic proportions throughout the Western world by 2030. With. Deadly. Effects. These are sobering statistics that further highlight the importance of social support in the daily fabric of our lives. [10]

WE SOMETIMES THINK WE WANT TO DISAPPEAR,
BUT ALL WE REALLY WANT IS TO BE FOUND.
—UNKNOWN

You may wonder—if my social support is so great, how'd I end up as emotional roadkill? Idiocy, really. I didn't take advantage of the social support that I'd cultivated over the years. Totally moronic when you think about it. It's like saving for a rainy day, having a safety cache of funds, and then when the crisis hits—just leaving it at the bank, unused, and then wondering why you're bankrupt. Not exactly a well-thought-out plan. But that's what sometimes happens in the downpour of depression and grief; you forget to open your umbrella.

All those friends and family—that social support—are to little avail when you don't self-disclose. This is where I went astray. I didn't talk about things. I deflected. I was too depressed, ashamed, or embarrassed to mention my issues. I was supposed to be strong. Many of my friends heard about my roadkill sojourn for the first time when proofreading this book.

Studies have found that without self-disclosure, people will still feel lonely even if they have friends. [11] It requires more than just discussing politics, the latest Netflix series, or sports. The sappy memes are often right—true intimacy is "into me you see." You must let people in. Self-disclosure is integral to the development and maintenance of relationships. And that means emotional disclosures, not just factual ones. In addition to combating loneliness, self-disclosure activates the parts of the brain associated with positive emotion and intrinsic rewards. [12] That's right: intimate disclosure lights up the same neuro hotspots as sex, food, and drugs without the risk of STDs, muffin-top, or addiction. In other words, self-disclosure with your intimate social support network is paramount to happiness. So, open up. Like they taught us in kindergarten, sharing is caring.

GROW YOUR GARDEN

Many years ago, there was a rather psychedelic children's show called *The Magic Garden*. Two wholesome hosts sang songs, told stories, and taught lessons among their blossoming buddies in the garden. There was a magic tree, a mischievous squirrel, and a patch of flowers called the chuckle patch that would tell jokes and giggle incessantly. In essence, the garden was their friend.

If we examined your garden of social support, what would we find? Is it a plethora of gorgeous flowers and magical trees designed to color and strengthen your world? Or is it a barren wasteland with the occasional stinkweed? Do you tend to it on a regular basis, or do you just show up when it suits you to find the garden in dire need of care and attendance? Perhaps you've been so MIA that the flowers have pollinated elsewhere, seeking friendlier soil.

The analogy may be simplistic, but really—our adult filters can get so polluted that we lose sight of the basics, the ABCs of life. Love. Friendship. Trust. So, tend your garden. If it's rather sparse, sprinkle more seeds. Water them. Grow your social support.

$\geq\!\!\backslash\!\!|\!\!/\!\!\leq$

THE BEST TIME TO MAKE FRIENDS IS BEFORE YOU NEED THEM.
—ETHEL BARRYMORE

There's no one way to cultivate your social support network, but no matter which approach you take, it's taking the first step that can be most daunting. I get it. *I really do.* For as extraverted (and loud) as I may appear, I hate going places where I don't know anyone. I can speak on stage in front of hundreds of people, yet entering a cocktail party where I know no one is like going for a root canal without anesthesia. I must push myself to do so. And when I do, I'm always better for it.

Everything that we want in life is on the other side of fear. You just need to push through. There are many ways to grow your garden [13]:

* Volunteer
* Take a class at a local community college
* Join a gym or a fitness group
* Join a church group
* Join a common interest club
* Find a support group (i.e., divorce, new baby, loss of a loved one)
* Attend book readings, gallery openings, recitals, workshops
* Keep your energy open and be approachable

You must be willing to make the investment. As studies show, it's the best deposit you can make as it pays off in spades—in increased happiness, life satisfaction, longevity, and stress management, to name a few. [14] Find me one study that finds the same benefits for sitting at home binge-watching a series. You can't. We're wired to be connected.

There was a recent study examining how many hours it takes to make a friend, the results of which I found fascinating and rather spot-on. Researchers found that it takes between forty to sixty hours to form a casual friendship, eighty to one hundred hours to transition to friend, and more than two hundred hours to become a really close friend. [15]

When I first moved to California, I attended a weekend workshop on personal development. We spent the entire weekend together, and then additional weekends as we took subsequent workshops together. I developed friendships at those workshops that are as intimate to me as those made in high school. Although a truncated period, we spent many hours together, which hastened the bonding process—hours that involved self-disclosure. My point being that if you just meet for coffee once a month, it may take a bit longer for a friendship to evolve. Like everything else in life, you must put in the time to get meaningful results. There are no shortcuts for anything worthwhile.

Once you have a social support system, you must continue to cultivate it. Friendships are a give and take, not a take-and-take (or a give-and-give, for that matter). It's about loving reciprocity. So, keep in touch. Answer the phone. Return the text or email. Be their cheering section. Be a good listener. Show them that their life events mean as much as yours. Show them how much they mean to you. As Walter Winchell said, "A real friend is someone who walks in when the rest of the world walks out." Be *that* kind of friend.

One last thing. Research has often found a positive relationship between marriage and happiness. One recent study offers an even more nuanced perspective in that people who consider their spouse to be their best friend were almost twice as satisfied in their marriages as other people. [16] Yes, other marriages can be happy, but it appears that being married to your bestie is an added bonus. As the German philosopher Nietzsche asserted over a century ago, "It is not a lack of love, but a lack of friendship that makes unhappy marriages."

REMOVE EMOTIONAL VAMPIRES FROM YOUR LIFE

Enough said. Just get rid of them.

BE YOUR OWN BFF

Okay, so we've established that love is the big kahuna of happiness. I'd be remiss if we didn't turn that focus inward as well. Yes, relationships are where it's at, but we can't ignore the importance of loving yourself. Many theorize that this is a necessary precursor to healthy relationships: to first love yourself. Your relationship with yourself is the longest relationship you'll ever have, so it's a good idea to actually enjoy the company, don't you think? This all starts with self-love and self-compassion.

IF YOU HAVE THE ABILITY TO LOVE, LOVE YOURSELF FIRST.
—CHARLES BUKOWSKI

This doesn't mean engaging in self-pitying parties, taking self-esteem to the precipice of narcissism, or self-indulgence to the point of gluttony. "Self-compassion is treating yourself with the same kindness and care you'd treat a friend," says Dr. Kristin Neff, a pioneer in the field of self-compassion. [17]

So how can you practice self-love and compassion? We've touched on several ways throughout the book thus far. Let's take a quick skip down memory lane (plus a few bonus tips we didn't cover earlier!):

- PERFECTLY IMPERFECT. Give up the quest for perfection. You're glorious in your imperfections. Remember *kintsugi*—the beauty is in the scars. Love yourself exactly as you are.

- SAY NO WHEN YOU NEED TO. Setting boundaries is healthy. Boundaries aren't meant to divide but rather to preserve. It's about being true to yourself. Balance being kind and helpful without sacrificing your self-worth.

- STOP THE COMPARISON. This destructive tendency has reached epic proportions with social media and its picture-perfect lives. It's all a carefully curated charade, really—an unhealthy one at that. No one is posting a picture of their ugly cry face or puffy, swollen eyes after fighting with their significant other. Nobody.

- FOCUS ON YOUR STRENGTHS. Write out a list of your strengths and accomplishments. Leave nothing out. You'll be surprised at what a f*cking rock star you really are.

- GIVE YOURSELF A PARDON. View yourself through more compassionate eyes. Forgive yourself and let it go. The past is merely a lesson and not a prison sentence. Learn and move on.

- IT'S OKAY IF NOT EVERYONE LIKES YOU. You're not going to be everyone's flavor, and that's okay. Some people like vanilla, some like Cherry Garcia, and some just prefer sherbet. Just try and stay away from rocky road. There's a flock for everyone.

- GRATITUDE. Be in it daily, folks. It changes the game each and every time.

- WORDS MATTER. Speak kindly about yourself to yourself and others. Silence the inner critic and stop the self-deprecating humor. Self-affirmations really do work.

- ACCEPT THE DARN COMPLIMENT ALREADY. When someone compliments you, don't pshaw, deflect, or deny it. Say thank you instead. That positive acceptance eventually takes root in your heart.

- REWARD YOURSELF. Do things you love doing. Buy yourself something special. I love rewarding myself after I reach a goal. It's also awesome to do so for no reason whatsoever. *Just because.*

- INDULGE IN SELF-CARE RITUALS. Meditate. Take a bath. Listen to music. Read a book. Get a massage. Go to the salon. Do an at-home facial. Pamper yourself with the love that you deserve.

- JOURNAL. Let it all out. It's more therapeutic than you realize.

- REACH OUT AND TOUCH SOMEONE. Call a friend. Catch up. Connect.

- TAKE A TECHNOLOGY BREAK. Try twenty-four hours without being on social media, the internet, or Netflix. Give yourself a breather. Just be.

- TAKE A WALK OUTSIDE. Hang out with Mother Nature for a while. Research shows that being in nature makes us feel better.

- TAKE CARE OF YOURSELF PHYSICALLY:

    EXERCISE. Sweat. Get the endorphins pumping on your behalf.

    NUTRITION. We really are a byproduct of what we consume. Make sure you're eating nutrient-dense meals. They call it nourishment for a reason.

    PRIORITIZE SLEEP. We've touched on this so many times. Zzzzz's are where it's at. It sets you up for success. (Naps rock too!)

IF YOU DON'T LOVE YOURSELF, NOBODY ELSE WILL.
NOT ONLY THAT—YOU WON'T BE GOOD AT LOVING ANYONE ELSE.
LOVING STARTS WITH THE SELF.
—DR. WAYNE DYER

Self-compassion has been the subject of scientific research in recent years. The results are in line with what you would expect. People who engage in self-compassion and are kinder to themselves are more resilient, happier, have less stress, greater life satisfaction, and healthier lifestyles. [18] Do yourself a favor and be good to yourself. Fall in love with yourself. It will transform you and your relationships. And it will help with future relationships too. As author and journalist Neill Stauss observed, "Perhaps the biggest mistake I made in the past was that I believed love was about finding the right person. In reality, love is about becoming the right person. Don't look for the person you want to spend your life with. Become the person you want to spend your life with." [19]

Be the energy you want to attract. You want to receive love? Love yourself first.

WHEN IN DOUBT, FOCUS OUT

Nineteenth-century American author Henry James observed, "Three things in human life are important. The first is to be kind. The second is to be kind. And the third is to be kind." Imagine what the world would be like if everyone embraced that philosophy. I've referenced Martin Seligman repeatedly throughout this journey because of his pioneering and game-changing research in positive psychology and happiness. His expertise and reach in this field are indisputable. He asserts in his book *Flourish*, "We scientists have found that doing a kindness produces the single most reliable momentary increase in well-being of any exercise we have tested." [20]

Research has found that acts of kindness can produce a positive feedback loop between kindness and happiness. In other words, doing acts of kindness makes us feel happier, and that happiness, in turn, promotes continued altruism. [21] Another study revealed that recipients of kindness become happier (of course, right?)—but they found that the *doers* of kindness benefited even *more* than the receivers. Not only did they report an increase in happiness but an increase in life and job satisfaction as well as a decrease in depression. [22] Apparently, when you are kind to another person, your brain's pleasure and awards center is activated as if you were the recipient of the kind act. In essence, giving has a boomerang effect on the brain, which researchers have called the "helper's high." Numerous studies have found greater psychological flourishing when people are giving to others as opposed to themselves. [23]

Studies have found that acts of kindness reduce inflammation, blood pressure, negative feelings, depression, stress, and anxiety. [24] In fact, it appears that kindness from the heart is good for the heart. According to Dr. Hamilton, author of *The Five Side Effects of Kindness*, being kind to others creates emotional warmth by releasing oxytocin (otherwise known as the love/attachment hormone), which in turn stimulates the release of nitric oxide, which dilates the blood vessels. [25] Kindness helps protect the heart by lowering blood pressure. It is cardioprotective.

Rather poetic irony, isn't it? Opening your heart can actually protect it. Acts of kindness are also linked to increased levels of happiness, longevity, life satisfaction, optimism, energy, and peer acceptance. [26]

If that doesn't convince you, I'll gladly appeal to your romantic side. Recent research reveals that kindness is the trait that people want most in a partner. [27] Kindness trumped physical looks, financial security, humor, and a whole host of other variables. Dr. John Gottman, the world-renowned researcher and clinician who has spent over forty years studying marriage stability and divorce, has found that kindness is the glue that holds marriages together. So, kindness is not only what draws you to a relationship; it's also apparently what keeps you there. [28] Fancy that. *Just. Being. Kind.*

≥\\//⁄

HAPPINESS IS THE NEW RICH. INNER PEACE IS THE NEW SUCCESS.
HEALTH IS THE NEW WEALTH. KINDNESS IS THE NEW COOL.

—SYED BALKHI

Researchers have found that kindness has a ripple effect, as recipients start to spontaneously pay it forward. [29] Simply stated, kindness is contagious, like a game of benevolent dominos. And every act of kindness counts—from a smile to a thank you, to buying the next customer's coffee, to volunteering, to humanitarian initiatives.

There are so many inspiring stories about kindness in this world. [30] One that immediately comes to mind is Chef José Andrés and his charity, World Central Kitchen, which has served over fifteen million meals to those in need during times of global crisis. You see him, his field kitchens, and his staff of forty-five thousand volunteers at the scene of pandemics, hurricanes, earthquakes, tornados, and floods worldwide. He and his team come in when most people are fleeing. The acclaimed chef has an insatiable appetite for kindness and serves as a beacon and role model to millions.

The late Princess Diana was another walking embodiment of kindness. In 1987, she was famously photographed shaking hands with an AIDS patient without gloves at a time ridden with misconceptions, prejudice, and fear about the nature of the disease and its transmission. She transformed the dialogue around AIDS with her single act of kindness. A handshake—piercing through the false narrative more effectively than any impassioned speech.

Another foot soldier of kindness is comedian Russell Brand who has been known to often spend time with the homeless—not just buying them food but spending *time* with them. It might seem like a small thing, but the truth is, time is often the greatest gift you can give—far more valuable, and meaningful, than any dollar amount ever could be. To reiterate, all acts of kindness matter. Big and small. The ripple effect produces a current of compassion that connects us all.

\\|//

TO STRENGTHEN THE MUSCLES OF YOUR HEART, THE BEST EXERCISE
IS LIFTING SOMEONE ELSE'S SPIRIT WHENEVER YOU CAN.
—DODINSKY

LOVE WITH A SIDE OF FURBALLS

Let me preface this by stating that I'm undoubtedly biased when it comes to this topic. I just couldn't discuss social support without giving a shout-out to our furry friends.

How does one even begin to capture with words the unconditional love, loyalty, and social support found in our beloved pets? As French literary figure and Nobel Prize recipient Anatole France observed, "Until one has loved an animal, a part of one's soul remains unawakened." While that may seem rather dramatic (Anatole was a poet as well as journalist and author), I can understand the sentimental hyperbole.

I hadn't owned a pet for a few years and had been toying with the idea for several months. The day my father died, after I hung up with my mother, I immediately looked at the online classifieds to see if any dogs were being rehomed. I was barely functioning, yet the move felt natural—I was almost on autopilot. A litter of maltipoos was listed in the Los Angeles area. I prefer a hypoallergenic dog that doesn't shed, so it was perfect. My daughter and I drove up, picked up the two-pound pup, and brought her home.

We named her Zuzu, after the little girl in one of my favorite movies of all time, *It's a Wonderful Life*. I watch that film every holiday season without fail and watched it many times with my father growing up. At the end of the movie, Zuzu famously says to her father (played by Jimmy Stewart), "Every time a bell rings, an angel gets his wings." We gave Zuzu her name in honor of my father getting his angel wings that day. She was our angel too.

Quite frankly, it was Zuzu who got me through that first week. I realized later we were kindred spirits, both experiencing loss of family on the same day. It was a bond born in sorrow and forged with love. I slept downstairs next to her crate for the first few nights. I'd like to say it was to help her acclimate, but I believe it may have been more for me in retrospect. Focusing on this new puppy, focusing outside of myself, was like a lifeline during those initial stages of grief. She brought an element of joy to our lives when it was needed most.

We found out later that she was anything but a maltipoo. Our guess is perhaps chihuahua/spaniel/corgi mix. A mutt, for sure, which suits our eccentric menagerie of personalities just fine. She certainly brings new meaning to the word "she-shed," as my anal-retentive self now vacuums daily.

Almost a year after adopting her, I felt that Zuzu needed a canine companion. A best bud. Someone to run the circuit course with her that she had created in our house. So we got another itsy-bitsy puppy (this time an actual maltipoo), and the girls named her Baby.

Both of these furballs of love reawakened a part of me and provided a type of support that I very much needed—and couldn't have gotten from another human. For that, I'm grateful.

And I believe anyone who has a pet can relate. They just seem to make life more colorful—full—*happy*.

✴

AN ANIMAL'S EYES HAVE THE POWER
TO SPEAK A GREAT LANGUAGE.
—MARTIN BUBER

Yes, I know my story is purely anecdotal. As you may have gathered, I'm somewhat fanatical about supporting theories with empirical research—so let's cite some studies! Unfortunately, this area of study can be rather murky; human-animal interaction (HAI) research has somewhat mixed findings given differing methodologies, measurements, and populations throughout the years. [31] Empirical research does, however, suggest that people facing serious health problems fare better with pets. [32] A good deal of this research focused on the positive relationship between pet interaction and cardiovascular disease and blood pressure. Nothing to sneeze at, for sure, as cardiovascular disease is the number one cause of death globally—an estimated 31 percent of all deaths worldwide. [33]

Research examining the effects of pet interaction with psychological well-being and happiness is more limited, but emerging. Recent studies have found a promising correlation between pet ownership and life satisfaction. [34] One study suggests that pets serve as an important source of social support. In fact, these researchers also found that pet owners had greater self-esteem, were in better shape, were less lonely, and were more outgoing. [35] Additional research has found that companion animals play a role in mitigating loneliness. [36] Specifically, 80 percent of pet owners say their pet makes them feel less lonely. Other research has found that animal-assisted therapy improved happiness and quality of life for residential psychiatric patients and cancer patients. [37]

Finally, a recent study showed that people are happier when they spend money on their pets instead of themselves or another person. [38] This makes sense, given that the US pet industry reached $99 billion in 2020. [39] To put that in perspective, the US cosmetic, beauty, and personal care market was $81.1 billion in 2019. [40] Pets are the hands-down winner.

One of my dearest friends often fosters orphan animals in addition to caring for her own household pets. Essentially, when you're a foster caretaker, you help socialize a shelter animal and ready them for eventual adoption. In opening your heart and home, you're buying them time and giving these animals a second chance—the helper's high but for furry creatures. You want to see gratitude in action? Just watch a tail wag.

There is no doubt that pet ownership comes with great responsibility and cost. And it may not be for everyone. Whatever the reason or the mechanism, though, pets are a source of happiness. Full stop. And that's worth all the effort—and fur—to me.

HAPPINESS CHECK

STRETCH

Let's try a random act of kindness. Smile at five strangers throughout your day—not just a half-smirk, but a full-blown genuine smile, eye contact and all. Not only will it improve those folks' day, it could also improve your *life*: smiling has been shown to reduce stress, boost your immunity, and increase longevity. [41] So, show some teeth and give your best Julia Roberts grin to five people.

CHALLENGE

Water your garden. Call a friend that you have not spoken to in a while, no matter how long it's been. Really engage and listen to what's been going on in their life. Make plans to meet up or Zoom call (if not local) within the next three weeks so you that can see each other in person. Put it on the calendar (otherwise the days just keep flying by). Make a point to let them know how much you've missed them.

DOUBLE-DOG DARE YA

Grow your garden. Ask someone that you'd like to get to know better to coffee, dinner, a walk, etc. Take the first step. The staircase will appear, promise. If literally no one comes to mind, it's time to get more proactive—take a class, join the gym, join a common-interest club, join a church group, volunteer, etc. Put yourself out there!

CHAPTER SEVEN

Success on the Daily

"IT'S IMPOSSIBLE,"
SAID PRIDE.
"IT'S RISKY,"
SAID EXPERIENCE.
"IT'S POINTLESS,"
SAID REASON.
"GIVE IT A TRY,"
WHISPERED THE HEART.
—ANONYMOUS

Have you ever received a package whose protected parcel was enshrined in those dreaded packing peanuts from hell? As soon I open such a box, a rather unladylike expletive (shocker) escapes my lips because I know what suckiness is about to ensue. These organized soldiers of hell have a mind of their own, and it seems designed to drive us out of *ours*.

Turns out these harbingers of OCD doom have an official title other than "bane of my existence." I discovered this not so long ago, when I saw a packing advertisement that labeled these hated foam shrapnel as "void-fill." I paused for a moment to really digest that concept. *Void-fill.* What an interesting name, right?

I indulgently philosophized about such an odd-sounding label. Void-fill is used in packages to protect what's on the inside. It fills up the space. With that in mind, I started to wonder, *What's my void-fill?*

LIFE AS A TREASURE CHEST

There will always be voids in life here and there, empty spaces that need filling. What you put in that void not only defines and predicts your happiness but also reveals how much you cherish that protected parcel of self. I want you to think of yourself as a treasure chest. There are twenty-four hours each day for you to find the most precious of treasures to put into it. What do you fill it with? What is your void-fill?

French philosopher, author, and Nobel Prize recipient Albert Camus once said, "Life is a sum of all your choices." So is your happiness. If you don't think your daily habits affect your happiness, you're fooling yourself. You can read every self-help book, keep a gratitude journal, and meditate daily, but if the rest of your lifestyle is junk food, sugary energy drinks, alcohol, little exercise, and poor sleep habits, it's a happiness house of cards. Life and happiness are the sum of *all* your choices.

HAPPINESS IS WHEN WHAT YOU THINK, WHAT YOU SAY,
AND WHAT YOU DO ARE IN HARMONY.
—MAHATMA GANDHI

As you may have noticed, healthy daily habits are often cited in differing areas of happiness research. Whether the research is about letting go, neuroplasticity, self-compassion, stress relief, hormones, etc., three things are a common thread throughout: nutrition, exercise, and sleep. Why? Because they're foundational—and without a solid foundation, we're all bound to tip over eventually.

We're going to start with sleep, since it really is the precursor to your day. It sets the stage for everything. We'll then touch on other daily habits, and you can decide for yourself if your void-fill is quality, meaningful, and the best love of self or if it perhaps needs an upgrade to something more sustainable—something that adds to the sum of your happiness as opposed to detracting from it.

Remember: happiness habits aren't inborn. They're created.

MR. SANDMAN, BRING ME A DREAM

Sleep gets a bad rap. Cartoon-wise, that is. From Homer Simpson to Garfield to Sleepy from *Snow White*, sleep is portrayed as laziness. And since I was pretty much raised by Looney Tunes, that misperception took root in my young mind.

It wasn't until I reached maturity that I realized sleep is the opposite of laziness. It's actually what sets you up for optimum productivity. In fact, given the abundance of research about the harmful effects of sleep deprivation, I'm always slightly confounded when someone wears their lack of sleep as a badge of honor. *Huh?*

According to the Centers for Disease Control and Prevention

(CDC), not getting enough sleep is associated with many chronic conditions such as obesity, type 2 diabetes, heart disease, high blood pressure, depression, anxiety, and risk of premature death. [1] Lack of sleep is also associated with impairment in memory, attention, and concentration; increased accidents and work mistakes; negative repetitive thought; taxed immunity and metabolism; and increased stress hormones. [2]

Sleep deprivation is dangerous both off and on the road. The National Highway Traffic Safety Administration estimated that ninety-one thousand police-reported automobile crashes were caused by drowsy driving in 2017. These crashes led to fifty thousand injuries and nearly eight hundred deaths, [3] along with millions in monetary losses. These results are mirrored annually. This isn't necessarily due to extremes in sleep deprivation. In fact, one researcher found that as little as a one-hour deficit can negatively affect driving. [4] A nationwide analysis of motor vehicle accidents between 1986 and 1995 examined the effects of daylight savings time when Americans put the clock forward one hour every spring. Researchers found a 17 percent increase in traffic deaths on the Monday following the time change compared to the week prior. [5] Not just accidents, *deaths*.

Lack of sleep and the ensuing human error have contributed to some of history's greatest disasters, such as Chernobyl, the Challenger explosion, the Exxon Valdez oil spill, and Three Mile Island. [6] If that's not a wake-up call, I'm not sure what is. Sadly, it's currently estimated that one in three adults don't get enough sleep. That means hundreds of millions of us are at risk for these adverse effects due to sleep deficit.

The National Sleep Foundation recommends seven to nine hours of sleep per night for adults. [7] There's a lot of research showing the positive link between sleep and happiness/life satisfaction. [8] Think about that. If I told you that you'd be happier, healthier, and more engaged by doing something daily that doesn't cost anything, would you say no? *Of course not.* It's like gratitude. Some of the most effective happiness builders are so simplistic and easy to facilitate.

Let's look at ways you can cozy up your relationship with Mr. Sandman. Sleep researchers recommend the following to cultivate optimal sleep [9]:

- Maintain a consistent sleep/wake schedule.

- Have a comfortable sleep environment (pillows, cozy blankets, optimal temperature, avoid bright lights).

- Do not watch TV or be on the computer in your sleep haven.

- Have a calming pre-sleep routine. I used to tell my kids it was "wind-down" time—whatever that may be for you (e.g., bath, light reading, etc.).

- Avoid caffeine, alcohol, nicotine, or other stimulants.

- Exercise promotes sleep (but not too close to bedtime).

- Don't eat or drink too much at least two hours before bedtime.

- Don't watch the clock! If you can't fall asleep, do something else (low-key) until you're tired.

- Engage in a little pre-sleep sexual intimacy.

There's nothing better than waking up refreshed and energized—so set yourself up for success!

EITHER YOU RUN THE DAY, OR THE DAY RUNS YOU.
—JIM ROHN

RISE AND SHINE

I love reading famous commencement speech addresses. Like, *love*. Commencement speakers seem to give significant thought to their words—I assume because they know their audiences are coming-of-age hopefuls about to embark on their next chapter in this glorious journey—and the resulting speeches are literal goldmines of wisdom and inspiration.

One of my favorite addresses is from Admiral William H. McRaven to the graduating class of the University of Texas at Austin in 2014. This speech by the incredibly decorated admiral (credited with overseeing the raid that killed Osama bin Laden) and former Navy SEAL later became a *New York Times* best-selling book of the same name, *Make Your Bed*. [10] On starting your day with a successful mindset:

"If you want to change the world, start off by making your bed. . . . If you make your bed every morning, you will have accomplished the first task of the day. It will give you a small sense of pride, and it will encourage you to do another task and another and another. And by the end of the day, that one task completed, will have turned into many tasks completed. Making your bed will also reinforce the fact that the little things in life matter."

Little things matter. Little habits can add up to health and happiness. *Or not*. You get to choose, right? Starting the day off on the right foot sets your tone for the day. Before I even get out of bed, I pause in gratitude for the day because every day is a gift. Every day is a new start, a fresh beginning. I'm not suggesting every day must be this epic, existential reckoning, but I am proposing that when we really view each new day as a gift, not to be taken for granted, there's less of a propensity to squander it.

So, yes, how you unwrap your day matters as much as how you wrap it up.

I recently read somewhere that we have approximately twenty-five thousand mornings in our adult life. (Being a Virgo, I did the math, and it adds up). *Let's make every morning matter.* Start each morning in gratitude. Make your bed. Have a morning routine. Research has found that morning routines increase happiness, reduce procrastination, and enhance performance. [11] As Tim Ferriss, one of my favorite authors and lifestyle guru, has asserted, "Win the morning, win the day." *How?* Start with the basics. Studies have found that exposure to morning light is a beneficial way to start your day. [12] Sunlight resets your circadian clock. It's your internal rise and shine. So, open up those blinds and let the sunshine in.

EACH DAY IS GOD'S GIFT TO YOU.
WHAT YOU DO WITH IT IS YOUR GIFT TO HIM.
—T. D. JAKES

Hal Elrod, author of *The Miracle Morning*, examined the morning routines of successful individuals and found common elements among them. [13] It's not rocket science. No one "discovered" the morning routine. Successful people tend to have similar habits because—*da-ta-da-da*—it sets them up for success. Whether Tony Robbins, Tim Ferriss, Richard Branson, Oprah Winfrey, or Warren Buffett, the common threads are [14]:

* Early rising

* Gratitude

- Meditation
- Journaling
- Light exercise
- Setting goals for the day
- Water and a healthy breakfast

Try to incorporate more of these habits into your morning routine. It will jumpstart your day and set the stage for success.

One of my favorite morning routine recommendations is attributed to the illustrious Mark Twain: "Eat a live frog first thing in the morning, and nothing worse will happen to you the rest of the day." He wasn't being literal, of course; he didn't mean turn Kermit into an omelet. What he was saying was, *Do your most undesirable task first*. Get it over with, and the rest of the day will be smooth sailing. I'm not saying it's easy; I mean, who typically wants to do a dreaded chore first? But is procrastinating so that task hangs over your head like an albatross all day really better?

Eat the frog. You'll have a feeling of accomplishment when you do so and get to enjoy the more pleasurable elements of your day a thousand times more.

CONSUME WISELY

"You are what you eat"—we've all heard that one before. But I only learned once I started researching for this book that the phrase's origin is attributed to French author Jean Anthelme Brillat-Savarin, who wrote in a work published in 1826 a line that translates as, "Tell me what you eat and I will tell you what you are." [15] Meaning: nutrition affects our mental and physical condition.

A recent study found that we make about two hundred food-, drink-, and snack-related decisions daily, though we aren't aware of most of these decisions (when, what, how much, where, with whom) or the environmental factors that influence these unconscious decisions. [16] Mindful, not mindless, eating is the key. The World Health Organization (WHO) recommends a diet rich in fruits, vegetables, legumes, and whole grains; moderate fats and oil; and reduced sodium and sugar levels than what's commonly found in mainstream diets. [17] This is very similar to the Mediterranean diet, which is associated with decreased depression. [18] Drinking good ole H_20 has also been linked to a reduced risk of depression and anxiety. [19]

Healthy food and water—lower incidence of depression. We typically assume food and drink only affect physical health or longevity, yet recent studies show there's a psychological well-being link as well.

Many people have a complicated relationship with food as it's often used as a means of emotional regulation. *We eat our feelings.* Ironically, the food we choose to make ourselves feel better (i.e., happier) tends to be the type of foods most nutritionists would argue have the opposite effect. I mean, when was the last time you were depressed and binged on broccoli or kale? It just doesn't happen. Our go-to is ice cream, cookies, chips, pasta, etc. In our house, it's pizza, dill-pickle chips (sounds gross, I know), and piña colada cookies. I felt unhealthy even typing that.

∖\∣//⁄

Comfort food, our supposed warm culinary embrace, is really a vise grip. Researchers recently examined the psychological benefits of comfort food and found that while it did improve mood, it was no greater than other food or no food at all. [20] Meanwhile, research has found that high glycemic index diets (typical comfort good) are linked to a higher incidence of depression. [21] So while it may give a temporary boost, it doesn't have staying power; in fact, it may just drag you further down afterward.

Good news, though: recent research has found that healthier food choices are indeed linked to happiness. [22] In fact, some researchers advocate a paradigm shift from viewing "food as health" to "food as well-being." [23] Research found that healthy food choices are happy choices too, totally eschewing the commonly held belief that healthy foods are a trade-off for tasty, feel-good foods. [24] It's not mutually exclusive. Moreover, a recent meta-analysis of twenty research papers found compelling evidence for a causal effect of a healthy diet on happiness. [25] Food for thought, right?! I'll let you chew on that for a while. (Sorry—couldn't resist.)

The bottom line is that recent research reveals that a healthy diet is associated with happiness and mental well-being, in addition to physical health and longevity. Think of it as feeding your body, mind, and soul. Consume happiness. Literally.

LET'S GET PHYSICAL

We all know that physical exercise has numerous health benefits, but did you know that it's positively associated with happiness and well-being as well? The Department of Health and Human Services recommends at least 150 to 300 minutes of moderate-intensity aerobic activity per week, plus muscle-strengthening activity on two or more days a week. [26] Despite the undisputed health benefits, 80 percent of adults aren't meeting recommended guidelines for aerobic and strength training activity—and that lack of physical activity is estimated to cost $117 billion in annual health care and is associated with 10 percent premature morbidity. *Yikes!*

The fact that physical activity helps with mental fitness in addition to physical fitness gives us added incentive to shake our booty. Physical activity is shown to [27]:

- Increase feel-good hormones and neurotransmitters such as endorphins, serotonin, dopamine, norepinephrine.
- Decrease stress hormones such as cortisol and adrenaline.
- Help alleviate depression.

Endorphins—also known as the happiness hormones—are responsible for that feeling of euphoria associated with physical activity. Given its structural similarity to morphine, endorphins also have an analgesic effect and help with pain relief. Explains why we feel so good after moving our bodies even just a little, doesn't it?

A systematic review of the scientific literature reveals a consistent relationship between physical activity and happiness. [28] As little as ten minutes of activity a day can boost mood, but the more movement, the greater the reported happiness. When people met the recommended guidelines of about thirty minutes per day, they were 30 percent more likely to consider themselves happy than those who did not meet the criteria. [29]

IF YOU DON'T MAKE TIME FOR EXERCISE,
YOU'LL PROBABLY HAVE TO MAKE TIME FOR ILLNESS.
—ROBIN SHARMA

A recent study by researchers at Yale and Oxford found that physical activity resulted in improved mood regardless of other variables such as income, age, and marital status. This cross-sectional analysis of 1.2 million participants found that the happiness boost from regular exercise was equivalent to a $25,000 bump in income! [30]

If you're just too busy to make mid-week workouts happen, don't despair. Another study found that weekend warriors— those who squeeze their fitness routine into two extended sessions over the weekend—report almost as many health benefits as those who exercise more often, as long as they met the recommended guidelines. According to the researchers, the key was to be "purposeful" in their exercise, with the intention to improve one's health. [31] There's that good ole mindfulness again. Mindful exercise. Really takes away the excuses, doesn't it?

I like to explain things to myself like I'm in kindergarten. Like Albert Einstein said, "If you can't explain it simply, you don't understand it well enough." So let's break it down: There are fourteen hundred minutes in each day. If you do some sort of physical activity for thirty minutes, it's only 2 percent of your day. Two percent! Yet those peeps are 30 percent more likely to consider themselves happy. Similar to a $25,000 bump in salary. I'll take those odds. We are always looking for that magic bullet, it seems; well, exercise is a pretty good one.

DON'T SIT ON IT

Remember my first crush, the Fonz from *Happy Days*? The gang had a common put-down phrase particular to their vernacular. If someone was bugging them, they would tell them to "sit on it." I never really understood that. What's so bad about sitting? How is that a slight? Well, I finally got my answer. This section of the book wasn't planned initially but rather came about as a function of the book. *Literally.* I ended up in urgent care with excruciating back and sciatica pain—all because I spent too many hours sitting while writing this book.

Sitting! That's it! No other extreme activity, accident, or fall. Just simply sitting. The doctor and subsequent physical therapists told me there's been an increase in back issues because so many people were sitting for longer periods while working from home. I was then thoroughly briefed on the health dangers of sitting.

SITTING IS THE NEW SMOKING.
—DR. JAMES LEVINE

The pain alone was enough for me to believe, but I wanted to review the research as well. My doctor had mentioned a famous study about double-decker buses, so I ferreted it out, and here's what I learned. On double-decker buses, there are two workers: the drivers (sedentary) and the conductors (active). The conductors walked between 500 to 750 steps collecting tickets, walking the stairs, etc., while on duty. Despite similar demographics in age and socioeconomic status, researchers found that the drivers had a higher incidence of cardiovascular disease than the conductors. [32] The conductors were half as likely to die from a sudden heart attack than the drivers. *Half!* These were landmark studies back in the 1950s before researchers readily embraced the link between physical activity and premature morbidity.

Recent research continues to show the deleterious association between sitting and health. A meta-analysis of studies involving eight hundred thousand participants revealed that sedentary behavior is linked to [33]:

* 112 percent increased risk of diabetes

* 147 percent increased risk of cardiovascular disease

* 90 percent increased risk of cardiovascular mortality

* 47 percent increased risk of all-cause mortality

What blew my mind was that these results were largely independent of physical activity. Meaning if you met the recommended guidelines for physical activity but spent the rest of your time in sedentary behavior (hello, desk job), it still negatively impacted health. Scientists make no bones about it: sitting is lethal. [34]

Honestly, this was rather shocking to me. I wanted to see if there was any link between happiness and sitting, in addition to the grim health associations, so I kept digging—and it turns out that recent research has indeed found that a reduction in sitting time is associated with improved mood. [35] Another study found that sit-stand workstations improved subjects' happiness as well as job performance. [36] Additionally, researchers at the University of Cambridge in England tracked activity and mood using a smartphone app over seventeen months and found that more active people were generally happier. [37] Other studies have found similar inverse results, with sedentary behaviors associated with increased risk of depression and anxiety. [38]

Apparently, "sit on it" can be a detriment to your subjective well-being as well as your health. I can tell you that reducing my back pain absolutely made me happier. A standing desk was a game-changer for me. Please be aware of the amount of sitting you're doing, even if you exercise, before it catches up with you. The Mayo Clinic recommends taking a break from sitting every thirty minutes. [39] Watch your posture. Make sure you are moving and stretching regularly. Move it or lose it. *Literally.*

KISS MY GRITS

When I was young, a TV show called *Alice* centered on the lives of waitresses at a local diner. A sassy Southern character named Flo coined the catchphrase, "Kiss my grits." A nice way of saying kiss my a$$—in a way that only Southerners can. Kinda like how "bless your heart" is really a covert insult, as it can cast more shade than the mightiest of Southern magnolia trees. Anyway, it appealed to my salty tongue, and I used to love to say, "Kiss my grits." This was before I developed a love/hate relationship with my grits, that is. I'm telling you all this for a reason; we'll get back to the grits in a minute.

While we're on the subject of diet and exercise, we've got to address the relationship between body image and happiness. This one hits close to home for me; it's been an ongoing struggle for me since adolescence.

Unfortunately, I'm not an anomaly. It's estimated that 91 percent of women are unhappy with their bodies. [40] Sad, but true. The unrealistic media images do not make it any easier. The fact that a "thigh gap" is a thing and heralded as a beauty ideal is pathetic—and scary. This quest for physical perfection is a driving factor behind body dysmorphia and eating disorders.

Research has found a positive correlation between body satisfaction and happiness. Conversely, body dissatisfaction has been linked to reduced well-being and depressive symptoms. [41] A national study by researchers at Chapman University highlighted the prevalence of body dissatisfaction among adults. [42] They surveyed over twelve thousand adults about their body image, happiness, and overall satisfaction with life, and the results were somewhat disconcerting. Overall, there was a positive correlation between body image and life satisfaction, but it differed between men and women. For women, satisfaction with their appearance was the third-largest predictor of overall life happiness, trailing behind financial satisfaction and satisfaction in their romantic relationships. Surprisingly, it was number two for men, second only to financial satisfaction.

The research is sobering, but I didn't need studies to validate this. I'm well-aware of this fact just from the conversations with my girlfriends. From personal experience. From my daughters' experiences. I dated a man who often said, "a little bit of an eating disorder is a good thing," and jokingly wanted it engraved on his tombstone. He thought he was funny. Yet, he was probably one of the greatest contributors to my body image woes. He had opinions about my boobs, my butt, my thighs. It was a nightmare.

STOP TRYING TO FIX YOUR BODY. IT WAS NEVER BROKEN.
—EVE ENSLER

He wasn't the only one. Apparently, I attracted men with a wide array of opinions about my body type. It was hard to keep up. Some liked me more voluptuous. Some more muscular. Some as skinny as I could get. I felt like a body dysmorphia ATM machine trying to spit out whatever their preference was. It. Was. Exhausting.

I wish I could say that I'm totally dialed in now, and these issues are a thing of the past. But that would be a fib. It's an ongoing struggle of which I get to be mindful. Positive affirmations really do help. As I've said before, it all starts with loving yourself. It's no wonder I attracted jackass men like that. I was just attracting what was on the inside. Energy doesn't lie. You change the energy; you change the vibration. *For yourself.*

Let's look at some ways to up your body appreciation game. [43] It will ultimately up your happiness game as well.

- Engage in positive body talk. Appreciate what your body can do. It's more than you realize.

- Surround yourself with positive, supportive peeps.

- Avoid having meals with people constantly on a diet. You know who they are.

- Stop the comparison! Just stop already.

- Minimize exposure to unrealistic body images on social media, advertising, and print. View it with a critical, discerning eye. Recognize the negative messaging.

- Wear clothing that you feel good in.

- True beauty comes from within. Nothing is more beautiful than self-confidence.

- Do nice things for your body. Get a massage. Take a bath. Love on it.

- You are more than your body. View yourself as a whole being: body, mind, and soul.

- Have the goal be a healthy lifestyle, not a body ideal.

Fast-forward to present day. There's no way I would consider having or make excuses for a partner who made critical comments about my body. *No. Way.* It would be the quintessential red flag and cause for a quick buh-bye. Take your body misogyny and kiss my grits, pal.

'Cause I love my grits. It was my grits that helped me climb back up the mountain and go from roadkill to redemption, after all. It was my grits that got me out of bed, both literally and figuratively. So, yes, I love *all* my grits. It's truly remarkable that when you change *how* you see, you change how you look—without actually changing how you look.

SUCCESS IS A FEW GOOD HABITS REPEATED EVERY DAY,
FAILURE IS A FEW BAD DECISIONS REPEATED EVERY DAY.
—JIM ROHN

SOLO SOBRIETY VS. SOLO CUPS OF WINE

I recently read a *New York Times* article in which the author characterized happiness as a subjective, squishy concept. [44] *Squishy.* It reminded me of one of Dr. Wayne Dyer's life lessons. The late Dr. Dyer was one of my most favorite authors and motivational speakers. He once made the analogy between an orange and people. When we squeeze an orange, orange juice comes out because that is what's on the inside. He observed, "What comes out when life squeezes you? When someone hurts or offends you? If anger, pain, and fear come out of you, it's because that's what's inside. It doesn't matter who does the squeezing—your mother, your brother, your children, your boss, the government. If someone says something about you that you don't like, what comes out of you is what's inside. And what's inside is up to you, it's your choice." [45]

There was a point in my grief spiral and sojourn as roadkill that if you'd squeezed me, I think chardonnay would've come out. I used to think social drinking was perfectly fine, even if to teenie-weenie excess at times, as long as that was the exception and not the rule. I would foolishly rationalize that it was the drinking alone, by oneself, that was the *real* problem. Isn't it curiously funny how we rationalize addictions or problems along a continuum, the moral arc of which always swings in favor of our innocence? *At least I'm not . . .* fill in your rationalization of choice. So, that was mine. At least, I didn't drink by myself. If I imbibed with like-minded peeps, I was cool. In fact, overly zealous wine consumption was almost a deserved badge of honor for harried suburban moms.

So, let's just say I had a very cozy relationship with the chardonnay grape.

Enter 2020. Isolation. Social distancing. Suddenly, Zoom happy hours are a "thing." It's not really drinking by yourself because you're talking and laughing to a screen, right? It was a slippery slope—and as the bleakness of 2020 started to slowly enshroud my life, I suddenly didn't need a Zoom call to rationalize a cocktail. I mean, everybody was drinking at home by themselves now—bars weren't even open! I downloaded a liquor delivery app because, of course, there would be an instantly gratified means to procure booze when too timid to venture outside.

My dad got sick. An evening drink helped calm the nerves. I always waited until at least five o'clock to stay within the societal guardrails of acceptance. My father passed. Overwhelming grief further exacerbated by isolation. I rationalized that I didn't want to have to wash my wine glasses, and it was easier and more efficient to use disposable Solo cups. That's right—an eighteen-ounce red freaking Solo cup for wine. Less mess. Fewer trips to the fridge. Less culpability in front of my teenagers.

I went from solo sobriety to Solo cups of wine—and very soon after that, to consuming an entire bottle of wine every night. It's still hard for me to wrap my mind around that one. And so very, very hard to admit.

FACING IT, ALWAYS FACING IT,
THAT'S THE WAY TO GET THROUGH. FACE IT.
—JOSEPH CONRAD

Much like we have our own triggers, we also have our own paths to recovery that work best for us. To each their own, right? I personally have never been good at the all-or-nothing thing. Typically, if I forbid myself from having something (e.g., cigarette, carb, sugar, bad boy love interest—you name it), I'm then tortuously consumed with thoughts and needs for said forbidden fruit (*white bear! white bear!*). So, although I know organized programs are the road to recovery for millions and am grateful for their profound contribution, my journey looked a little different. For me, it was about regaining self-control. If the ultimate destination is the same—a healthy relationship with whatever is your addiction temptress of choice—I'm cool with whatever your personal journey to get there looks like.

As I said at the beginning, my dad's passing brought me to my knees, but after several months of grieving, the time had come to eliminate alcohol as the recovery crutch. And, truth be told, it was anything but. I was essentially limping along in a dulled, numbed-out lethargy.

Sadly, the use of alcohol as a coping mechanism is more prevalent than not. Remember the longitudinal Harvard study and the beloved Dr. Vaillant who cited happiness as "love, full stop"? Guess what else he gleaned from the findings? In his estimation, "Alcoholism is a disorder of great destructive power." [46] It was the leading cause of divorce, correlated with neurosis and depression, and combined with cigarette smoking, was the single greatest contributor to early morbidity for participants.

Those Harvard grads are not an anomaly. According to the National Institute of Alcohol Abuse and Alcoholism, nearly fifteen million adults suffer from alcohol use disorder in the United States. In 2019, 25 percent of adults reported they engaged in binge drinking in the past month. [47] Alcohol consumption increased even more during the pandemic and lockdown, so much so that the WHO issued a warning about limiting consumption and access. [48] Apparently, I was not alone. A study found that women increased heavy drinking by 41 percent during the pandemic. [49] Ouch!

According to Nielsen, two-thirds of millennials are trying to consume less alcohol, citing overall health and wellness as their top motivator. [50] They are leading the way with a mindful drinking movement which is fantastic. For the sober or sober-curious, more and more nonalcoholic elixirs are finding their way into the marketplace. Hopefully, a course change is on the horizon. I've embraced the calming effects of CBD and theanine. More importantly, I dug my emotional regulation tool kit out of its padlocked storage and started engaging in positive, stress-relieving mechanisms in lieu of the easy five o'clock pour.

Our life is a series of decisions, good ones or bad ones. If you have healthy daily habits but your coping mechanisms are a masterclass in self-sabotage when you encounter stress, you're doing yourself a disservice. Because let's face it, stressors are a part of life, so if you don't have an emotional regulation tool kit mentally handy, it's like playing Russian roulette with your coping abilities.

You don't want to wait till the shit hits the fan. Prepare. Know your triggers and how you're going to proactively handle them. Engage in these practices during times of non-stress to prime the pump.

Let's look at some clinically proven ways to relieve stress, and hopefully you will find a few that resonate and work for you [51]:

* Deep breathing
* Meditation

- Yoga

- Exercise

- Getting a massage

- Progressive muscle relaxation

- Connecting with others

- Playing with your pet

- Journaling

- Reading a book

- Taking a walk outside

- Aromatherapy; light a candle

- Adult coloring books

These coping practices have been proven to help alleviate stress. Find which ones work best for you, and, the next time stress hits, indulge in these stress relievers as opposed to maladaptive coping mechanisms. Alcohol, food, drugs, shopping, gambling, and sex when used as a means to cope may provide temporary respite but are the ultimate false panacea. These wolves in sheep's clothing will consume you if you let them.

IT TAKES COURAGE . . . TO ENDURE THE SHARP PAINS OF SELF-DISCOVERY RATHER THAN CHOOSE TO TAKE THE DULL PAIN OF UNCONSCIOUSNESS THAT WOULD LAST THE REST OF OUR LIVES.
—MARIANNE WILLIAMSON

What's so maddening to me is that I didn't have to be roadkill. I knew better. In abandoning my emotional regulation tool kit, I abandoned myself. Instead of saving myself, I was instrumental in my own *SPLAT* and did little to scrape myself off the asphalt. I chose numbness over living. I buried my feelings along with my father.

I recently read something about grief that really resonated and touched my heart. Author Jamie Anderson observed, "Grief, I've learned, is really just love. It's all the love you want to give, but cannot. All of that unspent love gathers in the corners of your eyes, the lump in your throat, and in the hollow part of your chest. Grief is just love with no place to go." If I'd allowed myself to mourn healthily and not numb out, love—not chardonnay, not the ickies—is what would have come out when life squeezed me. All my love for my sweet dad. And I could have channeled that love toward my family, friends, or even myself—and saved myself a whole lotta heartache and hurt.

Lesson learned. Thank you, universe.

HAPPINESS CHECK

STRETCH

Eat the frog first. What is the activity/chore/task/project that you have been putting off? Whatever it is that you may be dreading, do it first today. Come on—rip off the Band-Aid. See what it's like to get the *yuck* out of the way early on and truly enjoy the rest of your day!

CHALLENGE

As the Borg said, resistance is futile. Instead of resisting cravings and impulses, lean into them. Urge surf. It's a mindfulness technique to help get through an urge without acting on the destructive impulse. When an urge hits, roll with it. Acknowledge the trigger. What's going on in your body? What are the physical sensations? Focus on the sensations. Pay attention to your breathing. Continue to deep breathe. Observe your breath as you ride the waves of the urge. Refocus on your body. Stay present and mindful, without judgment.

DOUBLE-DOG DARE YA

Commit to regular physical exercise for two weeks. Let's start out with minimum of 150 minutes of moderate-intensity aerobic activity per week. It can be as simple as brisk walking. Spread it out through the week or be a weekend warrior—whatever sets you up for success and eliminates excuses. Add two strength-training sessions for bonus points. I'm humming the *Rocky* theme song. You got this.

DEPRESSION IS NOT A CHOICE

It should go without saying that depression is a very real condition and not a choice. Depression is a clinical illness that leads to persistent feelings of sadness, deep despair, hopelessness, loss of interest, and suicidal ideation, all of which interfere with day-to-day life. To conflate depression with "being unhappy" minimizes and mischaracterizes a serious mood disorder and does a disservice to millions. The WHO's website states that approximately 280 million people suffer from depression globally. [1] It is an epidemic.

Depression is not something to just "snap out of." As I stated in the beginning, this book is an integrated model grounded in science to whip your mental ass and mojo back into shape. Depression, on the other hand, typically requires professional intervention. Fortunately, it is one of the most treatable mental disorders. According to the American Psychiatric Association, 80 to 90 percent of people with depression respond to treatment in time. [2]

If you or someone you know is suicidal, please contact your physician, ER, or local suicide prevention center. For the United States, the 988 Suicide & Crisis Lifeline is 800-273-TALK (8255) or call, text, or chat 988.

CHAPTER EIGHT

Your Past Prepares You

HAPPINESS IS A CHOICE, NOT A RESULT.
NOTHING WILL MAKE YOU HAPPY UNTIL YOU CHOOSE TO BE HAPPY.
NO PERSON WILL MAKE YOU HAPPY UNLESS
YOU DECIDE TO BE HAPPY.
YOUR HAPPINESS WILL NOT COME TO YOU.
IT CAN ONLY COME FROM YOU.
—RALPH MARSTON

A whopping 453 days after the start of the 2020 pandemic lockdowns, California officially reopened, and most state-wide restrictions were lifted. Businesses reopened at full capacity, and fully vaccinated citizens ditched their masks in most scenarios. The fact that I started writing the final chapter of this "road-  kill to redemption" narrative on the same day seemed poetically serendipitous. Our masks were coming off. The irony was not lost on me. We'd been wearing masks long before the virus ever came into the picture.

It's time to shed them.

Removing your "mask" may not be an easy, painless en- deavor. I get that, and I understand the discomfort that can accompany the removal of our masks—the shedding of the persona that is showcased on our social media. But when you show up authentically, without artifice or pretense, you open up the doors for others to reciprocate. You create a space that is safe, accessible, and true. And that is when the magic happens. When writing this book, I often felt extremely vulnerable. Raw. But rather than being imprisoned by fear or shame, the opposite happened. The telling of your story—the good, the bad, and the ugly—is *freeing*. The redemption is in the reveal— in the beautiful brokenness.

I feel like I'm starting to get it right, which wouldn't have happened without the messiness, without the lessons. Yes, there's pain and discomfort in shedding the multiple masks we wear—but every transformation requires a shedding. Just ask the butterfly.

THIS ISN'T A DRESS REHEARSAL

As you may have noticed by this point, I'm a sucker for inspirational soundbites. I'm totally here for it. One of my faves is:

> *You are not defined by your past.*
> *You are prepared by your past.*
> *It doesn't define you.*
> *It refines you.*

I believe this with all my heart. There's something so redemptive about it. It's why I love the story of Joseph in the Bible; it has the same message. Quick refresher (or introduction), in case you need it. A number of misfortunes befall Joseph (betrayal by brothers, sold into slavery, falsely accused, wrongly imprisoned, etc.), but ultimately, he discovers that everything that happened was preparing him for his ultimate destiny: to help rule over Egypt and save thousands of lives in the process. If not for the lessons learned from his trials and tribulations, he wouldn't have had the skills to do so—and through it all, he never lost faith.

I believe the same holds true for all of us. Your past prepares you. The good and the bad. You aren't a prisoner of your past. Your past liberates you. It sets you free—to become. And you never stop becoming. You never stop growing. You never stop learning. Every single day, you're a brand-new version of yourself. Updated. Refined. *Better.*

And since you are the star of your story, you're guaranteed a redemptive character arc. And who doesn't love a redemptive character arc? Those are the characters we end up loving the most because they grew beyond their flaws. From Theon Greyjoy in *Game of Thrones*, Michael in *The Good Place*, Snape in *Harry Potter*, Alex in *Grey's Anatomy*, to Loki in the Avengers franchise. We root for them and want them to triumph over circumstance. Just like the Big Guy wants us to triumph. And what plans He has for us! The best is yet to be.

Each chapter of your life is a new beginning. Think of it as micro tabula rasa—you aren't the same person you were ten chapters ago. As British writer C. S. Lewis observed, "You are never too old to set another goal or to dream a new dream." I'll add to that: . . . *or be a new you.* When you really start to believe that, possibility is everywhere. In everything. In everyone. In every moment.

I don't believe there's such a thing as a late bloomer. Late according to whom? Seems to me, the timing is exactly when it's supposed to be. And some harvests are just better with age. Just ask any sommelier. There are no timelines on possibility, no deadlines on potential. God didn't say, "I have plans for you to prosper, but it must be completed by the age of thirty or you are out of luck." I mean, that sounds ridiculous, right? Stop thinking *it's too late*; *that ship has sailed*, or whatever other defeatist or resigned thought you may be having. Live in the possibility of now. It's gorgeous here.

IT IS NEVER TOO LATE TO BE WHAT YOU MIGHT HAVE BEEN.
—UNKNOWN

Since I love anecdotal sources of inspiration, I'm going to share a few success stories here, with the hopes they'll inspire you. Each person bloomed in their own time and in their own way [1]:

* STAN LEE: Created his first comic book at thirty-nine years of age. He became Marvel Comic's primary creative leader, catapulting it into a multimedia corporation. Comic book writer, editor, publisher, and producer—he was master of the Marvel universe.

* VERA WANG: Originally wanted to be an Olympic figure skater. When that didn't come to fruition, she entered the fashion world at the age of forty. Brides around the world have rejoiced ever since.

* TONI MORRISON: This Nobel and Pulitzer Prize–winning author published her first novel, *The Bluest Eye*, when she was forty years old.

- JOY BEHAR: A former high school teacher, she didn't start her show biz career until after forty. From stand-up comedy to the longest cohost on *The View*. In her late seventies now, her views still crack me up every morning.

- BERNIE MARCUS AND ARTHUR BLACK: After being let go from their jobs, these gentlemen started The Home Depot at forty-nine years of age. It's now the largest home improvement retailer with over twenty-two hundred stores across North America.

- JULIA CHILD: Mainly worked in advertising her entire life. She didn't release her first cookbook until the age of fifty and is arguably the OG of celebrity chefs.

- MIGUEL DE CERVANTES: Miguel was fifty-eight when he wrote his most famous novel, *Don Quixote*, the second most translated book after the Bible.

- KATHRYN JOOSTEN: Was a nurse and stay-at-home mom until her divorce. She decided to pursue her acting dream, broke into the industry at the young age of sixty, and was seen on such shows as *The West Wing, Family Matters, My Name is Earl*, and *Desperate Housewives*. She won two Emmy Awards for her work.

- FRANK MCCOURT: A former teacher, he started writing at sixty-five, and his memoir, *Angela's Ashes*, won both the Pulitzer Prize and National Book Critics Circle Award.

- ANNA MARY ROBERTSON MOSES: Also known as Grandma Moses, this celebrated folk artist began her painting career at seventy-eight. Her paintings are beloved and sell for over $1 million.

Happy AF

YOU MISS 100 PERCENT OF THE SHOTS YOU DON'T TAKE.
—WAYNE GRETZKY

Pretty inspiring, right?

My Stoic sweetie, Marcus Aurelius, wrote that "what we do now echoes in eternity." When we think along those lines— that every action has a consequence, an echo—it puts everything in a sharper focus, don't you think? In his best-selling book *Atomic Habits*, James Clear asserts, "Every action you take is a vote for the type of person you wish to become. No single instance will transform your beliefs, but as the votes build up, so does the evidence of your new identity." [2] And everything we do *not* do or do *not* say also has an impact. Sometimes, it's the absence of action or words that strikes the loudest chord. Of harmony. *Or discord.*

Sometimes, I worry that my echo will be too damn loud. I want my echo to be powerful but not strident, harsh, or grating. I get to be mindful of my delivery. Of everything. My words, my actions. I do like to think in reverse when it comes to this. Play the movie backwards. Reverse echoes. How do I want my story to end? What do I want my echo to be? And whatever that looks like, am I on course—or do I need to recalibrate my compass?

I started thinking about this while researching the people whose work I've discussed and stories I've told in this book. I was fascinated by the titles after their names in their biographies—Philanthropist, Author, Entrepreneur, Spiritual Leader, Peace Activist, Lifestyle Guru, Philosopher, Life Nomad, etc. What would mine be? Of course, I want "Badass Mom" on my epitaph, but what else? When someone recently asked me what I did, I said I was a writer instead of my usual professional titles.

Its official inauguration spoken into the universe. Soon "author," I thought to myself, keeping my vision in top-of-mind awareness. But in playing my echo in reverse, I knew I didn't want it to end there. It didn't sound finished to me.

Then it hit me. I want my echo to be that of a weaver. I want to weave stories, parables, and musings that inspire transformation and growth. That leaves an echo for the next generation of echo-makers. Beautiful word tapestries. *And beauty lies in the eye of the beholder, right?*

Sounds grandiose? Not really. Your dreams are only limited by your imagination, and your imagination has no limits. So, dream without borders, without qualifiers. Dream to the end of the ocean and beyond. Did the Wright brothers think that their dream was "too big" when they invented the first aircraft? Did Carl Benz, whose patent for a "vehicle with gas engine operation" is considered the registration of birth for the automobile? Did Sir Alexander Fleming, who changed the course of medicine with the discovery of penicillin? Alexander Graham Bell and the telephone? Computer scientists Vinton Cerf and Bob Kahn and the internet? These individuals brought dreams and ideas to life that were unheard of, unimaginable even, in previous generations. I personally don't want "unimaginable" in my motivational lexicon.

Neither should you.

A quote I'm about to share is often attributed to Mark Twain (American writer, humorist, entrepreneur, publisher, and lecturer—otherwise known as dude with super cool titles). However, the Center for Mark Twain Studies stated that Mr. Twain never actually said or wrote this. According to the post, "There is perhaps no greater testament to Twain's lasting reputation than the habitual misattribution of miscellaneous wit and wisdom to his name." [3] I thought that was so remarkable. Imagine having an echo so big—so profound—so beloved—that great writings are misattributed to you? Assumptive greatness reverberating in conjunction with Mr. Twain's epic echo. That's so awesome.

Here's the quote:

> *Twenty years from now, you will be more disappointed by the things you didn't do than by the ones you did do. So throw off the bowlines! Sail away from safe harbor. Catch the trade winds in your sails. Explore. Dream. Discover!*
> —Not Mark Twain, but sure sounds like something cool he would say

THE IN-BETWEEN

Hopefully you've played your movie backwards by now, and it's given you a better idea of how you want your story to end. You can start making any necessary adjustments or plot twists to ensure that you're on the correct path. What about the in-between? What then? The in-between shouldn't affect your happiness. As I said in the introduction, there is no happiness destination. The journey is the destination. There is no happy *when* or happy *because* or happy *if.* The Deferred Happiness Plan sucks, my friends. Its compounding interest annihilates happiness in the now. Obliterates it, actually. Don't wait on something, someone, or some event to be happy. Just be happy. *Now.* Being fully immersed in the present—*hey, that sounds like mindfulness*—is integral to happiness. Happiness is a choice, not a result.

My learning curve in this arena is somewhat ironic. Okay,

maybe not ironic, but rather serendipitous, as is often the case in the poetry of life. I learned about love from my divorce—learned that it's a choice, not an emotion; that emotions are fleeting, capricious, whimsical, and sometimes cruel; and that's not love. Love is a commitment, a choice that you make every day.

From the pain of my grief, I learned that happiness, too, is a choice. When you fully embrace that, there is no happy *when*, happy *if* or happy *because*. You can be happy right now. There's incredible power in that.

Do you want to be happy? Are you ready to commit to that choice? Sometimes, the decision to do so can be daunting. It removes our excuses, our whataboutisms, our false rationales that we hide behind to perpetuate our misery, our self-pity, our mediocrity. "Our deepest fear is not that we are inadequate," said Marianne Williamson. "Our deepest fear is that we are powerful beyond measure. It is our light, not our darkness, that most frightens us." [4]

Surrender to your light. Surrender to happiness.

Say yes to you.

SOME WISHBONES DON'T BREAK

Did you ever break a wishbone as a kid? It's kinda gross when you think about it. When my grandmother would make chicken, she would save the wishbone so we could pull it apart and make a wish—a tradition that dates all the way back to the ancient Romans. [5]

The wishbone, otherwise known as the furcula (meaning "little fork" in Latin), is part of a unique structure in birds that assists in flight. It helps to lift the wings and breathe during aerial locomotion. A fresh wishbone won't break. It will simply bend, which makes sense given that anatomically it serves as an elastic spring for wings. It's super flexible and can expand up to 50 percent larger than its resting position in some species. That's why it needs to dry out for a few days and achieve its brittle state before it can break. This little rando nugget of information is quite profound for me, and that's because of an experience I had many years ago—one I've only shared with a handful of people before now.

I was in high school, and it was a typical Friday night—a bunch of us had just left a football game and congregated at the local pizza parlor. But that fateful Friday, a group of boys came to the pizza place, rather obnoxiously inebriated. I can't say what led up to this or even what happened after because, quite frankly, I can't remember—it's like a black void in my memory—but at some point these boys had this bright idea to play wishbone with my body and a telephone pole . . . to see if I would break. Their words, not mine. Picked me up spread-eagle against my will and proceeded to pull my body with all their might with a telephone pole between my legs.

All I can remember from this experience is the screaming, begging, and crying—and the humiliating pain. I don't remember anything else. In fact, I completely blocked the incident out and didn't think of it again until college. I was home visiting one weekend, and a former classmate brought it up while at a bar (because of course that's a fond recollection while drinking). I had no idea what she was talking about. *Until I did.* Suddenly, the memory pierced through my consciousness years after its deep-sea burial.

I must have buried the memory as a coping mechanism to get through high school. When the memory was unearthed, I wanted to rebury it as it was a Pandora's box that I didn't want opened. Such shame surrounding the incident. Such helplessness. I internalized it—that somehow, I must have done something to cause it. Because who would treat a person like that? You wouldn't even treat a dog like that. Such degradation. Humiliation. Pain. So, I didn't talk about it again until twenty-five years later—this time in a therapy session. Cried fresh tears like it happened yesterday, but finally processed it. The fresh tears washed and cleaned my misguided filters on the subject. I was able to reframe it. See it clearly. Those boys didn't break me. Just the opposite, in fact.

$$\geqslant\!\!\backslash\!\!|/\!\!\!/\!\!\leqslant$$

THEY TRIED TO BURY US. THEY DIDN'T KNOW WE WERE SEEDS.
—DINOS CHRISTIANOPOULOS

I recently thought about that incident again. Not in a "poor me" way, but instead in the resilient context of my recent climb back up the mountaintop, from roadkill to happy AF. One day, it struck me that in all my efforts to strengthen myself, to get stronger, I was getting softer as well—but in a good way. In a grateful way. In an empathic way. These days, I often get a lump of gratitude in my throat over a beautiful sunset, the ocean, or watching my girls laugh. I feel softer on the inside, but not weaker. On the contrary, the softness is making me stronger. I'm like a wishbone, which must be flexible and soft in order to not break. To help fly. To help soar.

I embraced this softness. This *soft-strong*. It's very similar to the willow tree. Despite its slim stature, the flexibility of the willow tree allows it to weather the most devastating of storms. The willow may appear frail compared to the mighty oak, yet it can't be easily broken. Its secret? The roots. The root system of the willow tree is vast, strong, and aggressive. The roots radiate far from the tree itself. In fact, the roots of the willow tree can spread over one hundred feet long.

Rooted.

I like that word. Everything discussed herein is essentially a rooting system for happiness. And we covered a lot—mind, body, and soul. We explored a whole host of strategies, all backed by research, that can help you up your happiness game. There's not a one-size-fits-all approach, thus why we examined so many different strategies. Try each one on and see what works best for you. Just like any road trip, there is more than one way to get there. Word to the wise: if you experience strong resistance to any suggestion, strategy, or practice, do that one first. Eat the damn frog. As the saying goes: *"What you resist, persists; what you accept, transforms."*

There *is* one common denominator for every strategy—one nonnegotiable: constant practice. Cultivating happiness is a constant practice. Your daily life, ergo your state of mind, is dictated by your daily choices, day in, day out. Small consistent steps are the foot soldiers that win this crusade for hope and champion a "happiness" happening. You gotta be in it, to win it. This means living with intention and not just operating on autopilot; creating a life based on choices, not habits; and each day practicing the sort of person you want to be.

So, unlike the willow, let's send our roots deep. Anchor yourself. Have happiness habits be the norm rather than the exception. That way, next time a storm comes (and it will come), your happiness will not be easily swayed, helpless like a leaf in the wind; you'll be firmly tethered, and only let go when and if you want to. Only when you decide it's time to fly. To soar. To feel the wind.

That's my wish for you.

UNTIL NEXT TIME

A few summers ago, I purchased a rather large linen canvas from one of the local beachfront stores in my town. It has two sentences screen printed on it. Nothing else. The words are the art, the beauty. I love things that speak to me. That touch my soul. I have it hanging next to my bedside, and it's literally the first thing I see upon waking every day. It simply says, *Let your story be your song. And sing it out for all to hear.* Rather prophetic, in hindsight.

Looks like I'm a singer, after all.

I'm so happy that you took this journey with me. Road trips are best with friends along for the ride. We've all felt like roadkill at some point, but it's the hike back up the mountaintop that defines the human spirit. Our unassailable ability to bounce. To keep on keepin' on. To be happy AF.

A BIRD SITTING ON A TREE IS NEVER AFRAID OF THE BRANCH
BREAKING BECAUSE HER TRUST IS NOT ON THE BRANCH
BUT ON ITS OWN WINGS. ALWAYS BELIEVE IN YOURSELF.
—ANONYMOUS

Don't shy away from the skinny branches in your happiness journey, my friends. I believe in you too. Sending X's and O's.

Until the next road trip.

LIKE A MOTH TO A FLAME,

AND SO I DANCE.

MY EMOTIONS UNDULATING

TO ITS CAPRICIOUS FLICKER.

SEARING,

IT SCORCHES MY WINGS.

YET I AM DRAWN TO ITS BLAZING LIGHT,

UNTIL IT CONSUMES ME.

ASHES ENVELOP ME,

LIKE A SHROUDED COCOON.

ITS DARKNESS,

A WELCOME RESPITE.

I RETREAT INTO THE HEALING ARMS OF TIME,

ITS EMBRACE ENDURING AND SECURE.

SEASONS PASS.

FROM THE HOLLOWS EMERGES A BUTTERFLY,

BOLDER, BRIGHTER, STRONGER.

WATCH ME SOAR.

—ME

ACKNOWLEDGMENTS

Where to even begin? Words alone cannot encompass my incredible gratitude to my family and friends who supported me on this journey. And it wasn't always an easy ride.

To my children, Mimi and Pavis, for being cool with getting takeout all the time so I could sit there and write late into the night and for always encouraging me to color outside the lines. I love you beyond belief. To my mom, Nancy Felker, who read every chapter and did not judge my confessed peccadilloes. (Although she *does* want me to stop cursing.) Her encouragement is everything. To my brothers, David and Matthew Felker, who are like my Rock(s) of Gibraltar. I love being your Jan. And to the rest of the Felker family—I love our messiness.

To my beta reader besties for taking the time and effort to read my draft book and send detailed comments and feedback. Ruth Agron, Jen Frankito, Angela Goodman, Kristy Hardesty, Kelly Sunday, Jen Tubley, Sione Tupou, and Tamar Waller. You guys (*Philly speak*) are my ride-or-die and bring so much color to my life. Special thanks to Tammy Weinstein, who would send pages and pages of feedback and took this on as if it were a job. You are just magnificent, sister of my heart.

To the incredible team at She Writes Press, particularly Brooke Warner, Lauren Wise, Krissa Lagos, Anne Durette, and Laura Matthews who wielded the editorial machete with Zorro-like grace and made this book so much better. Truly amazing . . . and I am forever grateful. Artistic kudos to Rebecca Lown and Stacey Aaronson for creating a beautiful cover and interior layout. So very talented. Many thanks to the wonderful PR team at

BookSparks, Crystal Patriarche, Tabitha Bailey, and Grace Fell, for helping to launch this labor of love. Your incredible efforts gave this book wings. Heartfelt thanks to Kiersten Armstrong for designing such a kick-ass website and to Eliana Seochand for helping to create an online presence despite my social media angst. You are my creative superheroes.

And, finally, to my sweet dad—who was always happy.

NOTES

Introduction: From Crappy to Happy and Everything in Between

POSITIVELY PSYCHO TO POSITIVE PSYCHOLOGY

1. Martin E. P. Seligman and Mihaly Csikszentmihalyi, "Positive Psychology: An Introduction," *American Psychologist* 55, no. 1 (2000): 5–14, https://doi.org/10.1037/0003-066x.55.1.5.

2. Sonja Lyubomirsky, Kennon M. Sheldon, and David Schkade, "Pursuing Happiness: The Architecture of Sustainable Change," *Review of General Psychology* 9, no. 2 (June 2005): 111–31, https://doi.org/10.1037/1089-2680.9.2.111.

CALL ME GRETCHEN

3. Zuzanna Stanska, "The Mysterious Street from Edvard Munch's 'The Scream,'" *DailyArt Magazine*, December 9, 2022, https://www.dailyart magazine.com/the-mysterious-road-of-the-scream-by-edvard-munch/.

SELF-HELP VS. SELF-HOPE

4. Ad Bergsma, "Do Self-Help Books Help?" *Journal of Happiness Studies* 9, no. 3 (February 28, 2007): 341–60, https://doi.org/10.1007/s10902-006-9041-2.

5. Acacia C. Parks and Rebecca K Szanto, "Assessing the Efficacy and Effectiveness of a Positive Psychology-Based Self-Help Book," *Terapia Psicológica* 31, no. 1 (April 2013): 141–49, https://doi.org/10.4067/s0718-48082013000100013.

6. Dawn M. Wilson and Thomas F. Cash, "Who Reads Self-Help Books?: Development and Validation of the Self-Help Reading Attitudes Survey," *Personality and Individual Differences* 29 (2000): 119–29.

Chapter 1: The Art of Letting Go, Bouncing Back, and Being

LET GO OR BE DRAGGED

1. Sarah Whitten, "'Frozen II' Is Now the Highest Grossing Animated Movie of All Time," CNBC.com, January 5, 2020, https://www.cnbc.com/2020/01/05/frozen-2-is-now-the-highest-grossing-animated-movie-of-all-time.html.

2. Matthew Solan, "The Secret to Happiness? Here's Some Advice from the Longest-Running Study on Happiness," *Harvard Health*, October 5, 2017, https://www.health.harvard.edu/blog/the-secret-to-happiness-heres-some-advice-from-the-longest-running-study-on-happiness-2017100512543.

3. Elisabeth Kübler-Ross and Ira Byock, MD, *On Death and Dying: What the Dying Have to Teach Doctors, Nurses, Clergy and Their Own Families*, Reissue (Scribner, 2014).

4. Jos F. Brosschot, William Gerin, and Julian F. Thayer, "The Perseverative Cognition Hypothesis: A Review of Worry, Prolonged Stress-Related Physiological Activation, and Health," *Journal of Psychosomatic Research* 60, no. 2 (February 2006): 113–24, https://doi.org/10.1016/j.jpsychores.2005.06.074; Elissa S. Epel et al., "Accelerated Telomere Shortening in Response to Life Stress," *Proceedings of the National Academy of Sciences of the United States of America* 101, no. 49 (2004): 17312–15, https://doi.org/10.1073/pnas.0407162101; Laura M. Glynn, Nicholas Christenfeld, and William Gerin, "The Role of Rumination in Recovery from Reactivity: Cardiovascular Consequences of Emotional States," *Psychosomatic Medicine* 64, no. 5 (September 1, 2002): 714–26, https://doi.org/10.1097/01.psy.0000031574.42041.23; Abiola Keller et al., "Does the Perception That Stress Affects Health Matter? The Association with Health and Mortality.," *Health Psychology* 31, no. 5 (2012): 677–84, https://doi.org/10.1037/a0026743; Kate A. Leger, Susan T. Charles, and David M. Almeida, "Let It Go: Lingering Negative Affect in Response to Daily Stressors Is Associated with Physical Health Years Later," *Psychological Science* 29, no. 8 (March 19, 2018): 1283–90, https://doi.org/10.1177/0956797618763097; T. C. Russ et al., "Association between Psychological Distress and Mortality: Individual Participant Pooled Analysis of 10 Prospective Cohort Studies," *BMJ* 345, no. jul31 4 (July 31, 2012): e4933–e4933, https://doi.org/10.1136/bmj.e4933.

5. N. S. Fagley, "Appreciation Uniquely Predicts Life Satisfaction above Demographics, the Big 5 Personality Factors, and Gratitude," *Personality and Individual Differences* 53, no. 1 (July 2012): 59–63, https://doi.org/10.1016/j.paid.2012.02.019; Wai Kai Hou et al., "Psychological Detachment and Savoring in Adaptation to Cancer Caregiving," *Psycho-Oncology* 25, no. 7 (October 30, 2015): 839–47, https://doi.org/10.1002/pon.4019; Paul E. Jose, Bee T. Lim, and Fred B. Bryant, "Does Savoring Increase Happiness? A Daily Diary Study," *The Journal of Positive Psychology* 7, no. 3 (May 2012): 176–87, https://doi.org/10.1080/17439760.2012.671345; Jennifer L. Smith and Fred B. Bryant, "The Benefits of Savoring Life," *The International Journal of Aging and Human Development* 84, no. 1 (September 22, 2016): 3–23, https://doi.org/10.1177/0091415016669146; Jennifer L. Smith and Agnieszka A. Hanni, "Effects of a Savoring Intervention on Resilience and Well-Being of Older Adults," *Journal of Applied Gerontology* 38, no. 1 (February 10, 2017): 137–52, https://doi.org/10.1177/07334648 17693375; Joanne V. Wood, Sara A. Heimpel, and John L. Michela, "Savoring versus Dampening: Self-Esteem Differences in Regulating Positive Affect.," *Journal of Personality and Social Psychology* 85, no. 3 (2003): 566–80, https://doi.org/10.1037/0022-3514.85.3.566.

ENTER THE GROWTH ZONE

6. Judith Bardwick, *Danger in the Comfort Zone: From Boardroom to Mailroom—How to Break the Entitlement Habit That's Killing American Business*, 2nd ed. (AMACOM, 1995).

7. Oliver Page MD, "How to Leave Your Comfort Zone and Enter Your 'Growth Zone,'" PositivePsychology.com, December 28, 2022, https://positivepsychology.com/comfort-zone.

8. R. Nicholas Carleton, "Fear of the Unknown: One Fear to Rule Them All?" *Journal of Anxiety Disorders* 41 (June 2016): 5–21, https://doi.org/10.1016/j.janxdis.2016.03.011.

9. Joel Osteen and Victoria Osteen, *Wake Up to Hope: Devotional*, Reprint (FaithWords, 2017), 82.

BE A WEEBLE

10. Karen E. Adolph et al., "How Do You Learn to Walk? Thousands of Steps and Dozens of Falls per Day," *Psychological Science* 23, no. 11 (October 19, 2012): 1387–94, https://doi.org/10.1177/0956797612446346.

11. Geert A. Buijze et al., "The Effect of Cold Showering on Health and Work: A Randomized Controlled Trial," ed. Jacobus van Wouwe, *PLOS ONE* 11, no. 9 (September 15, 2016): e0161749, https://doi.org/10.1371/journal.pone.0161749; Donatella Marazziti et al., "Thermal Balneotherapy Induces Changes of the Platelet Serotonin Transporter in Healthy Subjects," *Progress in Neuro-Psychopharmacology and Biological Psychiatry* 31, no. 7 (October 2007): 1436–39, https://doi.org/10.1016j.pnpbp.2007.06.025; Nikolai A. Shevchuk, "Adapted Cold Shower as a Potential Treatment for Depression," *Medical Hypotheses* 70, no. 5 (January 2008): 995–1001, https://doi.org/10.1016/j.mehy.2007.04.052; Masahiro Toda et al., "Change in Salivary Physiological Stress Markers by Spa Bathing," *Biomedical Research* 27, no. 1 (2006): 11–14, https://doi.org/10.2220/biomedres.27.11.

12. Yuna L. Ferguson and Kennon M. Sheldon, "Trying to Be Happier Really Can Work: Two Experimental Studies," *The Journal of Positive Psychology* 8, no. 1 (January 2013): 23–33, https://doi.org/10.1080/17439760.2012.747000; Myriam V. Thoma et al., "The Effect of Music on the Human Stress Response," ed. Robert L. Newton, *PLOS ONE* 8, no. 8 (August 5, 2013): e70156, https://doi.org/10.1371/journal.pone.0070156; Graham F. Welch et al., "Editorial: The Impact of Music on Human Development and Well-Being," *Frontiers in Psychology* 11 (June 17, 2020), https://doi.org/10.3389/fpsyg.2020.01246; "Music and the Brain: What Happens When You're Listening to Music," *Pegasus Magazine*, October 30, 2019, https://www.ucf.edu/pegasus/your-brain-on-music/.

LET'S GET WIRED

13. D. Hebb, *The Organization of Behavior: A Neuropsychological Theory*, 1st ed. (Psychology Press, 2012).

14. John T. Cacioppo, Stephanie Cacioppo, and Jackie K. Gollan, "The Negativity Bias: Conceptualization, Quantification, and Individual Differences," *Behavioral and Brain Sciences* 37, no. 3 (June 2014): 309–10, https://doi.org/10.1017/s0140525x13002537; Rick Hanson, *Hardwiring Happiness: The New Brain Science of Contentment, Calm, and Confidence* (Harmony, 2013).

15. Robert Leahy, *The Worry Cure: Seven Steps to Stop Worry from Stopping You*, (Harmony, 2006).

16. Deepak Chopra MD, *Quantum Healing (Revised and Updated): Exploring the Frontiers of Mind/Body Medicine* (New York: Penguin Random House, 2015); Raj Raghunathan, "How Negative Is Your 'Mental Chatter'?" *Psychology Today*, October 10, 2013, https://www.psychologytoday.com/intl/blog/sapient-nature/201310/how-negative-is-your-mental-chatter; Julie Tseng and Jordan Poppenk, "Brain Meta-State

Transitions Demarcate Thoughts across Task Contexts Exposing the Mental Noise of Trait Neuroticism," *Nature Communications* 11, no. 1 (July 13, 2020), https://doi.org/10.1038/s41467-020-17255-9.

17. Cristina M. Alberini, "Long-Term Memories: The Good, the Bad, and the Ugly," *Cerebrum: The Dana Forum on Brain Science*, August 31, 2010; John T. Cacioppo, Stephanie Cacioppo, and Jackie K. Gollan, "The Negativity Bias: Conceptualization, Quantification, and Individual Differences," *Behavioral and Brain Sciences* 37, no. 3 (June 2014): 309–10, https://doi.org/10.1017/s0140525x13002537.

18. John Gottman PhD, *Why Marriages Succeed or Fail: And How You Can Make Yours Last* (Simon & Schuster, 1995).

THE FRYING PAN OF STRESS

19. Spinal Research, "Chronic Stress—The Effects on Your Brain," *Australian Spinal Research Foundation*, February 18, 2021, https://spinalresearch.com.au/chronic-stress-effects-brain/; G. E. Tafet et al., "Correlation between Cortisol Level and Serotonin Uptake in Patients with Chronic Stress and Depression," *Cognitive, Affective, & Behavioral Neuroscience* 1, no. 4 (December 1, 2001): 388–93, https://doi.org/10.3758/cabn.1.4.388.

20. Deborah S. Hartz-Seeley, "Chronic Stress Is Linked to the Six Leading Causes of Death," *Miami Herald*, March 21, 2014, https://www.miamiherald.com/ living/ article1961770.html; Rajita Sinha, "Chronic Stress, Drug Use, and Vulnerability to Addiction," *Annals of the New York Academy of Sciences* 1141, no. 1 (October 2008): 105–30, https://doi.org/10.1196/annals.1441.030.

21. Egon Dejonckheere and Brock Bastian, "Perceiving Social Pressure Not to Feel Negative Is Linked to a More Negative Self-Concept," *Journal of Happiness Studies* 22, no. 2 (March 14, 2020): 667–79, https://doi.org/10.1007/s10902-020-00246-4; James J. Gross and Robert W. Levenson, "Hiding Feelings: The Acute Effects of Inhibiting Negative and Positive Emotion," *Journal of Abnormal Psychology* 106, no. 1 (February 1997): 95–103, https://doi.org/10.1037/0021-843x.106.1.95.

22. David Lewis, "Galaxy Stress Research." *Mindlab International* (UK: Sussex University 2009).

23. Erin Nrodwin, "24 Easy Habits That Psychologists Have Linked with Health and Happiness," *Business Insider*, July 26, 2019, https://www.businessinsider.com/science-backed-things-that-make-you-happier-2015-6; Tiffany Field et al., "Cortisol Decreases and Serotonin and Dopamine Increase following Massage Therapy," *International Journal of Neuroscience* 115, no. 10 (January 2005): 1397–1413, https://doi.org/10.1080/00207450590 956459; Rick Hanson and Richard Mendius, *Buddha's Brain: The Practical Neuroscience of Happiness, Love, and Wisdom*, 1st ed. (New Harbinger Publications, 2009); Xiao Ma et al., "The Effect of Diaphragmatic Breathing on Attention, Negative Affect and Stress in Healthy Adults," *Frontiers in Psychology* 8 (June 6, 2017), https://doi.org/10.3389/fpsyg.2017.00874; Michael Miller and William F. Fry, "The Effect of Mirthful Laughter on the Human Cardiovascular System," *Medical Hypotheses* 73, no. 5 (November 2009): 636–39, https://doi.org/10.1016/j.mehy.2009.02.044; Kelly Richards, C. Campenni, and Janet Muse-Burke, "Self-Care and Well-Being in Mental Health Professionals: The Mediating Effects of Self-Awareness and

Mindfulness," *Journal of Mental Health Counseling* 32, no. 3 (July 1, 2010): 247–64, https://doi.org/10.17744/mehc.32.3.0n31v8830 4423806; J. Thirthalli et al., "Cortisol and Antidepressant Effects of Yoga," *Indian Journal of Psychiatry* 55, no. 7 (2013): 405, https://doi.org/10.4103/0019-5545.116315.

Chapter 2: Change Your Thoughts, Change Your Life

1. Richard M. Wenzlaff and Daniel M. Wegner, "Thought Suppression," *Annual Review of Psychology* 51, no. 1 (February 2000): 59–91, https://doi.org/10.1146/annurev.psych.51.1.59.

2. Daniel M. Wegner et al., "Paradoxical Effects of Thought Suppression," *Journal of Personality and Social Psychology* 53, no. 1 (1987): 5–13, https://doi.org/10.1037/0022-3514.53.1.5.

3. Aditya Shukla, "Stop/Control Negative Thoughts with Cognitive Defusion and Cognitive Restructuring Techniques," *Cognition Today*, September 24, 2020, https://cognitiontoday.com/stop-negative-thoughts-with-cognitive-defusion-cognitive-restructuring-techniques/.

4. Daniel Siegel and Tina Payne Bryson, *The Whole-Brain Child: 12 Revolutionary Strategies to Nurture Your Child's Developing Mind*, Illustrated (Bantam, 2012).

5. University of California–Los Angeles. "Putting Feelings into Words Produces Therapeutic Effects in the Brain," ScienceDaily, www.sciencedaily.com/releases/2007/06/070622090727.htm (accessed January 12, 2021).

6. Pablo Briñol et al., "Treating Thoughts as Material Objects Can Increase or Decrease Their Impact on Evaluation," *Psychological Science* 24, no. 1 (November 26, 2012): 41–47, https://doi.org/10.1177/0956797612449176.

THE HORSEMAN OF THE HAPPINESS APOCALYPSE

7. The Seleni Institute, "7 Ways to Deal with Negative Thoughts," *Psychology Today* (blog), September 29, 2015, https://www.psychologytoday.com/us/blog/women-s-mental-health-matters/201509/7-ways-deal-negative-thoughts.

THE BEST DEFENSE IS A GOOD OFFENSE

8. David A. Clark, "Cognitive Restructuring" in *The Wiley Handbook for Cognitive Behavioral Therapy*, ed. Stefan G. Hofmann, First Edition (New York: John Wiley & Sons, Ltd. 2014): 23–44.

9. Brené Brown, *Daring Greatly: How the Courage to Be Vulnerable Transforms the Way We Live, Love, Parent, and Lead*, 1st ed. (Avery, 2012).

10. Robert A. Emmons and Michael E. McCullough, "Counting Blessings versus Burdens: An Experimental Investigation of Gratitude and Subjective Well-Being in Daily Life," *Journal of Personality and Social Psychology* 84, no. 2 (2003): 377–89, https://doi.org/10.1037/0022-3514.84.2.377; Alex Korb PhD and Daniel Siegel MD, *The Upward Spiral:*

Using Neuroscience to Reverse the Course of Depression, One Small Change at a Time, Illustrated (Oakland, CA: New Harbinger Publications, 2015); Roland Zahn et al., "The Neural Basis of Human Social Values: Evidence from Functional MRI," *Cerebral Cortex* 19, no. 2 (May 22, 2008): 276–83, https://doi.org/10.1093/cercor/bhn080.

11. Ryan Niemiec and Robert McGrath, *The Power of Character Strengths: Appreciate and Ignite Your Positive Personality* (New York: VIA Institute on Character, 2019); Martin Seligman, *Authentic Happiness: Using the New Positive Psychology to Realize Your Potential for Lasting Fulfillment,* Reprint (United States: Atria Books, 2004).

RETRAIN THE BRAIN

12. Shawn Achor, *The Happiness Advantage: The Seven Principles of Positive Psychology That Fuel Success and Performance at Work,* 1st ed. (New York: Crown Publishing, 2010).

13. Chad M. Burton and Laura A. King, "The Health Benefits of Writing about Intensely Positive Experiences," *Journal of Research in Personality* 38, no. 2 (April 2004): 150–63, https://doi.org/10.1016/s0092-6566(03)00058-8; Rick Hanson PhD, *Hardwiring Happiness: The New Brain Science of Contentment, Calm, and Confidence,* Reprint (Harmony, 2016); Korb, *The Upward Spiral: Using Neuroscience to Reverse the Course of Depression, One Small Change at a Time.*

14. Britta K. Hölzel et al., "Mindfulness Practice Leads to Increases in Regional Brain Gray Matter Density," *Psychiatry Research: Neuroimaging* 191, no. 1 (January 2011): 36–43, https://doi.org/10.1016/j.pscychresns.2010.08.006; Friederike Gundel et al., "Meditation and the Brain—Neuronal Correlates of Mindfulness as Assessed with Near-Infrared Spectroscopy," *Psychiatry Research: Neuroimaging* 271 (January 2018): 24–33, https://doi.org/10.1016/j.pscychresns.2017.04.002.

15. Kimberly Schaufenbuel, "Why Google, Target, and General Mills Are Investing in Mindfulness," *Harvard Business Review,* August 30, 2021, https://hbr.org/2015/12/why-google-target-and-general-mills-are-investing-in-mindfulness; University of California–San Diego, "War and Peace (of Mind): Mindfulness Training for Military Could Help Them Deal with Stress," ScienceDaily, www.sciencedaily.com/releases/2014/05/140516092519.htm.

16. Melissa Wozniak, "50 Famous People Who Meditate," *Meditation Wise,* n.d., https://www.meditationwise.com/50-famous-people-who-meditate.

17. Amy G. Lam, "Effects of Five-Minute Mindfulness Meditation on Mental Health Care Professionals," *Journal of Psychology & Clinical Psychiatry* 2, no. 3 (March 26, 2015), https://doi.org/10.15406/jpcpy.2015.02.00076.

18. Shana Cole, Emily Balcetis, and Sam Zhang, "Visual Perception and Regulatory Conflict: Motivation and Physiology Influence Distance Perception," *Journal of Experimental Psychology: General* 142, no. 1 (2013): 18–22, https://doi.org/10.1037/a0027882; Rebecca J. Compton, "The Interface between Emotion and Attention: A Review of Evidence from Psychology and Neuroscience," *Behavioral and Cognitive Neuroscience Reviews* 2, no. 2 (June 2003): 115–29, https://doi.org/10.1177/1534582303002002003.

19. Tiffany Field, "Touch for Socioemotional and Physical Well-Being: A Review," *Developmental Review* 30, no. 4 (December 2010): 367–83, https://doi.org/10.1016/j.dr.2011.01.001.

20. Ruth Feldman and Arthur I. Eidelman, "Skin-to-Skin Contact (Kangaroo Care) Accelerates Autonomic and Neurobehavioural Maturation in Preterm Infants," *Developmental Medicine & Child Neurology* 45, no. 04 (April 2003), https://doi.org/ 10.1017/s0012162203000525.

21. Fernando Gomez-Pinilla and Ethika Tyagi, "Diet and Cognition," *Current Opinion in Clinical Nutrition and Metabolic Care* 16, no. 6 (November 2013): 726–33, https://doi.org/ 10.1097/mco.0b013e328365aae3; Ruben Guzman-Marin and Dennis McGinty, "Sleep Deprivation Suppresses Adult Neurogenesis: Clues to the Role of Sleep in Brain Plasticity," *Sleep and Biological Rhythms* 4, no. 1 (February 2006): 27–34, https://doi.org/10.1111/ j.1479-8425. 2006.00203.x; Claudia Niemann, Ben Godde, and Claudia Voelcker-Rehage, "Not Only Cardiovascular, but Also Coordinative Exercise Increases Hippocampal Volume in Older Adults," *Frontiers in Aging Neuroscience* 6 (August 4, 2014), https://doi.org/ 10.3389/fnagi.2014.00170.

22. Christopher N. Cascio et al., "Self-Affirmation Activates Brain Systems Associated with Self-Related Processing and Reward and Is Reinforced by Future Orientation," *Social Cognitive and Affective Neuroscience* 11, no. 4 (November 5, 2015): 621–29, https://doi.org/ 10.1093/scan/nsv136; Janine M Dutcher et al., "Neural Mechanisms of Self-Affirmation's Stress Buffering Effects," *Social Cognitive and Affective Neuroscience* 15, no. 10 (April 4, 2020): 1086–96, https://doi.org/10.1093/scan/nsaa042; Emily B. Falk et al., "Self-Affirmation Alters the Brain's Response to Health Messages and Subsequent Behavior Change," *Proceedings of the National Academy of Sciences* 112, no. 7 (February 2, 2015): 1977–82, https://doi.org/10.1073/pnas.1500247112.

23. Muhammad Ali, *The Greatest: My Own Story*, Illustrated (United States: Graymalkin Media, 2015).

GO WITH THE FLOW

24. Mihaly Csikszentmihalyi, *Creativity: Flow and the Psychology of Discovery and Invention*, Reprint (United States: Harper Perennial, 2013); Yuri Hanin and Khanin, *Emotions in Sport* (United States: Human Kinetics, 2000).

25. John Geirland, "Go with the Flow," *Wired*, September 1, 1996, https:// www.wired.com/1996/09/czik/.

26. Arne Dietrich, "Neurocognitive Mechanisms Underlying the Experience of Flow," *Consciousness and Cognition* 13, no. 4 (December 2004): 746–61, https://doi.org/10.1016/ j.concog.2004.07.002; Joshua Gold and Joseph Ciorciari, "A Review on the Role of the Neuroscience of Flow States in the Modern World," *Behavioral Sciences* 10, no. 9 (September 9, 2020): 137, https://doi.org/10.3390/bs10090137; Kenji Katahira et al., "EEG Correlates of the Flow State: A Combination of Increased Frontal Theta and Moderate Frontocentral Alpha Rhythm in the Mental Arithmetic Task," *Frontiers in Psychology* 9 (March 9, 2018), https://doi.org/10.3389/fpsyg.2018.00300; "The Neuroscience of Flow," Brain Biz, August 31, 2018, https://brainbiz.com.au/the-neuroscience-of-flow/.

27. Lauren Effron, "Michael Jordan, Kobe Bryant's Meditation Coach on How to Be 'Flow Ready' and Get in the Zone," *ABC News*, April 7, 2016, https://abcnews.go.com/Health/ michael-jordan-kobe-bryants-meditation-coach-flow-ready/story?id=38175801.

28. Elaine Houston, "Flow State: 11+ Activities to Enter a Flow State of Mind," PositivePsychology.com, September 8, 2022, https://positivepsychology.com/flow-activities/.

29. Marino Bonaiuto et al., "Optimal Experience and Personal Growth: Flow and the Consolidation of Place Identity," *Frontiers in Psychology* 7 (November 7, 2016), https://doi.org/10.3389/fpsyg.2016.01654.

30. Tom Rath, *Strengths Finder 2.0: A New and Upgraded Edition of the Online Test from Gallup's Now, Discover Your Strengths* (New York: Gallup Press, 2007).

BOUNCE, BABY, BOUNCE

31. "Resilience," *Psychology Today*, n.d., https://www.psycho-logytoday.com/ us/basics/resilience.

32. Erin McDowell, "20 Rich and Famous People Who Were Once Homeless," *Business Insider Nederland*, August 20, 2020, https://www.businessinsider.nl/rich-and-famous-people-who-were-homeless-2015-10.?international= true&r=US; "10 Celebrities Who Were Homeless before Famous," *The Mind Circle*, December 29, 2015, https://themindcircle.com/homeless-celebrities/.

33. "Building Your Resilience," *American Psychological Association*, February 1, 2020, https://www.apa.org/topics/resilience/building-your-resilience.

34. Jessica Bennett, "On Campus, Failure Is on the Syllabus," *The New York Times*, July 2, 2017, https://www.nytimes.com/2017/06/24/fashion/fear-of-failure.html.

35. "How Coca-Cola, Netflix, and Amazon Learn from Failure," *Harvard Business Review*, September 17, 2021, https://hbr.org/2017/11/how-coca-cola-netflix-and-amazon-learn-from-failure; "Making Failure Work," Brightline Initiative, n.d., https://www.brightline.org/resources/making-failure-work/.

36. "5 Key Questions about Employee Resilience," BetterUp, n.d., https://grow.betterup.com/resources/5-key-questions-about-employee-resilience.

37. "Resilience," Feeling Good MN, n.d., https://www.feelinggoodmn. org/what-we-do/bounce-back-project-/resilience/.

38. Sheryl Sandberg, "University of California, Berkeley 2016 Commencement Address, May 14th, 2016," https://news.berkeley. edu/wp-content/uploads/2016/05/Sheryl-Sandberg-Berkeley-commencement-speech.pdf.

Chapter 3: The Game-Changing Trifecta— Gratitude, Faith, and Grace

1. "Discovering the Secret," Oprah.com, January 1, 2006, https://www.oprah.com/spirit/_75/7.

BE A GRATITUDE BALLER

2. Michael Craig Miller, "In Praise of Gratitude," *Harvard Health Blog* (blog), November 21, 2012, https://www.health.harvard.edu/blog/in-praise-of-gratitude-201211215561.

THANK U, NEXT

3. Dan Baker Ph.D. and Cameron Stauth, *What Happy People Know: How the New Science of Happiness Can Change Your Life for the Better* (New York: St. Martin's Griffin, 2004).

4. Alex Korb Ph.D., "The Grateful Brain: The Neuroscience of Giving Thanks," *Psychology Today Prefrontal Nudity: The Brain Exposed* (blog), November 20, 2012, https://www.psycho-logytoday.com/us/blog/prefrontal-nudity/201211/the-grateful-brain.

5. Mitchel G. Adler and N. S. Fagley, "Appreciation: Individual Differences in Finding Value and Meaning as a Unique Predictor of Subjective Well-Being," *Journal of Personality* 73, no. 1 (February 2005): 79–114, https://doi.org/10.1111/j.1467-6494. 2004.00305.x; Lung Hung Chen and Chia-Huei Wu, "Gratitude Enhances Change in Athletes' Self-Esteem: The Moderating Role of Trust in Coach," *Journal of Applied Sport Psychology* 26, no. 3 (May 8, 2014): 349–62, https://doi.org/10.1080/ 10413200.2014.889255; C. Nathan DeWall et al., "A Grateful Heart Is a Nonviolent Heart," *Social Psychological and Personality Science* 3, no. 2 (September 6, 2011): 232–40, https://doi.org/10.1177/1948550611416675; Robert Emmons, *Thanks!: How Practicing Gratitude Can Make You Happier* (New York: First Houghton Mifflin, 2007); Robert A. Emmons and Michael E. McCullough, "Counting Blessings versus Burdens: An Experimental Investigation of Gratitude and Subjective Well-Being in Daily Life," *Journal of Personality and Social Psychology* 84, no. 2 (2003): 377–89, https://doi.org/10.1037/0022-3514.84.2.377; N. S. Fagley, "Appreciation Uniquely Predicts Life Satisfaction above Demographics, the Big 5 Personality Factors, and Gratitude," *Personality and Individual Differences* 53, no. 1 (July 2012): 59–63, https://doi.org/10.1016/j.paid.2012.02.019; Alison Killen and Ann Macaskill, "Using a Gratitude Intervention to Enhance Well-Being in Older Adults," *Journal of Happiness Studies* 16, no. 4 (June 20, 2014): 947–64, https://doi.org/10.1007/s10902-014-9542-3; Najma Khorrami MPH, "Gratitude Is a Gateway to Positive Emotions," *Psychology Today : Comfort of Gratitude* (blog), December 1, 2020, https://www.psychologytoday.com/us/blog/comfort-gratitude/202012/gratitude-is-gateway-positive-emotions; Sonja Lyubomirsky, *The How of Happiness: A New Approach to Getting the Life You Want*, Reprint (New York: Penguin Books, 2008); Michael E. McCullough, Robert A. Emmons, and Jo-Ann Tsang, "The Grateful Disposition: A Conceptual and Empirical Topography," *Journal of Personality and Social Psychology* 82, no. 1 (2002): 112–27, https://doi.org/10.1037/0022-3514.82.1.112.

6. Emmons and McCullough, "Counting Blessings versus Burdens: An Experimental Investigation of Gratitude and Subjective Well-Being in Daily Life," 2003.

7. Emmons, *Thanks!: How Practicing Gratitude Can Make You Happier*, 2007; Martin E. P. Seligman et al., "Positive Psychology Progress: Empirical Validation of Interventions," *American Psychologist* 60, no. 5 (July–August, 2005): 410–21, https://doi.org/10.1037/0003-066x. 60.5.410.

8. Ed Diener and Robert Biswas-Diener, "Will Money Increase Subjective Well-Being?: A Literature Review and Guide to Needed Research," *Social Indicators Research Series* (2009): 119–54, https://doi.org/10.1007/978-90-481-2350-6_6.

9. Tim Kasser, *The High Price of Materialism* (Cambridge: MIT Press, 2002).

10. Nathaniel M. Lambert et al., "More Gratitude, Less Materialism: The Mediating Role of Life Satisfaction," *The Journal of Positive Psychology* 4, no. 1 (January 2009): 32–42, https://doi.org/10.1080/17439760802216311.

11. Max Slater-Robins, "15 Inspirational Quotes from Steve Jobs," *Insider* (blog), September 29, 2015, https://www.businessinsider.com/steve-jobs-quotes-life-advice-2015-9.

12. Chris Ogden, "China's Richest Man Says He Was Happier Earning $12 a Month," LADbible, March 19, 2018, https://www.ladbible.com/community/inspirational-chinas-richest-man-says-he-was-happier-earning-12-a-month-20180204.

THE GRATITUDE GOODY BAG

13. Mikaela Conley, "Thankfulness Linked to Positive Changes in Brain and Body," *ABC News*, November 23, 2011, https://abcnews.go.com/Health/science-thankfulness/story?id=15008148.

14. Anna L. Boggiss et al., "A Systematic Review of Gratitude Interventions: Effects on Physical Health and Health Behaviors," *Journal of Psychosomatic Research* 135 (August 2020): 110165, https://doi.org/10.1016/j.jpsychores. 2020.110165; Emmons and McCullough, "Counting Blessings versus Burdens: An Experimental Investigation of Gratitude and Subjective Well-Being in Daily Life," 2003; Patrick L. Hill, Mathias Allemand, and Brent W. Roberts, "Examining the Pathways between Gratitude and Self-Rated Physical Health across Adulthood," *Personality and Individual Differences* 54, no. 1 (January 2013): 92–96, https://doi.org/10.1016/j.paid.2012.08.011; Marta Jackowska et al., "The Impact of a Brief Gratitude Intervention on Subjective Well-Being, Biology and Sleep," *Journal of Health Psychology* 21, no. 10 (July 9, 2016), 2207–17, https://doi.org/10.1177/1359105315572455; Sunghyon Kyeong et al., "Effects of Gratitude Meditation on Neural Network Functional Connectivity and Brain-Heart Coupling," *Scientific Reports* 7, no. 1 (July 11, 2017), https://doi.org/10.1038/s41598-017-05520-9; Laura S. Redwine et al., "Pilot Randomized Study of a Gratitude Journaling Intervention on Heart Rate Variability and Inflammatory Biomarkers in Patients with Stage B Heart Failure," *Psychosomatic Medicine* 78, no. 6 (July 2016): 667–76, https://doi.org/10.1097/psy.0000000000000316.

15. Amie M. Gordon et al., "To Have and to Hold: Gratitude Promotes Relationship Maintenance in Intimate Bonds," *Journal of Personality and Social Psychology* 103, no. 2 (August 2012): 257–74, https://doi.org/10.1037/a0028723; Lisa A. Williams and Monica Y. Bartlett, "Warm Thanks: Gratitude Expression Facilitates Social Affiliation in New Relationships via Perceived Warmth," *Emotion* 15, no. 1 (2015): 1–5, https://doi.org/10.1037/emo0000017.

16. Rodger Dean Duncan, "How Campbell's Soup's Former CEO Turned the Company Around," *Fast Company*, September 18, 2014, https://www.fastcompany.com/3035830/how-campbells-soups-former-ceo-turned-the-company-around.

17. Sara B. Algoe, "Find, Remind, and Bind: The Functions of Gratitude in Everyday Relationships," *Social and Personality Psychology Compass* 6, no. 6 (May 31, 2012): 455–69, https://doi.org/10.1111/j.1751-9004.2012.00439.x.

EMBRACE YOUR UPPIE

18. Robert Emmons, "Why Gratitude Is Good," *Greater Good Magazine* (University of Berkeley, November 16 2010), https://greatergood.berkeley. edu/article/item/why_gratitude_is_good.

19. Christopher Peterson and Martin Seligman, *Character Strengths and Virtues: A Handbook and Classification*, 1st ed. (American Psychological Association/Oxford University Press, 2004).

20. Brené Brown, *The Gifts of Imperfection: Let Go of Who You Think You're Supposed to Be and Embrace Who You Are*, 1st ed. (Center City, Minnesota: Hazelden Publishing, 2010).

21. Harold G. Koenig, "Concerns about Measuring 'Spirituality' in Research," *Journal of Nervous & Mental Disease* 196, no. 5 (May 2008): 349–55, https://doi.org/10.1097/nmd.0b013e31816ff796.

22. Chaeyoon Lim and Robert D. Putnam, "Religion, Social Networks, and Life Satisfaction," *American Sociological Review* 75, no. 6 (December 2010): 914–33, https://doi.org/10.1177/0003122410 386686; Thomas Plante PhD, *Religion, Spirituality, and Positive Psychology: Understanding the Psychological Fruits of Faith* (Santa Barbara, CA: Praeger, 2012); Susana C. Marques, Shane J. Lopez, and Joanna Mitchell, "The Role of Hope, Spirituality and Religious Practice in Adolescents' Life Satisfaction: Longitudinal Findings," *Journal of Happiness Studies* 14, no. 1 (March 15, 2012): 251–61, https://doi.org/10.1007/s10902-012-9329-3; Sadhna kumari Sharma and O. P. Sharma, "Spirituality Leads to Happiness: A Correlative Study," *International Journal of Indian Psychology* 3, no. 2 (March 25, 2016), https://doi.org/10.25215/0302.177; Dirk van Dierendonck, "Spirituality as an Essential Determinant for the Good Life, Its Importance Relative to Self-Determinant Psychological Needs," *Journal of Happiness Studies* 13, no. 4 (August 19, 2011): 685–700, https://doi.org/10.1007/s10902-011-9286-2.

23. Arthur C. Brooks, "The 3 Equations for a Happy Life, Even during a Pandemic," *The Atlantic*, April 9, 2020, https://www.theatlantic. com/family/archive/2020/04/how-increase-happiness-according-research/609619/.

IN GRACE, FREEDOM

24. Karl Barth, Geoffrey Bromiley, and Thomas Forsyth Torrance, Church Dogmatics: The Doctrine of Reconciliation, Vol. 4, Pt. 1: The Subject-Matter and Problems of the Doctrine of Reconciliation, 1st Pbk. Ed (Bloomsbury T&T Clark, 2004), 41–42.

25. Michka Assayas, *Bono: In Conversation with Michka Assayas*, First Edition (New York: Riverhead Hardcover, 2005).

Chapter 4: Your Why Is the Way—
Goals, Vision, and Purpose

GET GOAL RICH

1. Napoleon Hill, *Think and Grow Rich: The Original Classic*, 1st ed. (West Sussex, UK: Capstone, 2010).

2. Sarah Gardner and Dave Albee, "Study Focuses on Strategies for Achieving Goals, Resolutions," Press Release, February 1, 2015, https://scholar.dominican.edu/news-releases/266; Gail Matthews, ed., *Goal Research Summary, 9th Annual International Conference of the Psychology Research Unit of Athens Institute for Education and Research (ATINER)*, 2015, https://boostprofits.com/wp-content/uploads/Goals-Research-Summary.pdf?x60870.

3. Laura A. King, "The Health Benefits of Writing about Life Goals," *Personality and Social Psychology Bulletin* 27, no. 7 (July 2001): 798–807, https://doi.org/10.1177/0146167201277003; Laura A. King and James W. Pennebaker, "Thinking about Goals, Glue, and the Meaning of Life" in *Ruminative Thoughts*, 10, ed. Wyer R. S. (Mahwah, NJ: Erlbaum): 97–106; Michaéla C. Schippers and Niklas Ziegler, "Life Crafting as a Way to Find Purpose and Meaning in Life," *Frontiers in Psychology* 10 (December 13, 2019), https://doi.org/10.3389/fpsyg.2019.02778; Henry David Thoreau, "Walking," in *The Making of the American Essay*, ed. John D'Agata (Minneapolis: Graywolf Press, 2016), 177–78.

4. Richard Koestner et al., "Attaining Personal Goals: Self-Concordance Plus Implementation Intentions Equals Success," *Journal of Personality and Social Psychology* 83, no. 1 (2002): 231–44, https://doi.org/10.1037/0022-3514.83.1.231; Edwin A. Locke and Gary P. Latham, "New Directions in Goal-Setting Theory," *Current Directions in Psychological Science* 15, no. 5 (October 2006): 265–68, https://doi.org/10.1111/j.1467-8721.2006.00449.x.

MAKE EVERY GOAL COUNT

5. Achor, *Before Happiness: The 5 Hidden Keys to Achieving Success, Spreading Happiness, and Sustaining Positive Change*, 2013; Bruce Headey, "Life Goals Matter to Happiness: A Revision of Set-Point Theory," No 639, *Discussion Papers of DIW Berlin*, DIW Berlin German Institute for Economic Research, (2006), https://EconPapers.repec.org/RePEc:diw:diwwpp:dp639; Ian McGregor and Brian R. Little, "Personal Projects, Happiness, and Meaning: On Doing Well and Being Yourself," *Journal of Personality and Social Psychology* 74, no. 2 (1998): 494–512, https://doi.org/10.1037/0022-3514.74.2.494; Kennon M. Sheldon, "The Self-Concordance Model of Healthy Goal Striving: When Personal Goals Correctly Represent the Person," *Handbook of Self-Determination Research* (New York: The University of Rochester Press, 2002), 65–86; Barry J. Zimmerman and T. Cleary, "Adolescents' Development of Personal Agency," *Adolescence and Education 5: Self-Efficacy Beliefs of Adolescents*, eds. F. Pajares and T. Urdan (Greenwich, CT: Information Age Publishing, 2006), 45-69.

6. Christopher P. Niemiec, Richard M. Ryan, and Edward L. Deci, "The Path Taken: Consequences of Attaining Intrinsic and Extrinsic Aspirations in Post-College Life," *Journal of Research in Personality* 43, no. 3 (June 2009): 291–306, https://doi.org/10.1016/j.jrp.2008.09.001; Peter Schmuck, Tim Kasser, and Richard M. Ryan, "Intrinsic and Extrinsic Goals: Their Structure and Relationship to Well-Being in German and US College Students," *Social Indicators Research* 50, no. 2 (2000): 225–41, https://doi.org/10.1023/a:1007084005278.

7. Luke Wayne Henderson, Tess Knight, and Ben Richardson, "An Exploration of the Well-Being Benefits of Hedonic and Eudaimonic Behaviour," *The Journal of Positive Psychology* 8, no. 4 (July 2013): 322–36, https://doi.org/10.1080/17439760.2013.803596.

8. Barbara L. Fredrickson et al., "A Functional Genomic Perspective on Human Well-Being," *Proceedings of the National Academy of Sciences* 110, no. 33 (July 29, 2013): 13684–89, https://doi.org/10.1073/pnas.1305419110.

9. Peter Schmuck, Tim Kasser, and Richard M. Ryan, "Intrinsic and Extrinsic Goals: Their Structure and Relationship to Well-Being in German and US College Students,"

Social Indicators Research 50, no. 2 (2000): 225–41, https://doi.org/10.1023/
a:1007084005278; Kennon M. Sheldon and Tim Kasser, "Pursuing Personal Goals: Skills
Enable Progress, but Not All Progress Is Beneficial," *Personality and Social Psychology
Bulletin* 24, no. 12 (December 1998): 1319–31, https://doi.org/10.1177/0146167
2982412006.

10. Hannah J. P. Klug and Günter W. Maier, "Linking Goal Progress and Subjective Well-
Being: A Meta-Analysis," *Journal of Happiness Studies* 16, no. 1 (January 9, 2014): 37–65,
https://doi.org/10.1007/s10902-013-9493-0.

VISION QUEST

11. Oprah Winfrey, interview with Dr. Michael Bernard Beckwith, *SuperSoul
Conversations Podcast by Oprah* podcast video, October 25, 2017, https://
www.youtube.com/watch?v=rorytN0jYt8.

12. John Maxwell, *Put Your Dream to the Test: 10 Questions to Help You See It and Seize It*,
CSM (Nashville, TN: Thomas Nelson, 2011).

13. Elliott T. Berkman and Matthew D. Lieberman, "The Neuroscience of Goal Pursuit:
Bridging Gaps between Theory and Data," in *The Psychology of Goals*, eds. G. Moskotwitz
and H. Grant (Guiford, 2009), 98–126.

14. William Fezler, *Creative Imagery: How to Visualize in All Five Senses*, Paperback
(Fireside, September 15, 1989); Kathleen A. Martin and Craig R. Hall, "Using Mental
Imagery to Enhance Intrinsic Motivation," *Journal of Sport & Exercise Psychology* 17
(1995): 54–69; Ronald Finke, *Creative Imagery: Discoveries and Inventions in
Visualization* (New York: Routledge, 2016).

15. George Sullivan, *Mary Lou Retton: America's Olympic Superstar* (Julian Messner, 1985).

16. Anna Williams, "8 Successful People Who Use the Power of Visualization,"
Mindbodygreen, September 22, 2022, https://www.mindbodygreen.com/articles/
successful-people-who-use-the-power-of-visualization.

17. Bang Hyun Kim and Peter R. Giacobbi, "The Use of Exercise-Related Mental
Imagery by Middle-Aged Adults," *Journal of Imagery Research in Sport and Physical
Activity* 4, no. 1 (January 30, 2009), https://doi.org/10.2202/ 1932-0191.1031.

A PICTURE REALLY IS WORTH A THOUSAND WORDS

18. Jade Scipioni, "Top Execs Use This Visualization Trick to Achieve Success—Here's
Why It Works, According to a Neuroscientist," CNBC, November 26, 2019, https://
www.cnbc.com/2019/11/22/visualization-that-helps-executives-succeed-neuroscientist-
tara-swart.html; Tara Swart, *The Source: The Secrets of the Universe, the Science of the
Brain* (New York: HarperOne, 2019).

19. "Is Tetris Good for the Brain?" ScienceDaily, n.d., https://www.science daily.com/
releases/2009/09/090901082851.htm; Jeffrey Goldsmith, "This Is Your Brain on
Tetris," *Wired*, May 1, 1994, https://www.wired.com/1994/05/tetris-2/; Richard J. Haier
et al., "Regional Glucose Metabolic Changes after Learning a Complex Visuospatial/
Motor Task: A Positron Emission Tomographic Study," *Brain Research* 570, no. 1–2
(January 1992): 134–43, https://doi.org/10.1016/0006-8993(92)90573-r; "The Tetris

Effect (Definition + Examples)," *Practical Psychology*, September 14, 2022, https://practicalpie.com/the-tetris-effect/.

20. Maxime Lagacé, "100 Focus Quotes to Improve Your Concentration Skills," Wisdom Quotes, October 27, 2022, https://wisdomquotes.com/focus-quotes/.

21. T. D. Bank, "Visualizing Goals Influences Financial Health and Happiness, Study Finds," *PR Newswire*, June 29, 2018, https://www.prnewswire.com/news-releases/visualizing-goals-influences-financial-health-and-happiness-study-finds-300207028.html.

22. Swapnil Dhruv Bose, "When Jim Carrey Wrote Himself a $10 Million Cheque," *Far Out*, September 8, 2022, https://faroutmagazine.co.uk/jim-carrey-wrote-himself-10-million-cheque/.

23. United We Care, "5 Celebrities Who Use Vision Boards for Feeling Focused," United We Care: A Super App for Mental Wellness, May 29, 2022, https://www.unitedwecare.com/5-celebrities-who-use-vision-boards-for-feeling-focused/.

A REASON FOR BEING

24. Rick Warren, *The Purpose Driven Life: What on Earth Am I Here For? 40 Days of Purpose Campaign Edition*, 1st ed. (Zondervan Press, 2002).

25. Michael Singer, *Living Untethered: Beyond the Human Predicament*, 1st ed. (Oakland, CA: New Harbinger Publications, 2022).

26. "Few Regrets in the Face of Death," University of Basel, n.d., https://www.unibas.ch/en/News-Events/Uni-Nova/Uni-Nova-125/Uni-Nova-125-Few-regrets-in-the-face-of-death.html.

27. Hadley Stern, "Steve Job's Stanford Commencement Address," *AppleMatters*, June 5, 2005, http://www.applematters.com/article/steve_jobs_standford_commencement_address/.

28. Deepak Chopra, MD, *The Seven Spiritual Laws of Success: A Pocketbook Guide to Fulfilling Your Dreams (One Hour of Wisdom)*, (San Rafael, CA: Amber-Allen Publishing, 2015).

29. Paulo Coelho and Alan Clarke, *The Alchemist*, 1st ed. (New York: HarperOne, 1993).

30. Daniel Pink, *Drive: The Surprising Truth about What Motivates Us* (New York: Riverhead Books, 2011).

31. Viktor Frankl, *By Viktor E. Frankl: Man's Search for Meaning (4th Edition)*, (Beacon Press, 1992).

32. Patricia A. Boyle et al., "Purpose in Life Is Associated with Mortality Among Community-Dwelling Older Persons," *Psychosomatic Medicine* 71, no. 5 (June 2009): 574–79, https://doi.org/10.1097/psy.0b013e3181a5a7c0; Kendall Cotton Bronk et al., "Purpose, Hope, and Life Satisfaction in Three Age Groups," *The Journal of Positive Psychology* 4, no. 6 (November 2009): 500–510, https://doi.org/10.1080/17439760903271439; Dan Buettner and Sam Skemp, "Blue Zones," *American Journal of Lifestyle Medicine* 10, no. 5 (July 7, 2016): 318–21, https://doi.org/10.1177/1559827616637066; Pia Hedberg et al., "Depression in Relation to Purpose in Life Among a Very Old Population: A Five-Year Follow-up Study," *Aging & Mental Health* 14, no. 6 (August 2010): 757–63, https://doi.org/10.1080/1360786 1003713216; Patrick L. Hill et al., "Purpose in Life in Emerging Adulthood: Development and Validation of a

New Brief Measure," *The Journal of Positive Psychology* 11, no. 3 (June 3, 2015): 237–45, https://doi.org/10.1080/17439760.2015.1048817; Yoona Kang et al., "Purpose in Life and Conflict-Related Neural Responses during Health Decision-Making," *Health Psychology* 38, no. 6 (June 2019): 545–52, https://doi.org/10.1037/hea0000729; Eric S. Kim, Victor J. Strecher, and Carol D. Ryff, "Purpose in Life and Use of Preventive Health Care Services," *Proceedings of the National Academy of Sciences* 111, no. 46 (November 3, 2014): 16331–36, https://doi.org/10.1073/pnas.1414826111; Rosemarie Kobau et al., "Well-Being Assessment: An Evaluation of Well-Being Scales for Public Health and Population Estimates of Well-Being among US Adults," *Applied Psychology: Health and Well-Being* 2, no. 3 (May 25, 2010): 272–97, https://doi.org/10.1111/j.1758-0854.2010.01035.x; Nathan A. Lewis et al., "Purpose in Life and Cognitive Functioning in Adult-hood," *Aging, Neuropsychology, and Cognition* 24, no. 6 (November 7, 2016): 662–71, https://doi.org/10.1080/13825585. 2016.1251549; Shirley Musich et al., "Purpose in Life and Positive Health Outcomes Among Older Adults," *Population Health Management* 21, no. 2 (April 2018): 139–47, https://doi.org/10.1089/pop.2017.0063; Toshimasa Sone et al., "Sense of Life Worth Living (Ikigai) and Mortality in Japan: Ohsaki Study," *Psychosomatic Medicine* 70, no. 6 (July 2008): 709–15, https://doi.org/10.1097/psy.0b013e31817e7e64.

33. Dan Buettner, *The Blue Zones: Lessons for Living Longer from the People Who've Lived the Longest*, Illustrated (National Geographic, 2010).

Chapter 5: Mind Over Matter and Choosing the Right Hard

SWIPE ON, SWIPE OFF

1. Frank J. Bernieri and Kristen N. Petty, "The Influence of Handshakes on First Impression Accuracy," *Social Influence* 6, no. 2 (April 2011): 78–87, https://doi.org/10.1080/15534510.2011.566706; William F. Chaplin et al., "Handshaking, Gender, Personality, and First Impressions," *Journal of Personality and Social Psychology* 79, no. 1 (2000): 110–17, https://doi.org/10.1037/0022-3514.79.1.110; Greg L. Stewart et al., "Exploring the Handshake in Employment Inter-views," *Journal of Applied Psychology* 93, no. 5 (2008): 1139–46, https://doi.org/10.1037/0021-9010.93.5.1139.

STAND IN THE GAP

2. Colette M. Smart and Sidney J. Segalowitz, "Respond, Don't React: The Influence of Mindfulness Training on Performance Monitoring in Older Adults," *Cognitive, Affective, & Behavioral Neuroscience* 17, no. 6 (October 2, 2017): 1151–63, https://doi.org/10.3758/s13415-017-0539-3.

3. Yingmin Zou et al., "The Mediating Role of Non-Reactivity to Mindfulness Training and Cognitive Flexibility: A Randomized Controlled Trial," *Frontiers in Psychology* 11 (June 26, 2020), https://doi.org/10.3389/fpsyg.2020.01053.

EQ OVER IQ

4. Daniel Goleman, *Emotional Intelligence: Why It Can Matter More Than IQ*, 10th Anniversary (New York: Random House Publishing Group, 2005).

5. Travis Bradberry, Jean Greaves, and Patrick Lencioni, *Emotional Intelligence 2.0* (San Diego, CA: TalentSmart, 2009).

6. Virginia K. Bratton, Nancy G. Dodd, and F. William Brown, "The Impact of Emotional Intelligence on Accuracy of Self-awareness and Leadership Performance," *Leadership & Organization Development Journal* 32, no. 2 (March 8, 2011): 127–49, https://doi.org/ 10.1108/01437731111112971; Abraham Carmeli, Meyrav Yitzhak-Halevy, and Jacob Weisberg, "The Relationship between Emotional Intelligence and Psychological Wellbeing," *Journal of Managerial Psychology* 24, no. 1 (January 16, 2009): 66–78, https:// doi.org/10.1108/02683940910922546; Edwin Carrillo et al., "Examining the Impact of Emotional Intelligence on Workplace Stress," *International Journal of Management and Human Resources* 6 (1), (January 7, 2020): 1–16; Mary Heffernan et al., "Self-Compassion and Emotional Intelligence in Nurses," *International Journal of Nursing Practice* 16, no. 4 (July 22, 2010): 366–73, https://doi.org/10.1111/j.1440-172x.2010.01853.x; Carolyn MacCann et al., "Emotional Intelligence Predicts Academic Performance: A Meta-Analysis," *Psychological Bulletin* 146, no. 2 (February 2020): 150–86, https://doi.org/ 10.1037/bul0000219; John D. Mayer, Richard D. Roberts, and Sigal G. Barsade, "Human Abilities: Emotional Intelligence," *Annual Review of Psychology* 59, no. 1 (January 1, 2008): 507–36, https://doi.org/10.1146/annurev.psych.59.103006. 093646; Ernest H. O'Boyle et al., "The Relation between Emotional Intelligence and Job Performance: A Meta-Analysis," *Journal of Organizational Behavior* 32, no. 5 (June 29, 2010): 788–818, https:// doi.org/10.1002/job.714; Kalpana Srivastava, "Emotional Intelligence and Organizational Effectiveness," *Industrial Psychiatry Journal* 22, no. 2 (2013): 97–99, https://doi.org/ 10.4103/0972-6748.132912.

7. Lori Nathanson et al., "Creating Emotionally Intelligent Schools with RULER," *Emotion Review* 8, no. 4 (August 20, 2016): 305–10, https://doi.org/10.1177/1754073916650495

8. Fred Rogers, *The World According to Mister Rogers: Important Things to Remember* (New York: Hyperion, *2003).*

GREAT EXPECTATIONS

9. Robb B. Rutledge et al., "A Computational and Neural Model of Momentary Subjective Well-Being," *Proceedings of the National Academy of Sciences* 111, no. 33 (August 4, 2014): 12252–57, https://doi.org/10.1073/pnas.1407535111.

STOICISM, OPTIMISM, AND WINNIE THE POOH

10. Marcus Aurelius and Gregory Hays, *Meditations: A New Translation*, First American PB Edition (New York: Random House Publishing Group, 2003).

11. Aurelius and Hays, *Meditations: A New Translation*; A. Milne and Ernest Shepard, *The Complete Tales and Poems of Winnie-the-Pooh*, 75th Anniversary (New York: Dutton Books for Young Readers, 2001).

12. Martin Seligman, *Learned Optimism: How to Change Your Mind and Your Life*, Reprint (New York: Vintage, 2006).

13. Charles S. Carver and Michael F. Scheier, "Dispositional Optimism," *Trends in Cognitive Sciences* 18, no. 6 (June 2014): 293–99, https://doi.org/10.1016/j.tics.2014.02.003; Charles S. Carver, Michael F. Scheier, and Suzanne C. Segerstrom, "Optimism," *Clinical Psychology Review* 30, no. 7 (November 2010): 879–89, https://doi.org/10.1016/j.cpr.2010.01.006; Ciro Conversano et al., "Optimism and Its Impact on Mental and Physical Well-Being," *Clinical Practice & Epidemiology in Mental Health* 6, no. 1 (May 14, 2010): 25–29, https://doi.org/10.2174/1745017901006010025; Baki Duy and Mehmet Ali Yıldız, "The Mediating Role of Self-Esteem in the Relationship Between Optimism and Subjective Well-Being," *Current Psychology* 38, no. 6 (September 30, 2017): 1456–63, https://doi.org/10.1007/s12144-017-9698-1; James J. Gross and Oliver P. John, "Individual Differences in Two Emotion Regulation Processes: Implications for Affect, Relationships, and Well-Being," *Journal of Personality and Social Psychology* 85, no. 2 (2003): 348–62, https://doi.org/10.1037/0022-3514.85.2.348; Man Yee Ho, Fanny M. Cheung, and Shu Fai Cheung, "The Role of Meaning in Life and Optimism in Promoting Well-Being," *Personality and Individual Differences* 48, no. 5 (April 2010): 658–63, https://doi.org/10.1016/j.paid.2010.01.008; Lewina O. Lee et al., "Optimism Is Associated with Exceptional Longevity in Two Epidemiologic Cohorts of Men and Women," *Proceedings of the National Academy of Sciences* 116, no. 37 (August 26, 2019): 18357–62, https://doi.org/10.1073/pnas.1900712116; Yvo M. C. Meevissen, Madelon L. Peters, and Hugo J. E. M. Alberts, "Become More Optimistic by Imagining a Best Possible Self: Effects of a Two Week Intervention," *Journal of Behavior Therapy and Experimental Psychiatry* 42, no. 3 (September 2011): 371–78, https://doi.org/10.1016/j.jbtep.2011.02.012; Heather N. Rasmussen, Michael F. Scheier, and Joel B. Greenhouse, "Optimism and Physical Health: A Meta-Analytic Review," *Annals of Behavioral Medicine* 37, no. 3 (June 2009): 239–56, https://doi.org/10.1007/s12160-009-9111-x; Michael F. Scheier and Charles S. Carver, "Effects of Optimism on Psychological and Physical Well-Being: Theoretical Overview and Empirical Update," *Cognitive Therapy and Research* 16, no. 2 (April 1992): 201–28, https://doi.org/10.1007/bf01173489; Seligman, *Learned Optimism: How to Change Your Mind and Your Life*; Aehsan Ahmad Dar and Mohammad Amin Wani, "Optimism, Happiness, and Self-Esteem Among University Students," *Indian Journal of Positive Psychology* 8, no. 3 (August 31, 2017): 300–304, https://doi.org/10.15614/ijpp/2017/v8i3/161893.

Chapter 6: All You Need Is Love

1. George Vaillant, *Triumphs of Experience: The Men of the Harvard Grant Study*, Reprint (United States: Belknap Press: An Imprint of Harvard University Press, 2015).

2. George Vaillant, "Happiness Is Love: Full Stop," *Harvard Medical School and Brigham and Women's Hospital* (Boston, MA), https://www.duodecim.fi/xmedia/duo/pilli/duo99210x.pdf; George Vaillant, "Yes, I Stand By My Words, 'Happiness Equals Love—Full Stop,'" *Positive Psychology News* (July 16, 2009), https://positivepsychologynews.com/news/george-vaillant/200907163163.

SOCIAL SUPPORT, NOT SOCIAL MEDIA

3. Ed Diener and Martin E. P. Seligman, "Very Happy People," *Psychological Science* 13, no. 1 (January 2002): 81–84, https://doi.org/10.1111/ 1467-9280.00415; Martin Seligman, *Flourish: A Visionary New Understanding of Happiness and Well-Being*, Reprint (New York: Free Press, 2011).

4. "Key Constructs of Social Support," *University of Pennsylvania Medical School*, Health Behavior and Health Education, Part 3, Chapter 9, https://www.med.upenn.edu/hbhe4/part3-ch9-key-constructs-social-support.shtml; Hsiu-Chia Ko, Li-Ling Wang, and Yi-Ting Xu, "Understanding the Different Types of Social Support Offered by Audience to A-List Diary-Like and Informative Bloggers," *Cyberpsychology, Behavior, and Social Networking* 16, no. 3 (March 2013): 194–99, https://doi.org/10.1089/cyber.2012.0297.

5. Melikşah Demir et al., "Friendship and Happiness among Young Adults," *Friendship and Happiness* (April 2015):117–35, https://doi.org/10.1007/ 978-94-017-9603-3_7; Richard M. Ryan and Edward L. Deci, "On Happiness and Human Potentials: A Review of Research on Hedonic and Eudaimonic Well-Being," *Annual Review of Psychology* 52, no. 1 (February 2001): 141–66, https://doi.org/10.1146/annurev.psych.52.1.141; Bert N. Uchino, John T. Cacioppo, and Janice K. Kiecolt-Glaser, "The Relationship between Social Support and Physiological Processes: A Review with Emphasis on Underlying Mechanisms and Implications for Health," *Psychological Bulletin* 119, no. 3 (May 1996): 488–531, https://doi.org/10.1037/0033-2909.119.3.488.

6. Y. K. Chan and Rance P. L. Lee, "Network Size, Social Support and Happiness in Later Life: A Comparative Study of Beijing and Hong Kong," *Journal of Happiness Studies* 7, no. 1 (March 2006): 87–112, https://doi.org/10.1007/s10902-005-1915-1; Melikşah Demir et al., "Friendship and Happiness among Young Adults" in *Friendship and Happiness,* ed. M. Denir (New York: Springer, 2015):117–135; Maria Fastame et al., "Resilience in Elders of the Sardinian Blue Zone: An Explorative Study," *Behavioral Sciences* 8, no. 3 (February 26, 2018): 30, https://doi.org/10.3390/bs8030030; Sheldon Cohen et al., "Sociability and Susceptibility to the Common Cold," *Psychological Science* 14, no. 5 (September 2003): 389–95, https://doi.org/10.1111/1467-9280.01452; Julianne Holt-Lunstad, Timothy B. Smith, and J. Bradley Layton, "Social Relationships and Mortality Risk: A Meta-Analytic Review," ed. Carol Brayne, *PLoS Medicine* 7, no. 7 (July 27, 2010): e1000316, https://doi.org/10.1371/journal.pmed.1000316; Elżbieta Kasprzak, "Perceived Social Support and Life-Satisfaction," *Polish Psychological Bulletin* 41, no. 4 (January 1, 2010): 144–54, https://doi.org/10.2478/v10059-010-0019-x; Candyce H. Kroenke et al., "Social Networks, Social Support, and Survival after Breast Cancer Diagnosis," *Journal of Clinical Oncology* 24, no. 7 (March 1, 2006): 1105–11, https://doi.org/10.1200/jco.2005.04.2846; N. Leigh-Hunt et al., "An Overview of Systematic Reviews on the Public Health Consequences of Social Isolation and Loneliness," *Public Health* 152 (November 2017): 157–71, https://doi.org/10.1016/j.puhe.2017.07.035; Andrew Levula, Michael Harré, and Andrew Wilson, "Social Network Factors as Mediators of Mental Health and Psychological Distress," *International Journal of Social Psychiatry* 63, no. 3 (February 1, 2017): 235–43, https://doi.org/10.1177/0020764017695575; Babak Moeini et al., "The Association between Social Support and Happiness among Elderly in Iran," *Korean Journal of Family Medicine* 39, no. 4 (July 20, 2018): 260–65, https://doi.org/10.4082/kjfm.17.0121; Kemal Öztemel and Elvan Yıldız-Akyol, "The Predictive Role of Happiness, Social Support, and Future Time Orientation

in Career Adaptability," *Journal of Career Development* 48, no. 3 (April 2, 2019): 199–212, https://doi.org/10.1177/0894845319840437; Carla M. Perissinotto, Irena Stijacic Cenzer, and Kenneth E. Covinsky, "Loneliness in Older Persons," *Archives of Internal Medicine* 172, no. 14 (July 23, 2012), https://doi.org/10.1001/archinternmed.2012.1993; Yang Claire Yang et al., "Social Relationships and Physiological Determinants of Longevity across the Human Life Span," *Proceedings of the National Academy of Sciences* 113, no. 3 (January 4, 2016): 578–83, https://doi.org/10.1073/pnas.1511085112.

7. Julianne Holt-Lunstad et al., "Loneliness and Social Isolation as Risk Factors for Mortality," *Perspectives on Psychological Science* 10, no. 2 (March 2015): 227–37, https://doi.org/10.1177/1745691614568352.

8. Cigna US Report, "Loneliness and the Workplace," Cigna.com/CombattingLoneliness (2020), www.cigna.com/static/www-cigna-com/docs/about-us/newsroom/studies-and-reports/combatting-loneliness/cigna-2020-loneliness-factsheet.pdf.

9. Ali Cashin, "Loneliness in America: How the Pandemic Has Deepened an Epidemic of Loneliness," Making Caring Common Project, October 20, 2022, https://mcc.gse.harvard.edu/reports/loneliness-in-america.

10. Thomas K. M. Cudjoe and Ashwin A. Kotwal, "'Social Distancing' amid a Crisis in Social Isolation and Loneliness," *Journal of the American Geriatrics Society* 68, no. 6 (May 15, 2020), https://doi.org/10.1111/jgs.16527; Julianne Holt-Lunstad, "The Potential Public Health Relevance of Social Isolation and Loneliness: Prevalence, Epidemiology, and Risk Factors," *Public Policy & Aging Report* 27, no. 4 (2017): 127–30, https://doi.org/10.1093/ppar/prx030; Kerstin Gerst-Emerson and Jayani Jayawardhana, "Loneliness as a Public Health Issue: The Impact of Loneliness on Health Care Utilization among Older Adults," *American Journal of Public Health* 105, no. 5 (May 2015): 1013–19, https://doi.org/10.2105/ajph.2014.302427.

11. John K. Antill and Sandra Cotton, "Self-Disclosure between Husbands and Wives: Its Relationship to Sex Roles and Marital Happiness," *Australian Journal of Psychology* 39, no. 1 (April 1, 1987): 11–24, https://doi.org/10.1080/ 00049538708259032; Nancy L. Collins and Lynn Carol Miller, "Self-Disclosure and Liking: A Meta-Analytic Review," *Psychological Bulletin* 116, no. 3 (1994): 457–75, https://doi.org/10.1037/0033-2909.116.3.457; Jean-Philippe Laurenceau, Lisa Feldman Barrett, and Paula R. Pietromonaco, "Intimacy as an Interpersonal Process: The Importance of Self-Disclosure, Partner Disclosure, and Perceived Partner Responsiveness in Interpersonal Exchanges," *Journal of Personality and Social Psychology* 74, no. 5 (1998): 1238–51, https://doi.org/10.1037/0022-3514. 74.5.1238.

12. Netta Horesh and Alan Apter, "Self-Disclosure, Depression, Anxiety, and Suicidal Behavior in Adolescent Psychiatric Inpatients," *Crisis* 27, no. 2 (March 2006): 66–71, https://doi.org/10.1027/0227-5910.27.2.66; Diana I. Tamir and Jason P. Mitchell, "Disclosing Information about the Self Is Intrinsically Rewarding," *Proceedings of the National Academy of Sciences* 109, no. 21 (May 7, 2012): 8038–43, https://doi.org/10.1073/pnas.1202129109; ShanShan Wang et al., "A Voxel-Based Morphometry Study of Regional Gray and White Matter Correlate of Self-Disclosure," *Social Neuroscience* 9, no. 5 (June 5, 2014): 495–503, https://doi.org/10.1080/17470919.2014.925502.

GROW YOUR GARDEN

13. "Making Good Friends," HelpGuide.org, n.d., https://www.helpguide.org/articles/relationships-communication/making-good-friends.htm; "Manage Stress: Strengthen Your Support Network," *American Psychological Association*, October 8, 2019, https://www.apa.org/topics/stress/manage-social-support; "Social Support: Tap This Tool to Beat Stress," *Mayo Clinic*, April 25, 2020, https://www.mayoclinic.org/img-20006145.

14. Anne G. Danielsen et al., "School-Related Social Support and Students' Perceived Life Satisfaction," *The Journal of Educational Research* 102, no. 4 (May 2009): 303–20, https://doi.org/10.3200/joer.102.4.303-320; Guro Engvig Løseth et al., "Stress Recovery with Social Support: A Dyadic Stress and Support Task," *Psychoneuroendocrinology* 146 (December 2022): 105949, https://doi.org/10.1016/j.psyneuen.2022.105949; Babak Moeini et al., "The Association between Social Support and Happiness among Elderly in Iran," *Korean Journal of Family Medicine* 39, no. 4 (July 20, 2018): 260–65, https://doi.org/10.4082/kjfm.17.0121; Jaime Vila, "Social Support and Longevity: Meta-Analysis-Based Evidence and Psychobiological Mechanisms," *Frontiers in Psychology* 12 (September 13, 2021), https://doi.org/10.3389/fpsyg.2021.717164.

15. Jeffrey A. Hall, "How Many Hours Does It Take to Make a Friend?" *Journal of Social and Personal Relationships* 36, no. 4 (March 15, 2018): 1278–96, https://doi.org/10.1177/0265407518761225.

16. Shawn Grover and John Helliwell, "How's Life at Home? New Evidence on Marriage and the Set Point for Happiness," *National Bureau of Economic Research* (December 2014), https://doi.org/10.3386/w20794.

BE YOUR OWN BFF

17. Marina Krakovsky, "Self-Compassion Fosters Mental Health," *Scientific American*, July 1, 2012, https://www.scientificamerican.com/article/self-compassion-fosters-mental-health/.

18. Madeleine Ferrari et al., "Self-Compassion Moderates the Perfectionism and Depression Link in Both Adolescence and Adulthood," ed. Therese van Amelsvoort, *PLOS ONE* 13, no. 2 (February 21, 2018): e0192022, https://doi.org/10.1371/journal.pone.0192022; Fuschia M. Sirois, "Procrastination and Stress: Exploring the Role of Self-Compassion," *Self and Identity* 13, no. 2 (February 6, 2013): 128–45, https://doi.org/10.1080/15298868.2013. 763404; Allison C. Kelly et al., "Who Benefits from Training in Self-Compassionate Self-Regulation? A Study of Smoking Reduction," *Journal of Social and Clinical Psychology* 29, no. 7 (September 2010): 727–55, https://doi.org/10.1521/jscp.2010.29.7.727; Kristin Neff, "Self-Compassion: An Alternative Conceptualization of a Healthy Attitude toward Oneself," *Self and Identity* 2, no. 2 (April 2003): 85–101, https://doi.org/10.1080/15298860309032; Kristin D. Neff, "Self-Compassion, Self-Esteem, and Well-Being," *Social and Personality Psychology Compass* 5, no. 1 (January 2011): 1–12, https://doi.org/10.1111/j.1751-9004.2010.00330.x; Kristin D. Neff, "The Science of Self-Compassion," in *Compassion and Wisdom in Psychotherapy*, eds. C. Germer and R. Siegel (New York: Guilford Press 2012); 79–92; David A. Sbarra, Hillary L. Smith, and Matthias R. Mehl, "When Leaving Your Ex, Love Yourself," *Psychological Science* 23, no. 3 (January 26, 2012): 261–69, https://doi.org/

10.1177/0956797611429466; "Self-Acceptance Could Be the Key to a Happier Life, yet It's the Happy Habit Many People Practice the Least," ScienceDaily, n.d., https://www.sciencedaily.com/releases/2014/03/140307111016.htm; Lisa M. Yarnell and Kristin D. Neff, "Self-Compassion, Interpersonal Conflict Resolutions, and Well-Being," *Self and Identity* 12, no. 2 (March 2013): 146–59, https://doi.org/10.1080/15298868.2011.649545.

19. Neil Strauss, "Love in the Age of Hyperbole: Our Culture vs. Love," Neil Strauss, February 14, 2018, https://www.neilstrauss.com/neil/valentinesday message/.

WHEN IN DOUBT, FOCUS OUT

20. Seligman, *Flourish: A Visionary New Understanding of Happiness and Well-Being*, 2011.

21. Lara B. Aknin, Elizabeth W. Dunn, and Michael I. Norton, "Happiness Runs in a Circular Motion: Evidence for a Positive Feedback Loop between Prosocial Spending and Happiness," *Journal of Happiness Studies* 13, no. 2 (April 24, 2011): 347–55, https://doi.org/10.1007/s10902-011-9267-5; Julia K. Boehm and Sonja Lyubomirsky, "The Promise of Sustainable Happiness," in *Oxford Handbook of Positive Psychology*, eds., S. J. Lopez and C. R. Snyder (Oxford University Press 2009): 667–677; Keiko Otake et al., "Happy People Become Happier through Kindness: A Counting Kindnesses Intervention," *Journal of Happiness Studies* 7, no. 3 (September 2006): 361–75, https://doi.org/10.1007/s10902-005-3650-z.

22. Joseph Chancellor et al., "Everyday Prosociality in the Workplace: The Reinforcing Benefits of Giving, Getting, and Glimpsing," *Emotion* 18, no. 4 (June 2018): 507–17, https://doi.org/10.1037/emo0000321.

23. Elizabeth W. Dunn, Lara B. Aknin, and Michael I. Norton, "Spending Money on Others Promotes Happiness," *Science* 319, no. 5870 (March 21, 2008): 1687–88, https://doi.org/10.1126/science.1150952; James H. Fowler and Nicholas A. Christakis, "Cooperative Behavior Cascades in Human Social Networks," *Proceedings of the National Academy of Sciences* 107, no. 12 (March 8, 2010): 5334–38, https://doi.org/10.1073/pnas.0913149107; Allan Luks and Peggy Payne, *The Healing Power of Doing Good* (Lincoln, NE: iUniverse, 2001); S. Katherine Nelson et al., "Do unto Others or Treat Yourself? The Effects of Prosocial and Self-Focused Behavior on Psychological Flourishing," *Emotion* 16, no. 6 (September 2016): 850–61, https://doi.org/10.1037/emo0000178.

24. Lynn E. Alden and Jennifer L. Trew, "If It Makes You Happy: Engaging in Kind Acts Increases Positive Affect in Socially Anxious Individuals," *Emotion* 13, no. 1 (February 2013): 64–75, https://doi.org/10.1037/a0027761; Seoyoun Kim and Kenneth F. Ferraro, "Do Productive Activities Reduce Inflammation in Later Life? Multiple Roles, Frequency of Activities, and C-Reactive Protein," *The Gerontologist* 54, no. 5 (August 22, 2013): 830–39, https://doi.org/10.1093/geront/gnt090; Myriam Mongrain et al., "Acts of Kindness Reduce Depression in Individuals Low on Agreeableness," *Translational Issues in Psychological Science* 4, no. 3 (September 2018): 323–34, https://doi.org/10.1037/tps0000168; Rachel L. Piferi and Kathleen A. Lawler, "Social Support and Ambulatory Blood Pressure: An Examination of Both Receiving and Giving," *International Journal of Psychophysiology* 62, no. 2 (November 2006): 328–36, https://doi.org/10.1016/j.ijpsycho.2006.06.002; Elizabeth B. Raposa, Holly B. Laws, and Emily B. Ansell,

"Prosocial Behavior Mitigates the Negative Effects of Stress in Everyday Life," *Clinical Psychological Science* 4, no. 4 (June 23, 2016): 691–98, https://doi.org/10.1177/2167702615611073; T. O. N. G. Zhi-qing, "The Study between Blood Pressure Fluctuation in Pre-Operation and Post-Operation of Coronary Artery Angiography and Kindness Nursing," *Practical Clinical Medicine*, 07 (2008).

25. Hamilton David PhD, *The Five Side Effects of Kindness: This Book Will Make You Feel Better, Be Happier & Live Longer* (UK: Hay House, 2017).

26. John-Tyler Binfet, "Not-So Random Acts of Kindness: A Guide to Intentional Kindness in the Classroom," *International Journal of Emotional Education*, 7 (2) (2015), 49–62; Boehm and Lyubomirsky, "The Promise of Sustainable Happiness"; Kathryn E. Buchanan and Anat Bardi, "Acts of Kindness and Acts of Novelty Affect Life Satisfaction," *The Journal of Social Psychology* 150, no. 3 (April 30, 2010): 235–37, https://doi.org/10.1080/00224540903365554; Carter Christine Ph.D., *Raising Happiness: 10 Simple Steps for More Joyful Kids and Happier Parents*, Reprint (New York: Ballantine Books, 2011); Elizabeth A. Hoge et al., "Loving-Kindness Meditation Practice Associated with Longer Telomeres in Women," *Brain, Behavior, and Immunity* 32 (August 2013): 159–63, https://doi.org/10.1016/j.bbi.2013.04.005; Filip Drozd et al., "Better Days—A Randomized Controlled Trial of an Internet-Based Positive Psychology Intervention," *The Journal of Positive Psychology* 9, no. 5 (April 22, 2014): 377–88, https://doi.org/10.1080/17439760.2014.910822; W. G. Ganser, "Pursuing Happiness with Gratitude and Kindness: An Experimental Intervention Comparing Cognitive and Behavioral Activities," *Doctoral Dissertation, Northern Arizona University* (2012); Shelley L. Kerr, Analise O'Donovan, and Christopher A. Pepping, "Can Gratitude and Kindness Interventions Enhance Well-Being in a Clinical Sample?" *Journal of Happiness Studies* 16, no. 1 (January 19, 2014): 17–36, https://doi.org/10.1007/s10902-013-9492-1; Kristin Layous et al., "Kindness Counts: Prompting Prosocial Behavior in Preadolescents Boosts Peer Acceptance and Well-Being," ed. Frank Krueger, *PLOS ONE* 7, no. 12 (December 26, 2012): e51380, https://doi.org/10.1371/journal.pone.0051380; Elisabetta Magnani and Rong Zhu, "Does Kindness Lead to Happiness? Voluntary Activities and Subjective Well-Being," *Journal of Behavioral and Experimental Economics* 77 (December 2018): 20–28, https://doi.org/10.1016/j.socec.2018.09.009; Keiko Otake et al., "Happy People Become Happier through Kindness: A Counting Kindnesses Intervention," *Journal of Happiness Studies* 7, no. 3 (September 2006): 361–75, https://doi.org/10.1007/s10902-005-3650-z; Aneka J. Piavin, "Doing Well by Doing Good: Benefits for the Benefactor," in *Flourishing: Positive Psychology and the Life Well-lived*, eds. L. M. Keyes and J. Haid (2003): 227–247, https://cupola.gettysburg.edu/gssr/vol2/iss1/3; Michael J. Poulin et al., "Giving to Others and the Association between Stress and Mortality," *American Journal of Public Health* 103, no. 9 (September 2013): 1649–55, https://doi.org/10.2105/ajph.2012.300876; Sarah D. Pressman, Tara L. Kraft, and Marie P. Cross, "It's Good to Do Good and Receive Good: The Impact of a 'Pay It Forward' Style Kindness Intervention on Giver and Receiver Well-Being," *The Journal of Positive Psychology* 10, no. 4 (October 16, 2014): 293–302, https://doi.org/10.1080/17439760.2014.965269; Lee Rowland and Oliver Scott Curry, "A Range of Kindness Activities Boost Happiness," *The Journal of Social Psychology* 159, no. 3 (May 15, 2018): 340–43, https://doi.org/10.1080/00224545.2018.1469461; Helen Y. Weng et al., "Compassion Training Alters Altruism and Neural Responses to Suffering," *Psychological Science* 24, no. 7 (May 21, 2013): 1171–80, https://doi.org/10.1177/0956797612469537.

27. Andrew G. Thomas et al., "Mate Preference Priorities in the East and West: A Cross-Cultural Test of the Mate Preference Priority Model," *Journal of Personality* 88, no. 3 (September 13, 2019): 606–20, https://doi.org/10.1111/jopy.12514.

28. Kori Miller, "What Is Kindness in Psychology? (Incl. Activities + Quotes)," *Positive Psychology*, July 25, 2022, https://positive psychology.com/character-strength-kindness/.

29. Amit Kumar and Nicholas Epley, "A Little Good Goes an Unexpectedly Long Way: Underestimating the Positive Impact of Kindness on Recipients," *Journal of Experimental Psychology: General* (August 18, 2022): https://doi.org/10.1037/xge0001271.

30. Sean Gregory, "'Without Empathy, Nothing Works.' Chef José Andrés Wants to Feed the World through the Pandemic," *Time*, March 26, 2020, https://time.com/collection/apart-not-alone/5809169/jose-andres-coronavirus-food/; Alice Johnston, "11 Small Acts of Kindness That Changed the World Forever," *Culture Trip*, November 10, 2017, https://theculturetrip.com/europe/articles/10-small-acts-of-kindness-that-changed-the-world/; Winkgo Staff, "These 17 Celebrities Are Great but Here Is Something You Probably Didn't Know about Them," Winkgo, February 15, 2020, https://winkgo.com/17-celebrities-random-acts-of-kindness/.

LOVE WITH A SIDE OF FURBALLS

31. Harold Herzog, "The Impact of Pets on Human Health and Psychological Well-Being," *Current Directions in Psychological Science* 20, no. 4 (August 2011): 236–39, https://doi.org/10.1177/0963721411415220.

32. Karen Allen, Barbara E. Shykoff, and Joseph L. Izzo, "Pet Ownership, but Not ACE Inhibitor Therapy, Blunts Home Blood Pressure Responses to Mental Stress," *Hypertension* 38, no. 4 (October 2001): 815–20, https://doi.org/10.1161/hyp.38.4.815; "Dog Ownership Associated with Longer Life, Especially among Heart Attack and Stroke Survivors," ScienceDaily, n.d., https://www.sciencedaily.com/releases/2019/10/191008083121.htm; Erika Friedmann and Sue A. Thomas, "Pet Ownership, Social Support, and One-Year Survival after Acute Myocardial Infarction in the Cardiac Arrhythmia Suppression Trial (CAST)," *The American Journal of Cardiology* 76, no. 17 (December 1995): 1213–17, https://doi.org/10.1016/s0002-9149(99)80343-9; Nancy R. Gee et al., "Dogs Supporting Human Health and Well-Being: A Biopsychosocial Approach," *Frontiers in Veterinary Science* 8 (March 30, 2021): https://doi.org/10.3389/fvets.2021.630465; Cheryl A. Krause-Parello, "Pet Ownership and Older Women: The Relationships among Loneliness, Pet Attachment Support, Human Social Support, and Depressed Mood," *Geriatric Nursing* 33, no. 3 (May 2012), 194–203, https://doi.org/10.1016/j.gerinurse.2011.12.005; Mwenya Mubanga et al., "Dog Ownership and Survival after a Major Cardiovascular Event," *Circulation: Cardiovascular Quality and Outcomes* 12, no. 10 (October 2019), https://doi.org/10.1161/circoutcomes.118.005342; Mwenya Mubanga et al., "Dog Ownership and the Risk of Cardiovascular Disease and Death—A Nationwide Cohort Study," *Scientific Reports* 7, no. 1 (November 17, 2017), https://doi.org/10.1038/s41598-017-16118-6; Ruth A. Parslow et al., "Pet Ownership and Health in Older Adults: Findings from a Survey of 2,551 Community-Based Australians Aged 60–64," *Gerontology* 51, no. 1 (December 6, 2004): 40–47, https://doi.org/10.1159/000081433; Adnan I. Qureshi et al. "Cat Ownership and the Risk of Fatal Cardiovascular Diseases. Results from the Second National Health and Nutrition Examination Study Mortality Follow-Up Study," *Journal of Vascular and Interventional*

Neurology vol. 2,1 (2009): 132-135; Parminder Raina et al., "Influence of Companion Animals on the Physical and Psychological Health of Older People: An Analysis of a One-Year Longitudinal Study," *Journal of the American Geriatrics Society* 47, no. 3 (March 1999): 323–29, https://doi.org/10.1111/j.1532-5415.1999.tb02996.x.

33. "Cardiovascular Diseases," *World Health Organization*, June 11, 2019, https://www.who.int/health-topics/cardiovascular-diseases.

34. Katherine Jacobs Bao and George Schreer, "Pets and Happiness: Examining the Association between Pet Ownership and Wellbeing," *Anthrozoös* 29, no. 2 (May 3, 2016): 283–96, https://doi.org/10.1080/08927936.2016.1152721.

35. Allen R. McConnell et al., "Friends with Benefits: On the Positive Consequences of Pet Ownership," *Journal of Personality and Social Psychology* 101, no. 6 (2011): 1239–52, https://doi.org/10.1037/a0024506.

36. Human-Animal Bond Research Institute, "New Report on Addressing the Loneliness Crisis through the Power of Pets," HABRI, February 20, 2020, https://habri.org/pressroom/20200220.

37. Stewart Fleishman et al., "Beneficial Effects of Animal-Assisted Visits on Quality of Life during Multimodal Radiation-Chemotherapy Regimens," *The Journal of Community and Supportive Oncology* 13, no. 1 (January 2015): 22–26, https://doi.org/10.12788/jcso.0102; Mohammad Sahebalzamani, Omid Rezaei, and Ladan Fattah Moghadam, "Animal-Assisted Therapy on Happiness and Life Quality of Chronic Psychiatric Patients Living in Psychiatric Residential Care Homes: A Randomized Controlled Study," *BMC Psychiatry* 20, no. 1 (December 2020), https://doi.org/10.1186/s12888-020-02980-8.

38. Michael W. White et al., "Give a Dog a Bone: Spending Money on Pets Promotes Happiness," *The Journal of Positive Psychology* 17, no. 4 (March 13, 2021): 589–95, https://doi.org/10.1080/17439760.2021. 1897871.

39. "Pet Industry Market Size, Trends & Ownership Statistics," American Pet Products Association, n.d., https://www.american petproducts.org/press_IndustryTrends.asp.

40. P&S Intelligence, "US Beauty and Personal Care Products Market to Surpass $128.7 Billion Revenue by 2030," *PR Newswire,* November 16, 2020, https://www.prnewswire.com/news-releases/us-beauty-and-personal-care-products-market-to-surpass-128-7-billion-revenue-by-2030-ps-intelligence-301172677.html.

HAPPINESS CHECK

41. Ernest L. Abel and Michael L. Kruger, "Smile Intensity in Photographs Predicts Longevity," *Psychological Science* 21, no. 4 (February 26, 2010): 542–44, https://doi.org/10.1177/0956797 610363775; Fulvio D'Acquisto, Lorenza Rattazzi, and Giuseppa Piras, "Smile—It's in Your Blood!" *Biochemical Pharmacology* 91, no. 3 (October 2014): 287–92, https://doi.org/10.1016/j.bcp.2014.07.016; Tara L. Kraft and Sarah D. Pressman, "Grin and Bear It," *Psychological Science* 23, no. 11 (September 24, 2012): 1372–78, https://doi.org/10.1177/0956797612445312; Anthony C. Little, Benedict C. Jones, and Lisa M. DeBruine, "Facial Attractiveness: Evolutionary Based Research," *Philosophical Transactions of the Royal Society B: Biological Sciences* 366, no. 1571 (June 12, 2011): 1638–59, https://doi.org/10.1098/rstb.2010.0404.

Chapter 7: Success on the Daily

MR. SANDMAN, BRING ME A DREAM

1. "Sleep and Chronic Disease," Centers for Disease Control and Prevention, September 13, 2022, https://www.cdc.gov/sleep/about_sleep/chronic_disease.html.

2. Mathias Basner et al., "Sleep Deprivation and Neurobehavioral Dynamics," *Current Opinion in Neurobiology* 23, no. 5 (October 2013): 854–63, https://doi.org/10.1016/j.conb.2013.02.008; Naomi Breslau et al., "Sleep Disturbance and Psychiatric Disorders: A Longitudinal Epidemiological Study of Young Adults," *Biological Psychiatry* 39, no. 6 (March 1996): 411–18, https://doi.org/10.1016/0006-3223 (95)00188-3; D. F. Dinges, et al. "Cumulative Sleepiness, Mood Disturbance, and Psychomotor Vigilance Performance Decrements during a Week of Sleep Restricted to 4–5 Hours per Night," *Sleep: Journal of Sleep Research & Sleep Medicine* vol. 20, 4 (1997): 267–77; Megan E. Jewett et al., "Dose-Response Relationship between Sleep Duration and Human Psychomotor Vigilance and Subjective Alertness," *Sleep* 22, no. 2 (March 1999): 171–79, https://doi.org/10.1093/sleep/22.2.171; Ronald C. Kessler et al., "Insomnia and the Performance of US Workers: Results from the America Insomnia Survey," *Sleep* 34, no. 9 (September 2011): 1161–71, https://doi.org/10.5665/sleep.1230; Adam J. Krause et al., "The Sleep-Deprived Human Brain," *Nature Reviews Neuroscience* 18, no. 7 (May 18, 2017): 404–18, https://doi.org/10.1038/nrn.2017.55; Dag Neckelmann, Arnstein Mykletun, and Alv A. Dahl, "Chronic Insomnia as a Risk Factor for Developing Anxiety and Depression," *Sleep* 30, no. 7 (July 2007): 873–80, https://doi.org/10.1093/sleep/30.7.873; "Don't Worry, Be Happy: Just Go to Bed Earlier," ScienceDaily, n.d., https://www.sciencedaily.com/releases/2014/12/141204091129.htm; Hans P. A. Van Dongen et al., "The Cumulative Cost of Additional Wakefulness: Dose-Response Effects on Neurobehavioral Functions and Sleep Physiology from Chronic Sleep Restriction and Total Sleep Deprivation," *Sleep* 26, no. 2 (March 2003): 117–26, https://doi.org/10.1093/sleep/26.2.117; Myrna M. Weissman et al., "The Morbidity of Insomnia Uncomplicated by Psychiatric Disorders," *General Hospital Psychiatry* 19, no. 4 (July 1997): 245–50, https://doi.org/10.1016/s0163-8343(97)00056-x.

3. "Drowsy Driving," NHTSA, n.d., https://www.nhtsa.gov/risky-driving/drowsy-driving.

4. Austin C. Smith, "Spring Forward at Your Own Risk: Daylight Saving Time and Fatal Vehicle Crashes," *American Economic Journal: Applied Economics* 8, no. 2 (April 1, 2016): 65–91, https://doi.org/10.1257/app.20140100.

5. Stanley Coren, *Sleep Thieves: An Eye-Opening Exploration into the Science and Mysteries of Sleep* (New York: Free Press, 1996).

6. "5 Other Disastrous Accidents Related to Sleep Deprivation," HuffPost, December 7, 2017, https://www.huffpost.com/entry/sleep-deprivation-accidents-disasters_n_4380349.

7. Max Hirshkowitz et al., "National Sleep Foundation's Sleep Time Duration Recommendations: Methodology and Results Summary," *Sleep Health* 1, no. 1 (March 2015): 40–43, https://doi.org/10.1016/j.sleh.2014.12.010.

8. A. A. Borbély, "A Two Process Model of Sleep Regulation." *Human Neurobiology* vol. 1, 3 (1982): 195–204; Daniel Kahneman and Alan B. Krueger, "Developments in the

Measurement of Subjective Well-Being," *Journal of Economic Perspectives* 20, no. 1 (February 1, 2006): 3–24, https://doi.org/10.1257/089533006776526030; "More Sleep Would Make Us Happier, Healthier and Safer," *American Psychological Association* (February 2014), https://www.apa.org/action/resources/research-in-action/sleep-deprivation; Anthony D. Ong et al., "Linking Stable and Dynamic Features of Positive Affect to Sleep," *Annals of Behavioral Medicine* 46, no. 1 (March 13, 2013): 52–61, https://doi.org/10.1007/s12160-013-9484-8; Edward F. Pace-Schott and J. Allan Hobson, "The Neurobiology of Sleep: Genetics, Cellular Physiology and Subcortical Networks," *Nature Reviews Neuroscience* 3, no. 8 (August 1, 2002): 591–605, https://doi.org/10.1038/nrn895; Ji-eun Shin and Jung Ki Kim, "How a Good Sleep Predicts Life Satisfaction: The Role of Zero-Sum Beliefs about Happiness," *Frontiers in Psychology* 9 (August 28, 2018), https://doi.org/10.3389/fpsyg.2018.01589; Nicole K. Y. Tang et al., "Changes in Sleep Duration, Quality, and Medication Use Are Prospectively Associated with Health and Well-Being: Analysis of the UK Household Longitudinal Study," *Sleep* 40, no. 3 (January 6, 2017), https://doi.org/10.1093/sleep/zsw079.

9. "Adopt Good Sleep Habits | Need Sleep," n.d., https://healthysleep. med.harvard.edu/need-sleep/what-can-you-do/good-sleep-habits; Mounir Chennaoui et al., "Sleep and Exercise: A Reciprocal Issue?" *Sleep Medicine Reviews* 20 (April 2015): 59–72, https://doi.org/10.1016/j.smrv.2014.06.008; Angela M. DeSilva Mousseau et al., "Stressed and Losing Sleep: Sleep Duration and Perceived Stress among Affluent Adolescent Females," *Peabody Journal of Education* 91, no. 5 (August 22, 2016): 628–44, https://doi.org/10.1080/0161956x.2016.1227186; Kathryn J. Reid et al., "Aerobic Exercise Improves Self-Reported Sleep and Quality of Life in Older Adults with Insomnia," *Sleep Medicine* 11, no. 9 (October 2010): 934–40, https://doi.org/10.1016/j.sleep.2010.04.014; Nicole K. Y. Tang, D. Anne Schmidt, and Allison G. Harvey, "Sleeping with the Enemy: Clock Monitoring in the Maintenance of Insomnia," *Journal of Behavior Therapy and Experimental Psychiatry* 38, no. 1 (March 2007): 40–55, https://doi.org/10.1016/j.jbtep.2005.07.0.

RISE AND SHINE

10. Admiral William McRaven, *Make Your Bed: Little Things That Can Change Your Life . . . and Maybe the World*, 1st ed. (New York: Grand Central Publishing, 2017).

11. "Morningness is a Predictor of Better Grades in College," ScienceDaily, n.d., https://www.sciencedaily.com/releases/2008/06/080609071331.htm; Katherine R. Arlinghaus and Craig A. Johnston, "The Importance of Creating Habits and Routine," *American Journal of Lifestyle Medicine* 13, no. 2 (December 29, 2018): 142–44, https://doi.org/10.1177/1559827618818044; Katherine A. Kaplan, David C. Talavera, and Allison G. Harvey, "Rise and Shine: A Treatment Experiment Testing a Morning Routine to Decrease Subjective Sleep Inertia in Insomnia and Bipolar Disorder," *Behaviour Research and Therapy* 111 (December 2018): 106–12, https://doi.org/10.1016/j.brat.2018.10.009; Christoph Randler, "Proactive People Are Morning People," *Journal of Applied Social Psychology* 39, no. 12 (December 2009): 2787–97, https://doi.org/10.1111/j.1559-1816.2009.00549.x; Nancy P. Rothbard and Steffanie L. Wilk, "Waking Up on the Right or Wrong Side of the Bed: Start-of-Workday Mood, Work Events, Employee Affect, and Performance," *Academy of Management Journal* 54, no. 5 (October 2011): 959–80, https://doi.org/10.5465/amj.2007. 0056.

12. Patrick M. Fuller, Joshua J. Gooley, and Clifford B. Saper, "Neurobiology of the Sleep-

Wake Cycle: Sleep Architecture, Circadian Regulation, and Regulatory Feedback," *Journal of Biological Rhythms* 21, no. 6 (December 2006): 482–93, https://doi.org/10.1177/0748730406294627; Cassie J. Hilditch, Jillian Dorrian, and Siobhan Banks, "Time to Wake up: Reactive Countermeasures to Sleep Inertia," *Industrial Health* 54, no. 6 (2016): 528–41, https://doi.org/10.2486/indhealth.2015-0236; Afshin Shirani and Erik K. St. Louis, "Illuminating Rationale and Uses for Light Therapy," *Journal of Clinical Sleep Medicine* 05, no. 02 (April 15, 2009): 155–63, https://doi.org/10.5664/jcsm.27445; L. Thorn et al., "The Effect of Dawn Simulation on the Cortisol Response to Awakening in Healthy Participants," *Psychoneuroendocrinology* 29, no. 7 (August 2004): 925–30, https://doi.org/10.1016/j.psyneuen.2003.08.005.

13. Hal Elrod, *The Miracle Morning* (Hal Elrod International, Incorporated, 2012).

14. Travis Bradberry, "14 Things Ridiculously Successful People Do Every Day," *Inc.com*, n.d., https://www.inc.com/travis-bradberry/14-things-ridiculously-successful-people-do-every-day.htm.; Elrod, *The Miracle Morning*; "Tony Robbins Starts Every Morning with an 'Adrenal Support Cocktail,' a 'Priming' Meditation Exercise, and a Workout Involving a 'Torture Machine,'" *Business Insider Nederland*, October 13, 2017, https://www.businessinsider.nl/tony-robbins-morning-routine-meditation-and-workout-2017-10?international =true&r=US; Cody McLain, "The Importance of a Morning Routine: Cody McLain," Medium, December 7, 2021, https://neocody. medium.com/the-importance-of-a-morning-routine-b64ec1b642f1; "12 Morning Habits of Celebrities You Can Adopt to Set Up Each Day for a Win," Bright Side, May 6, 2022, https://brightside.me/wonder-people/12-morning-habits-of-celebrities-you-can-adopt-to-set-up-each-day-for-a-win-652060/.

CONSUME WISELY

15. Jean-Anthelme Brillat-Savarin, *Physiologie Du Goût, Ou Méditations de Gastronomie Transcendante (Éd. 1826) (French Edition)*, 1826 ed. (Hachette Livre-BNF, 2018).

16. Brian Wansink and Jeffery Sobal, "Mindless Eating," *Environment and Behavior* 39, no. 1 (January 2007): 106–23, https://doi.org/10.1177/ 0013916506295573.

17. World Health Organization, "Healthy Diet," April 29, 2020, https://www.who.int/news-room/fact-sheets/detail/healthy-diet.

18. Areni Altun et al., "The Mediterranean Dietary Pattern and Depression Risk: A Systematic Review," *Neurology, Psychiatry and Brain Research* 33 (September 2019): 1–10, https://doi.org/10.1016/j.npbr.2019.05.007; Jessica Bayes, Janet Schloss, and David Sibbritt, "Effects of Polyphenols in a Mediterranean Diet on Symptoms of Depression: A Systematic Literature Review," *Advances in Nutrition* 11, no. 3 (May 2020): 602–15, https://doi.org/10.1093/advances/nmz117; Ujué Fresán et al., "Does the MIND Diet Decrease Depression Risk? A Comparison with Mediterranean Diet in the SUN Cohort," *European Journal of Nutrition* 58, no. 3 (March 7, 2018): 1271–82, https://doi.org/10.1007/s00394-018-1653-x; Felice N. Jacka et al., "Association of Western and Traditional Diets with Depression and Anxiety in Women," *American Journal of Psychiatry* 167, no. 3 (March 2010): 305–11, https://doi.org/10.1176/appi.ajp.2009.09060881; Ole Köhler-Forsberg, Cristina Cusin, and Andrew A. Nierenberg, "Evolving Issues in the Treatment of Depression," *JAMA* 321, no. 24 (June 25, 2019): 2401, https://doi.org/10.1001/jama.2019.4990; Almudena Sanchez-Villegas and Miguel

A. Martínez-González, "Diet, a New Target to Prevent Depression?" *BMC Medicine* 11, no. 1 (January 3, 2013), https://doi.org/10.1186/1741-7015-11-3; Kimberly A. Skarupski et al., "Mediterranean Diet and Depressive Symptoms among Older Adults over Time," *The Journal of Nutrition, Health & Aging* 17, no. 5 (February 19, 2013): 441–45, https://doi.org/10.1007/s12603-012-0437-x.

19. Fahimeh Haghighatdoost et al., "Drinking Plain Water Is Associated with Decreased Risk of Depression and Anxiety in Adults: Results from a Large Cross-Sectional Study," *World Journal of Psychiatry* 8, no. 3 (September 20, 2018): 88–96, https://doi.org/10.5498/wjp.v8.i3.88.

20. Heather Scherschel Wagner et al., "The Myth of Comfort Food," *Health Psychology* 33, no. 12 (2014): 1552–57, https://doi.org/10.1037/hea0000068.

21. James E. Gangwisch et al., "High Glycemic Index Diet as a Risk Factor for Depression: Analyses from the Women's Health Initiative," *The American Journal of Clinical Nutrition* 102, no. 2 (June 24, 2015): 454–63, https://doi.org/10.3945/ajcn.114.103846; Anika Knüppel et al., "Sugar Intake from Sweet Food and Beverages, Common Mental Disorder and Depression: Prospective Findings from the Whitehall II Study," *Scientific Reports* 7, no. 1 (July 27, 2017), https://doi.org/10.1038/s41598-017-05649-7; J. Monroe Jr., "The Impact of Sugar and Poor Diet on Teen Mental Health," *U.S. News & World Report* (2018), https://health.usnews.com/health-care/for-better/articles/2018-10-24/how-sugar-and-poor-diet-affect-teen-mental-health.

22. David Blanchflower, "Is Psychological Well-Being Linked to the Consumption of Fruit and Vegetables?" NBER, October 18, 2012, https://www.nber.org/papers/w18469; Tamlin S. Conner et al., "Let Them Eat Fruit! The Effect of Fruit and Vegetable Consumption on Psychological Well-Being in Young Adults: A Randomized Controlled Trial," ed. Jacobus P. van Wouwe, *PLOS ONE* 12, no. 2 (February 3, 2017): e0171206, https://doi.org/10.1371/journal.pone.0171206; Patricia A. Ford et al., "Intake of Mediterranean Foods Associated with Positive Affect and Low Negative Affect," *Journal of Psychosomatic Research* 74, no. 2 (February 2013): 142–48, https://doi.org/10.1016/j.jpsychores.2012.11.002; Dominika Głąbska et al., "Fruit and Vegetable Intake and Mental Health in Adults: A Systematic Review," *Nutrients* 12, no. 1 (January 1, 2020): 115, https://doi.org/10.3390/nu12010115; Débora Godoy-Izquierdo et al., "Association of a Mediterranean Diet and Fruit and Vegetable Consumption with Subjective Well-Being among Adults with Overweight and Obesity," *Nutrients* 13, no. 4 (April 17, 2021): 1342, https://doi.org/10.3390/nu13041342; Redzo Mujcic and Andrew J. Oswald, "Evolution of Well-Being and Happiness after Increases in Consumption of Fruit and Vegetables," *American Journal of Public Health* 106, no. 8 (August 2016): 1504–10, https://doi.org/10.2105/ajph.2016.303260; Ciara Rooney, Michelle C. McKinley, and Jayne V. Woodside, "The Potential Role of Fruit and Vegetables in Aspects of Psychological Well-Being: A Review of the Literature and Future Directions," *Proceedings of the Nutrition Society* 72, no. 4 (September 11, 2013): 420–32, https://doi.org/10.1017/s0029665 113003388; Nicola-Jayne Tuck, Claire Farrow, and Jason M. Thomas, "Assessing the Effects of Vegetable Consumption on the Psychological Health of Healthy Adults: A Systematic Review of Prospective Research," *The American Journal of Clinical Nutrition* 110, no. 1 (June 1, 2019): 196–211, https://doi.org/10.1093/ajcn/nqz080; Ruut Veenhoven, "Will Healthy Eating Make You Happier? A Research Synthesis Using an Online Findings Archive," *Applied Research in Quality of Life* 16, no. 1 (August 14, 2019): 221–40, https://doi.org/10.1007/s11482-019-09748-7; Deborah R. Wahl et al., "Healthy Food Choices Are Happy Food Choices: Evidence from a Real Life

Sample Using Smartphone Based Assessments," *Scientific Reports* 7, no. 1 (December 6, 2017), https://doi.org/10.1038/s41598-017-17262-9; Rebecca M. Warner et al., "Fruit and Vegetable Intake Predicts Positive Affect," *Journal of Happiness Studies* 18, no. 3 (May 12, 2016): 809–26, https://doi.org/10.1007/s10902-016-9749-6; Bonnie A. White, Caroline C. Horwath, and Tamlin S. Conner, "Many Apples a Day Keep the Blues Away—Daily Experiences of Negative and Positive Affect and Food Consumption in Young Adults," *British Journal of Health Psychology* 18, no. 4 (January 24, 2013): 782–98, https://doi.org/10.1111/bjhp.12021.

23. Lauren G. Block et al., "From Nutrients to Nurturance: A Conceptual Introduction to Food Well-Being," *Journal of Public Policy & Marketing* 30, no. 1 (April 2011): 5–13, https://doi.org/10.1509/jppm.30.1.5.

24. Deborah R. Wahl et al., "Healthy Food Choices Are Happy Food Choices: Evidence from a Real Life Sample Using Smartphone Based Assessments," *Scientific Reports* 7, no. 1 (December 6, 2017), https://doi.org/10.1038/s41598-017-17262-9.

25. Ruut Veenhoven, "Will Healthy Eating Make You Happier? A Research Synthesis Using an Online Findings Archive," *Applied Research in Quality of Life* 16, no. 1 (August 14, 2019): 221–40, https://doi.org/10.1007/s11482-019-09748-7.

LET'S GET PHYSICAL

26. US Department of Health & Human Services, "Physical Activity Guidelines. 2nd Edition," Health.gov, https://health.gov/sites/default/files/2019-09/Physical_Activity_Guidelines_2nd_edition.pdf.

27. Peter J. Carek, Sarah E. Laibstain, and Stephen M. Carek, "Exercise for the Treatment of Depression and Anxiety," *The International Journal of Psychiatry in Medicine* 41, no. 1 (January 2011): 15–28, https://doi.org/10.2190/pm.41.1.c; Gary M Cooney et al., "Exercise for Depression," *Cochrane Database of Systematic Reviews* 2013, no. 9 (September 12, 2013) https://doi.org/10.1002/ 14651858.cd004366.pub6; Kenneth R. Fox, "The Influence of Physical Activity on Mental Well-Being," *Public Health Nutrition* 2, no. 3a (March 1999): 411–18, https://doi.org/10.1017/s13689800 99000567; K. T. Hallam, S. Bilsborough, and M. de Courten, "'Happy Feet': Evaluating the Benefits of a 100-Day 10,000 Step Challenge on Mental Health and Wellbeing," *BMC Psychiatry* 18, no. 1 (January 24, 2018), https://doi.org/10.1186/s12888-018-1609-y; Amanda L. Hyde, Jaclyn P. Maher, and Steriani Elavsky, "Enhancing Our Understanding of Physical Activity and Wellbeing with a Lifespan Perspective," *International Journal of Wellbeing* 3, no. 1 (March 7, 2013): 98–115, https://doi.org/10.5502/ijw.v3i1.6; Lyubomirsky, *The How of Happiness: A New Approach to Getting the Life You Want*; Nansook Park et al., "Positive Psychology and Physical Health," *American Journal of Lifestyle Medicine* 10, no. 3 (September 26, 2014): 200–206, https://doi.org/10.1177/1559827614550277; W. Jack Rejeski et al., "Effects of Baseline Responses, In-Task Feelings, and Duration of Activity on Exercise-Induced Feeling States in Women," *Health Psychology* 14, no. 4 (1995): 350–59, https://doi.org/10.1037/0278-6133.14.4.350; Peter Salmon, "Effects of Physical Exercise on Anxiety, Depression, and Sensitivity to Stress," *Clinical Psychology Review* 21, no. 1 (February 2001): 33–61, https://doi.org/10.1016/s0272-7358(99)00032-x; Felipe B. Schuch et al., "Physical Activity and Incident Depression: A Meta-Analysis of Prospective Cohort Studies," *American Journal of Psychiatry* 175, no. 7 (July 2018): 631–48, https://doi.org/10.1176/appi.ajp.2018.17111194; Timothy W. Smith, "Blood, Sweat, and Tears: Exercise in the Management of Mental and Physical Health

Problems," *Clinical Psychology: Science and Practice* 13, no. 2 (2006): 198–202, https://doi.org/ 10.1111/j.1468-2850.2006.00023.x; Justin C. Strickland and Mark A. Smith, "The Anxiolytic Effects of Resistance Exercise," *Frontiers in Psychology* 5 (July 10, 2014), https://doi.org/ 10.3389/fpsyg. 2014.00753; Andreas Ströhle, "Physical Activity, Exercise, Depression and Anxiety Disorders," *Journal of Neural Transmission* 116, no. 6 (August 23, 2008): 777–84, https://doi.org/10.1007/s00702-008-0092-x; Robert E. Thayer, J. Robert Newman, and Tracey M. McClain, "Self-Regulation of Mood: Strategies for Changing a Bad Mood, Raising Energy, and Reducing Tension," *Journal of Personality and Social Psychology* 67, no. 5 (1994): 910–25, https://doi.org/10.1037/0022-3514.67.5.910.

28. Robert E. Thayer, J. Robert Newman, and Tracey M. McClain, "Self-Regulation of Mood: Strategies for Changing a Bad Mood, Raising Energy, and Reducing Tension," *Journal of Personality and Social Psychology* 67, no. 5 (1994): 910–25, https://doi.org/ 10.1037/0022-3514.67.5.910; Zhanjia Zhang and Weiyun Chen, "A Systematic Review of the Relationship between Physical Activity and Happiness," *Journal of Happiness Studies* 20, no. 4 (March 24, 2018): 1305–22, https://doi.org/10.1007/s10902-018-9976-0; Chris Tkach and Sonja Lyubomirsky, "How Do People Pursue Happiness?: Relating Personality, Happiness-Increasing Strategies, and Well-Being," *Journal of Happiness Studies* 7, no. 2 (June 2006): 183–225, https://doi.org/10.1007/ s10902-005-4754-1.

29. "How Can I Influence Happiness in Lives of My Surroundings?" FH;P, n.d., https:// fhp.incom.org/project/10563.

30. Sammi R. Chekroud et al., "Association between Physical Exercise and Mental Health in 1.2 Million Individuals in the USA between 2011 and 2015: A Cross-Sectional Study," *The Lancet Psychiatry* 5, no. 9 (September 2018): 739–46, https://doi.org/10.1016/ s2215-0366 (18)30227-x.

31. Gary O'Donovan et al., "Association of 'Weekend Warrior' and Other Leisure Time Physical Activity Patterns with Risks for All-Cause, Cardiovascular Disease, and Cancer Mortality," *JAMA Internal Medicine* 177, no. 3 (March 1, 2017): 335, https://doi.org/ 10.1001/jamainternmed.2016.8014.

DON'T SIT ON IT

32. J. N. Morris et al., "Coronary Heart-Disease and Physical Activity of Work," *The Lancet* 262, no. 6796 (November 1953): 1111–20, https://doi.org/10.1016/ s0140-6736(53)91495-0; *U.S. News & World Report*, "What Do Double-Decker Buses Tell Us about Our Health?" WTOP News, October 13, 2015, https://wtop.com/news/ 2015/10/what-do-double-decker-buses-tell-us-about-our-health/.

33. E. G. Wilmot et al., "Sedentary Time in Adults and the Association with Diabetes, Cardiovascular Disease and Death: Systematic Review and Meta-Analysis," *Diabetologia* 55, no. 11 (August 14, 2012): 2895–2905, https://doi.org/10.1007/s00125-012-2677-z.

34. Keith M. Diaz et al., "Potential Effects on Mortality of Replacing Sedentary Time with Short Sedentary Bouts or Physical Activity: A National Cohort Study," *American Journal of Epidemiology* 188, no. 3 (January 14, 2019): 537–44, https://doi.org/10.1093/ aje/kwy271; David W. Dunstan et al., "Too Much Sitting—A Health Hazard," *Diabetes Research and Clinical Practice* 97, no. 3 (September 2012): 368–76, https://doi.org/ 10.1016/j.diabres.2012.05.020; Earl S. Ford and Carl J. Caspersen, "Sedentary Behaviour

and Cardiovascular Disease: A Review of Prospective Studies," *International Journal of Epidemiology* 41, no. 5 (May 25, 2012): 1338–53, https://doi.org/10.1093/ije/dys078; James A. Levine, "Sick of Sitting," *Diabetologia* 58, no. 8 (May 24, 2015): 1751–58, https://doi.org/10.1007/s00125-015-3624-6; Deborah Rohm Young et al., "Sedentary Behavior and Cardiovascular Morbidity and Mortality: A Science Advisory from the American Heart Association," *Circulation* 134, no. 13 (September 27, 2016), https://doi.org/10.1161/cir.0000000000000440.

35. Nicolaas P. Pronk et al., "Reducing Occupational Sitting Time and Improving Worker Health: The Take-a-Stand Project, 2011," *Preventing Chronic Disease* 9 (October 11, 2012), https://doi.org/10.5888/pcd9.110323.

36. Charlotte L. Edwardson et al., "Effectiveness of the Stand More AT (SMArT) Work Intervention: Cluster Randomised Controlled Trial," *BMJ* (October 10, 2018): k3870, https://doi.org/10.1136/bmj.k3870.

37. Neal Lathia et al., "Happier People Live More Active Lives: Using Smartphones to Link Happiness and Physical Activity," ed. Rebecca A. Krukowski, *PLOS ONE* 12, no. 1 (January 4, 2017): e0160589, https://doi.org/10.1371/journal.pone.0160589.

38. Megan Teychenne, Sarah A. Costigan, and Kate Parker, "The Association between Sedentary Behaviour and Risk of Anxiety: A Systematic Review," *BMC Public Health* 15, no. 1 (June 19, 2015), https://doi.org/10.1186/s12889-015-1843-x;

39. "Sitting Risks: How Harmful Is Too Much Sitting?" Mayo Clinic, July 13, 2022, https://www.mayoclinic.org/healthy-lifestyle/adult-health/expert-answers/sitting/faq-20058005?reDate=20012023.

KISS MY GRITS

40. Cristin D. Runfola et al., "Body Dissatisfaction in Women across the Lifespan: Results of the UNC-*SELF* and Gender and Body Image (GABI) Studies," *European Eating Disorders Review* 21, no. 1 (September 5, 2012): 52–59, https://doi.org/10.1002/erv.2201; "11 Facts about Body Image," DoSomething.org, n.d., https://www.dosomething.org/us/facts/11-facts-about-body-image.

41. Thomas F. Cash, Tejal A. Jakatdar, and Emily Fleming Williams, "The Body Image Quality of Life Inventory: Further Validation with College Men and Women," *Body Image* 1, no. 3 (September 2004): 279–87, https://doi.org/10.1016/s1740-1445(03)00023-8; Leanne L. Davis et al., "The Role of Body Image in the Prediction of Life Satisfaction and Flourishing in Men and Women," *Journal of Happiness Studies* 21, no. 2 (February 26, 2019): 505–24, https://doi.org/10.1007/s10902-019-00093-y; Ngaire Donaghue, "Body Satisfaction, Sexual Self-Schemas and Subjective Well-Being in Women," *Body Image* 6, no. 1 (January 2009): 37–42, https://doi.org/10.1016/j.bodyim. 2008.08.002; Meghan M. Gillen, "Associations between Positive Body Image and Indicators of Men's and Women's Mental and Physical Health," *Body Image* 13 (March 2015): 67–74, https://doi.org/10.1016/j.bodyim.2015.01.002; Amy C. Iannantuono and Tracy L. Tylka, "Interpersonal and Intrapersonal Links to Body Appreciation in College Women: An Exploratory Model," *Body Image* 9, no. 2 (March 2012): 227–35, https://doi.org/10.1016/j.bodyim. 2012.01.004; Jonathan Mond et al., "Obesity, Body Dissatisfaction, and Emotional Well-Being in Early and Late Adolescence: Findings from the Project EAT Study," *Journal of Adolescent Health* 48, no. 4 (April 2011): 373–78, https://doi.org/10.1016/

j.jadohealth.2010.07.022; Oktan Vesile and Mehmet Palanci. "Body Image, Subjective Happiness and Eating Attitudes among 19- to 63-Years-Old Turkish Women," (December 2018); Susan J. Paxton et al., "Body Dissatisfaction Prospectively Predicts Depressive Mood and Low Self-Esteem in Adolescent Girls and Boys," *Journal of Clinical Child & Adolescent Psychology* 35, no. 4 (December 2006): 539–49, https://doi.org/10.1207/s15374424 jccp3504_5; Rachel Stokes and Christina Frederick-Recascino, "Women's Perceived Body Image: Relations with Personal Happiness," *Journal of Women & Aging* 15, no. 1 (February 2003): 17–29, https://doi.org/10.1300/j074v15n01_03; Viren Swami et al., "Associations between Women's Body Image and Happiness: Results of the YouBeauty.Com Body Image Survey (YBIS)," *Journal of Happiness Studies* 16, no. 3 (April 26, 2014): 705–18, https://doi.org/10.1007/s10902-014-9530-7; Viren Swami et al., "Positive Body Image Is Positively Associated with Hedonic (Emotional) and Eudaimonic (Psychological and Social) Well-Being in British Adults," *The Journal of Social Psychology* 158, no. 5 (November 21, 2017): 541–52, https://doi.org/10.1080/00224545.2017.1392278; Rebecca E. Wilson, Janet D. Latner, and Kentaro Hayashi, "More than Just Body Weight: The Role of Body Image in Psychological and Physical Functioning," *Body Image* 10, no. 4 (September 2013): 644–47, https://doi.org/10.1016/j.bodyim.2013.04.007.

42. David A. Frederick et al., "Correlates of Appearance and Weight Satisfaction in a US National Sample: Personality, Attachment Style, Television Viewing, Self-Esteem, and Life Satisfaction," *Body Image*, 17, (June 2016):191–203, https://doi:10.1016/j.bodyim.2016.04.001.

43. "Infographic: 14 Ways to Improve Your Body Image Right Now," happify.com, n.d., https://www.happify.com/hd/improve-body-image-infographic/; Yvette Brazier, "What Is Body Image?" *Medical News Today*, August 15, 2022, https://www.medicalnewstoday.com/articles/249190; Healthy Women Editors, "9 Tips for Improving Body Image and Intimacy," Healthy Women, March 29, 2021, https://www.healthywomen.org/content/article/9-tips-improving-body-image-and-intimacy; "10 Steps to Positive Body Image," national eatingdisorders.org, n.d., https://www.nationaleating disorders.org/learn/general-information/ten-steps.

SOLO SOBRIETY VS. SOLO CUPS OF WINE

44. "How Can I Influence Happiness in Lives of My Surroundings?" n.d., https://fhp.incom.org/project/10563; Gretchen Reynolds, "Even a Little Exercise Might Make Us Happier," *National Library of Medicine*) May 2, 2018), https://www.ncbi.nlm.nih.gov/search/research-news/2097/.

45. "How to Forgive Someone Who Has Hurt You: In 15 Steps," *Dr. Wayne Dyer: Wayne's Blog* (blog), n.d., https://www.drwaynedyer.com/blog/.

46. Vaillant, *Triumphs of Experience: The Men of the Harvard Grant Study*, 2015.

47. "Alcohol Facts and Statistics | National Institute on Alcohol Abuse and Alcoholism (NIAAA)," n.d., https://www.niaaa.nih.gov/publications/brochures-and-fact-sheets/alcohol-facts-and-statistics.

48. "Alcohol Does Not Protect against COVID-19 and Its Access Should Be Restricted during Lock Down," World Health Organization, April 14, 2020, https://www.emro.who.int/mnh/news/alcohol-does-not-protect-against-covid-19-and-its-access-should-be-restricted-during-lock-down.html.

49. Michael S. Pollard, Joan S. Tucker, and Harold D. Green, "Changes in Adult Alcohol Use and Consequences during the COVID-19 Pandemic in the US," *JAMA Network Open* 3, no. 9 (September 29, 2020): e2022942, https://doi.org/10.1001/jamanetworkopen.2020.22942.

50. NielsenIQ, "Many Americans Are Looking for a Bar Experience without the Buzz," May 19, 2021, https://nielseniq.com/global/en/insights/analysis/2019/many-americans-are-looking-for-a-bar-experience-without-the-buzz/.

51. Karen Armstrong et al., "Anxiety Reduction in Patients Undergoing Cardiac Catheterization following Massage and Guided Imagery," *Complementary Therapies in Clinical Practice* 20, no. 4 (November 2014): 334–38, https://doi.org/10.1016/j.ctcp.2014.07. 009; Adam Burke et al., "Prevalence and Patterns of Use of Mantra, Mindfulness and Spiritual Meditation among Adults in the United States," *BMC Complementary and Alternative Medicine* 17, no. 1 (June 15, 2017), https://doi.org/10.1186/s12906-017-1827-8; Alberto Chiesa and Alessandro Serretti, "Mindfulness-Based Stress Reduction for Stress Management in Healthy People: A Review and Meta-Analysis," *The Journal of Alternative and Complementary Medicine* 15, no. 5 (May 2009): 593–600, https://doi.org/10.1089/acm.2008.0495; Michael de Vibe et al., "Mindfulness Training for Stress Management: A Randomised Controlled Study of Medical and Psychology Students," *BMC Medical Education* 13, no. 1 (August 13, 2013), https://doi.org/10.1186/1472-6920-13-107; Alisha L. Francis and Rhonda Cross Beemer, "How Does Yoga Reduce Stress? Embodied Cognition and Emotion Highlight the Influence of the Musculoskeletal System," *Complementary Therapies in Medicine* 43 (April 2019): 170–75, https://doi.org/10.1016/j.ctim.2019.01.024; Hon K. Yuen and Gavin R. Jenkins, "Factors Associated with Changes in Subjective Well-Being Immediately after Urban Park Visit," *International Journal of Environmental Health Research* 30, no. 2 (February 13, 2019): 134–45, https://doi.org/10.1080/09603123.2019.1577368; Lisa A. Kilpatrick et al., "Impact of Mindfulness-Based Stress Reduction Training on Intrinsic Brain Connectivity," *NeuroImage* 56, no. 1 (May 2011): 290–98, https://doi.org/10.1016/j.neuroimage.2011.02.034; Mi-kyoung Lee et al., "The Effects of Aromatherapy Essential Oil Inhalation on Stress, Sleep Quality and Immunity in Healthy Adults: Randomized Controlled Trial," *European Journal of Integrative Medicine* 12 (June 2017): 79–86, https://doi.org/10.1016/j.eujim. 2017.04.009; David Lewis, Galaxy Stress Research, *Mindlab International*, (Sussex University, UK: 2009); Xiao Ma et al., "The Effect of Diaphragmatic Breathing on Attention, Negative Affect and Stress in Healthy Adults," *Frontiers in Psychology* 8 (June 6, 2017), https://doi.org/10.3389/fpsyg.2017.00874; Michail Mantzios and Kyriaki Giannou, "When Did Coloring Books Become Mindful? Exploring the Effectiveness of a Novel Method of Mindfulness-Guided Instructions for Coloring Books to Increase Mindfulness and Decrease Anxiety," *Frontiers in Psychology* 9 (January 30, 2018), https://doi.org/10.3389/fpsyg.2018.00056; Franziska Matzer et al., "Combining Walking and Relaxation for Stress Reduction—A Randomized Cross-Over Trial in Healthy Adults," *Stress and Health* 34, no. 2 (August 25, 2017): 266–77, https://doi.org/10.1002/smi.2781; Genevive R. Meredith et al., "Minimum Time Dose in Nature to Positively Impact the Mental Health of College-Aged Students, and How to Measure It: A Scoping Review," *Frontiers in Psychology* 10 (January 14, 2020), https://doi.org/10.3389/fpsyg.2019.02942; "Mind and Body Approaches for Stress," NCCIH, n.d., https://www.nccih.nih.gov/health/providers/digest/mind-and-body-approaches-for-stress; Paolla Gabrielle Nascimento Novais et al., "The Effects of Progressive Muscular Relaxation as a Nursing Procedure Used for Those Who Suffer from Stress Due to

Multiple Sclerosis," *Revista Latino-Americana De Enfermagem* 24, no. 0 (2016), https://doi.org/10.1590/1518-8345. 1257.2789; Michaela C. Pascoe and Isabelle E. Bauer, "A Systematic Review of Randomised Control Trials on the Effects of Yoga on Stress Measures and Mood," *Journal of Psychiatric Research* 68 (September 2015): 270–82, https://doi.org/10.1016/j.jpsychires.2015.07.013; Renée van der Vennet and Susan Serice, "Can Coloring Mandalas Reduce Anxiety? A Replication Study," *Art Therapy* 29, no. 2 (June 2012): 87–92, https://doi.org/10.1080/07421656. 2012.680047; Marc A. Russo, Danielle M. Santarelli, and Dean O'Rourke, "The Physiological Effects of Slow Breathing in the Healthy Human," *Breathe* 13, no. 4 (November 30, 2017): 298–309, https://doi.org/10.1183 /20734735.009817; Ashish Sharma, Vishal Madaan, and Frederick D. Petty, "Exercise for Mental Health," *The Primary Care Companion to the Journal of Clinical Psychiatry* 08, no. 02 (April 15, 2006): 106, https://doi.org/10.4088/pcc.v08n0208a; Milad Azami et al., "The Effect of Yoga on Stress, Anxiety, and Depression in Women," *International Journal of Preventive Medicine* 9, no. 1 (2018): 21, https://doi.org/10.4103/ijpvm.ijpvm_242_16; "Stress Management," WebMD, January 1, 2000, https://www.webmd.com/balance/stress-management/stress-management; Kandhasamy Sowndhararajan and Songmun Kim, "Influence of Fragrances on Human Psychophysiological Activity: With Special Reference to Human Electroencephalographic Response," *Scientia Pharmaceutica* 84, no. 4 (November 29, 2016): 724–51, https://doi.org/10.3390/scipharm84040724; Chris C. Streeter et al., "Effects of Yoga versus Walking on Mood, Anxiety, and Brain GABA Levels: A Randomized Controlled MRS Study," *The Journal of Alternative and Complementary Medicine* 16, no. 11 (November 2010): 1145–52, https://doi.org/10.1089/acm.2010.0007; "Stress Relievers: Tips to Tame Stress," Mayo Clinic, March 18, 2021, https://www.mayoclinic.org/healthy-lifestyle/stress-management/in-depth/stress-relievers/art-20047257?reDate=20012023; Myriam V. Thoma et al., "The Effect of Music on the Human Stress Response," ed. Robert L. Newton, *PLOS ONE* 8, no. 8 (August 5, 2013): e70156, https://doi.org/10.1371/journal. pone.0070156; Liza Varvogli and Christina Darviri, "Stress Management Techniques: Evidence-Based Procedures That Reduce Stress and Promote Health," *Health Science Journal* 5, no. 2 (2011), 74-89;

DEPRESSION IS NOT A CHOICE

1. "Depression," World Health Organization, September 13, 2021, https://www.who.int/news-room/fact-sheets/detail/depression.

2. "What is Depression?" *American Psychiatric Association*, accessed February 2, 2023, https://www.psychiatry.org/patients-families/depression/what-is-depression.

Chapter 8: Your Past Prepares You

THIS ISN'T A DRESS REHEARSAL

1. Danielle McCarthy, "7 Famous People Who Found Success Later in Life," *OverSixty*, n.d., https://www.oversixty.com.au/lifestyle/retirement-life/famous-post-60s-achievements; Bill Murphy Jr., "14 Inspiring People who Found Crazy Success Later in Life," *Inc.Com*, n.d., https://www.inc.com/bill-murphy-jr/14-inspiring-people-who-

found-crazy-success-later-in-life.html; Kaye Ramos, "9 Late Bloomer Success Stories Who Prove It's Never Too Late to Achieve Your Dreams," Medium, June 5, 2020, https://medium.com/the-mission/9-late-bloomer-success-stories-who-prove-its-never-too-late-to-achieve-your-dreams-b036688da6f; Matt Valentine, "8 Highly Successful People Who Only Found Success Later in Life," Goalcast, July 14, 2021, https://www.goalcast.com/8-successful-people-found-success-later-life/.

2. James Clear, *Atomic Habits: An Easy & Proven Way to Build Good Habits & Break Bad Ones* (New York: Avery: An Imprint of Penguin Random House LLC, 2018).

3. Matt Seybold, "The Apocryphal Twain: 'The Things You Didn't Do,'" Center for Mark Twain Studies, June 28, 2019, https://marktwainstudies.com/the-apocryphal-twain-the-things-you-didnt-do/.

4. Marianne Williamson, *A Return to Love: Reflections on the Principles of "A Course in Miracles"* (New York: HarperOne, 1996).

SOME WISHBONES DON'T BREAK

5. Kim Ode, "No Bones about It, Breaking the Wishbone Is a Family Tradition," *Star Tribune*, November 26, 2014, https://www.startribune.com/no-bones-about-it-breaking-the-wishbone-is-a-family-tradition/283837301/.

ABOUT THE AUTHOR

BETH ROMERO was born and raised in Bethlehem, Pennsylvania. After a thirty-year sojourn on the West Coast, she recently moved back to Philadelphia. In addition to having made her a pizza aficionado, her Italian American, East Coast background inspires the straightforward, humorous, and self-deprecating narrative style that characterizes her writing. (As every good cook knows, the secret *is* the salt.) With a background and degree in psychology, Beth channeled her creativity into a successful sales and branding career. From Veep to Boss to Happiness Junkie—persuasive storytelling is her superpower. She showcases those skills to their fullest in this practical and entertaining how-to guide for happiness.

SCAN ME

SELECTED TITLES FROM SHE WRITES PRESS

She Writes Press is an independent publishing company founded to serve women writers everywhere. Visit us at www.shewritespress.com.

Negatively Ever After: A Skeptic's Guide to Finding Happiness by Deanna K. Willmon. $16.95, 978-1-63152-312-0. From achieving self-adoration and learning what gratitude truly means to determining whether sharing happiness is really a good idea, this realistic and accessible guide will help you harness your negativity and find your own inner happiness.

Stop Giving it Away: How to Stop Self-Sacrificing and Start Claiming Your Space, Power, and Happiness by Cherilynn Veland. $16.95, 978-1-63152-958-0. An empowering guide designed to help women break free from the trappings of the needs, wants, and whims of other people—and the self-imposed limitations that are keeping them from happiness.

The Buddha Sat Right Here: A Family Odyssey Through India and Nepal by Dena Moes. 16.95, 978-1-63152-561-2. Stressed-out midwife Dena Moes longed to escape the hamster wheel of modern motherhood—so she tore off her Supermom cape, shuttered the house, and took her husband and preteen daughters on a yearlong odyssey through India and Nepal.

Happier At Work by Gayle van Gils. $16.95, 978-1-63152-204-8. Practical applications of mindfulness and compassion, along with inspiring stories of companies who apply these principles, for the more than 70 percent of people in US workplaces who are disengaged and stressed.

The Self-Care Solution: A Modern Mother's Must-Have Guide to Health and Well-Being by Julie Burton. $16.95, 978-1-63152-068-6. Full of essential physical, emotional and relational self-care tools—and based on research by the author that includes a survey of hundreds of moms—this book is a life raft for moms who often feel like they are drowning in the sea of motherhood.